The Promise of Group Therapy

Bill Roller

The Promise
of Group Therapy

How to Build a Vigorous
Training and Organizational Base
for Group Therapy in
Managed Behavioral Healthcare

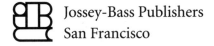
Jossey-Bass Publishers
San Francisco

Copyright acknowledgments are on pp. 223–224.

Substantial discounts on bulk quantities of Jossey-Bass books are available to corporations, professional associations, and other organizations. For details and discount information, contact the special sales department at Jossey-Bass Inc., Publishers (415) 433–1740; Fax (800) 605–2665.

For sales outside the United States, please contact your local Simon & Schuster International Office.

Jossey-Bass Web address: http://www.josseybass.com

 Manufactured in the United States of America on Lyons Falls Turin Book. This paper is acid-free and 100 percent totally chlorine-free.

Library of Congress Cataloging-in-Publication Data

Roller, Bill.
    The promise of group therapy : how to build a vigorous training
and organizational base for group therapy in managed behavioral
healthcare / Bill Roller. — 1st ed.
      p.   cm.
    Includes bibliographical references and index.
    ISBN 0-7879-0842-8 (alk. paper)
    1. Group psychotherapy—Practice.   2. Managed mental health care.
3. Group psychotherapists—Training of.   4. Group psychotherapy—
Study and teaching.   I. Title
RC488.R645   1997
616.89'152'023—dc21   96-48494
                                                CIP

FIRST EDITION
HB Printing   10 9 8 7 6 5 4 3 2 1

—m— Contents

Dedicated to Donald A. Shaskan, M.D.

(1912–1995)

Teacher, Mentor, Colleague, Friend

"It is the same with people," thought Nekhludoff. *"The whole trouble lies in that people think there are conditions excluding the necessity of love in their intercourse with man, but such conditions do not exist. Things may be treated without love; one may chop wood, make bricks, forge iron without love, but one can no more deal with people without love than one can handle bees without care. The nature of bees is such that if you handle them carelessly you will harm them as well as yourself. It is the same with people. And it cannot be different, because mutual love is the basic law of life."*

—*Leo Tolstoy*
Resurrection

~~~ Introduction

It was my good fortune to be the first group psychotherapy coordinator for the Group Health Cooperative of Puget Sound, a health maintenance organization (HMO) in Washington state and one of the pioneers in the consumer cooperative and prepaid healthcare movement. Since that time, various mental health institutions have asked me to share the secrets of our successful group therapy program in the Northwest. These secrets can be stated rather succinctly: appropriate organizational structure plus competent personnel in a context of ongoing professional training yield a successful operation that will be flexible enough to adjust with changing conditions. As I will show, the ingenuity and creativity of any group program lies in both the details of daily operation and the purposes and values on which the program is based. Given the recent acceleration of change in the financing of mental health delivery, there are now powerful incentives to use group therapy as never before.

Group therapy in managed care systems nationwide currently constitutes less than 10 percent of all patient mental health visits. In the next ten years, the use of group therapy will rise, primarily for economic reasons, to nearly 40 percent of all patient visits. During that same period, the demand for qualified group psychotherapists will increase so dramatically that we will have to train more than thirty thousand new group clinicians.

How will this change come about? And why is it happening now? The first is a question of how we conceptualize the training needs of the new group therapists and plan for the groups their patients will need in the future. The second is a question of why consumer demand for treatment and corporate marketing of health plans are now converging in a particular historical context.

WHY GROUP THERAPY?

The field of group psychotherapy is being tested more strenuously now than at any time in its young life. Having emerged from psychoanalysis and its Viennese and New York practitioners in the 1930s, group psychotherapy has survived a number of crises, cultural transmissions, and long periods of neglect by mental health professionals. Group therapists are now challenged in unprecedented ways, ironically, because the discipline they practice has met with success beyond their expectations.

Not so long ago, group therapy was considered a secondary (at best), ancillary form of treatment to be employed for reasons not well understood. Though regarded as theoretically inferior at that time, in this age of cost management group therapy has risen to the stature of a primary form of psychotherapeutic intervention. Some might say this change in status has occurred for the wrong reason, namely that in terms of industrial output, group therapy is a less labor-intensive way to deliver a product to consumers. A group therapist can treat from two to three times as many patients in one-half to one-third the time.

Capitation and Cost Control

These figures have enormous financial consequences for capitated systems, that is, cost management systems that undertake to cover a certain number of people for limited mental health benefits at a predetermined price per person. Capitation is a calculated risk that a mental health managed care system takes in writing a contract for employers who seek benefits for their employees. Because 93 percent of mental health delivery costs are personnel related, this wager will work for managed care systems only if the cost of delivery is reduced by methods that use less personnel. Thus it becomes clear why there is an urgent and extraordinary demand for group therapists to deliver their product.

Capitation is one of the driving forces behind the rise of group psychotherapy. The marketing strategy of selling capitated contracts to industry and business has become increasingly popular because it sets cost limits on the mental health benefits of employees. Under capitated contracts, a certain dollar amount is assigned to each employee with the guarantee that all necessary treatment will be given and no extra fees will be assessed regardless of the treatment needed. Under capitation, an employer can plan for the exact cost of mental health benefits for all employees and can shop around for the best mental health bargain. This situation gives rise to competition among managed care corporations to provide contracts at lower capitated rates.

Managed care corporations make a gamble when they enter into capitated contracts with employers. They bet that they can meet the mental health needs of the covered populations within the dollar amount they have bid. This financial risk motivates those managed care operations to provide lower-cost mental health alternatives. Group psychotherapy becomes a highly desirable treatment option under these conditions, and the development of group psychotherapy programs becomes paramount as a cost containment strategy. Group psychotherapy also becomes part of the marketing strategy. If a flourishing group therapy program is a component of my managed care operation, I can afford to sell a company a capitated mental health-care package at a lower price. As utilization increases, I can make my payroll by providing group therapy.

There are other ways to control costs besides using capitated contracts. Some managed care corporations control patient utilization rates by limiting access to mental health services through such formal and informal "gate keeping" procedures as proving medical necessity, allowing lengthy patient waiting lists, and remaining inaccessible by phone. In systems that do not sell capitated contracts, there are fewer incentives to provide group therapy.

Market Demand

Another driving force behind the desire to increase the implementation of group therapy is the prospect of a vast population using mental health services. In recent history, all industrialized nations in the world (with the exception of the United States) have found it a necessary element of their social organization to provide for the health needs of their citizens. In the near future, 300 million Americans, including the underserved population of poor and uninsured citizens, could be fully covered under the health plans of managed care corporations, HMOs, or government-sponsored single-payer plans. If we subtract 50 million because of unsuitability for mental health treatment (for instance, infants, as well as certain portions of the infirm and aged population), we have 250 million people eligible for potential mental health benefits. Managed care systems currently estimate that 3 to 6 percent of covered populations will use mental health services each year.

I find this estimate unrealistic over the long term, because it does not take into account the skyrocketing utilization rates that occur after natural disasters and other catastrophes. For example, one earthquake in California could treble utilization rates there for years to come. Especially pertinent in that regard is the proven efficacy of group treatment in the wake of calamities that bring large-scale trauma to the public. A more realistic figure is obtained by examining utilization rates in HMOs over the past few decades. The HMO industry has found that across its history 10 percent of their populations sought or required mental health treatment in a given contract year. A 10 percent utilization rate means some 25 million Americans will need or want mental health services in the United States annually.

Members of the American Association of Health Plans, formerly the Group Health Association of America (GHAA), who have developed state-of-the-art group therapy delivery systems for their capitated or otherwise covered populations, have discovered that 40 percent of the people who seek or require mental health treatment are appropriate for treatment by the full range of services provided by a comprehensive group therapy program. That means that 10 million Americans are suitable for treatment in appropriate therapy groups each year.

So what will it take to provide service for such a market? Dr. Michael Freeman, president of the Institute for Behavioral Health, estimates that the ratio of mental healthcare providers to patients in a managed care environment is between 1 to 3,000 and 1 to 6,000. Taking the lower end of Dr. Freeman's estimate, we can allow one provider for every 5,000 people fully capitated. If we take the 1 to 5,000 ratio of providers to capitated population, and assume that 10 percent will seek or require mental health services, then each provider will need to treat 500 patients each year. A competently trained and skilled group therapist can conduct about eight 90-minute groups every week. Each group can treat 32 patients per year (because the average stay of each group member in an 8-member group is 8 to 12 sessions), for a grand total of 256 patients. In this manner, a skilled group therapist could deliver service to more than half his yearly patient load in only 12 clinical hours per week.

At 250 patients in group treatment per year—the very maximum for highly trained and competent group therapists—we will need 40,000 group therapists in order to provide groups for 10 million people each year. The current membership of the American Group Psychotherapy Association, the premier association for group psychotherapists in the United States, is approximately 4,000 practitioners nationwide. There are probably another 4,000 therapists in the nation qualified by training and experience to practice group therapy. That means we will need to train 32,000 competent group therapists to meet the needs of the nation—assuming that all of the current group therapists continue practicing.

TRAINING THE GROUP THERAPIST

At the present time, there is no university or college in the United States that offers a comprehensive training program in group therapy. In the absence of educational institutions able to prepare qualified group therapists, I believe the HMO and managed care industry will have to train their own group therapists in comprehensive on-the-job training programs of one to three years' duration, depending on the level of skill required. The pressing need to develop programs to educate the next generation of group therapists is one of the chief motivations for writing this book.

In this book, I will set forth the necessary conditions for the training of competent group therapists in an organizational setting and the necessary conditions for the organization to provide a context in which the group therapist can succeed. Competence is defined in terms of functional tasks that must be accomplished. The question of mastery—always an elusive one in any high craft or art—remains open and is the subject of another work in progress, *The Pursuit of Paradox: Group Therapy, Equality, and Other Experiments With Democracy in America.*

Research has shown that a person's first exposure to group therapy leaves lasting impressions. If we want our patients to learn the purposes and values of group therapy, it is incumbent on us that we help to make the patient's first experience a positive one without minimizing the struggle that often occurs. The therapist's responsibility to be competent as group leader is paramount.

Paradoxically, the clinician who intends to practice short-term therapy and time-limited groups, as often mandated in managed care settings, must be *better* trained and prepared than her counterpart who conducts long-term groups. This is true for three reasons. First, the leader has less time to learn from mistakes in short-term treatment. She must read group situations rapidly and accurately, and respond appropriately within the time allotted. Second, the potential to harm patients is increased because there is less time for the leader to correct mistakes. The phenomenon of scapegoating alone—the most fre-quently encountered crisis in group—carries the possibility for harm. Although scapegoating must be processed and integrated by every group, the scarring of individuals is not necessary and can be averted by skillful leadership. Third, because the bond the group therapist makes with the patient may be minimal, the group cannot rely on the strength of the patient-therapist relationship to make up for a lack of skills or facility with the group.

HISTORICAL BACKGROUND

One of the practical breakthroughs of social psychology in this cen-tury has been the development of group psychotherapy as the primary method for addressing the individual's problems of isolation and alienation and for meeting the human needs of socialization, accep-tance, and healthy adaptation in the community.

There are many geniuses and pioneers who have contributed con-ceptually and pragmatically to the founding and advancement of group psychotherapy—I will name but a few here.

Joseph Pratt, an internist, met with tuberculosis patients in groups as early as 1905 in Boston, to give them information and help them cope with their illness. Trigant Burrow was a pioneer of training groups and the laboratory approach to the study of individual behav-ior in groups in the 1920s. In Vienna during the 1920s, Jacob Moreno applied dramatic methods to a form of group treatment he called psy-chodrama, and Alfred Adler met with children and adult patients in group settings.

Paul Schilder, a Viennese emigré in New York, extended the psy-choanalytic concepts of transference and dream interpretation to the practice of group therapy in 1936, and developed the idea of the body image as it related to group interactions. Also in New York, Louis Wen-der linked Sigmund Freud's ideas on group psychology with the appearance of family transferences in the treatment groups he con-ducted in the 1930s. About that time, S. R. Slavson began helping chil-dren become more spontaneous in the context of group activity. In 1947, Kurt Lewin brought the Gestalt notion of studying whole pat-terns to self-study groups at the National Training Laboratory at Bethel, Maine, leading the way to action research in the social sciences.

The need to provide treatment to thousands of psychologically impaired Allied soldiers during World War Two took the medical and psychiatric profession by surprise and introduced them to the benefits of group therapy for a large patient population. The necessity to treat so many combatants and the goal to return as many as possible to active duty spurred the evolution of creative methods in group intervention. Psychiatrists trained in psychoanalysis were obliged to improvise with their patients. American and British military hospitals provided training opportunities and advanced the professional careers of many who later became authorities in the field.

With the passage of the Community Mental Health Center Act of 1963, group therapy was given yet another stimulus, as thousands of citizens used the newly founded community mental health centers. Reflecting on the pressures of that time, Saul Scheidlinger reminds us that the current temptation for managed care organizations to employ unprepared clinicians as group therapists has an historical precedent. "The knowledge and the experience of group therapists in outpatient, inpatient, and preventive contexts were in demand. In fact, lacking a sufficient number of skilled group therapy practitioners, harassed administrators began to resort to rash solutions, among them assigning untrained staff persons to work with groups" (p. 4).

The community mental health movement in the 1960s and the human potential movement in the 1970s, with its burgeoning group modalities, found encouragement in the idea that the individual might gain insights into the self by meeting with a group of peers. Psychological research has since shown the effectiveness of group therapy in overcoming isolation and promoting socialization among varied patient populations.

GROUP PSYCHOTHERAPY AT PUGET SOUND

In the early 1980s, my colleagues and I at the Mental Health Service of Group Health Cooperative of Puget Sound created a state-of-the-art program for the delivery of group psychotherapy to a large population (300,000 members) covered under a prepaid comprehensive health plan. This was a staff model HMO, meaning that our mental health service had a salaried staff of sixty-plus support personnel functioning at five different sites in western Washington state. Within a four-year period, we had developed the largest group therapy delivery system in the nation, serving a diverse population of patients in one hundred psychotherapy groups each week. Ninety percent of these groups were designed as short-term group therapy, which we defined for the individual as a course of treatment consisting of eight to twenty sessions over a three- to six-month period.

I have distilled much of what we learned in that development process in the pages of this book. Of particular note is the way in which we applied the principles of organization development to the task. Organization development is the study and practice of how the organization and the individual interact in a specific context. Understanding the context in which both individual and organization interact is essential to shaping a group therapy program.

Motivation

The motives for the Mental Health Service to expand the group therapy program were threefold.

1. We wanted to reduce the costs for out-of-plan referrals, that is, the additional cost necessary to send a plan enrollee to a clinician outside the Mental Health Service because of our lack of services or capacity to treat the patient.

2. Use of mental health services by consumers was increasing for a number of reasons, including medical staff recognition that appropriate and timely referral of a patient could result in lower medical costs overall by preventing injury, illness, or death. (See the discussion of the offset effect in Chapter Seven.) In the face of increased utilization, group therapy became a practical and clinically sound solution to providing treatment in-house.

3. Although required by regulation to provide mental health services (as was every government-qualified HMO of the time), the management of the Group Health Cooperative of Puget Sound did not want to continue to do so, and actively lobbied at the state and national levels to be relieved of that responsibility. To management, the savings of the offset effect seemed vague, and would show only in the long term, whereas the savings of removing the mental health benefit, including the Mental Health Service, were immediate. The chief political factor that kept the mental health benefit alive was a small but dedicated group of citizens—members of the HMO who were highly vocal and effective in lobbying their elected representatives to keep their

mental health benefit. With the help of consumer allies, the Mental Health Service was allowed the time to expand its group program and significantly limit its out-of-plan referrals to a handful of extraordinary cases.

What Corporate Management Needs to Know

My experience at Puget Sound illustrates the three elements essential to the managed care system: (1) a financial organization that makes contracts with employers and hires professionals to provide treatment, (2) professionals highly qualified to deliver services, and (3) consumers who receive professional treatment as part of their contracted benefit. These elements have remained constant for nearly a century of developing prepaid, capitated health plans. However, the relative power that each element held has shifted extensively in the last five years in the direction of the corporation and its financial imperatives.

Although the recent transformation of American healthcare management has taken many in the field by surprise, it was not unanticipated. As early as 1982, Paul Starr predicted in a chapter entitled "The Coming of the Corporation" in *The Social Transformation of American Medicine* the rise of corporate control in medical and related fields:

> The emergence of corporate enterprise in health services is part of two broad currents in the political economy of contemporary societies. The older of these two movements is the steady expansion of the corporation into sectors of the economy traditionally occupied by self-employed small businessmen or family enterprises. In this respect, the growth of corporate medical care is similar to the growth of corporate agriculture. The second and more recent movement is the transfer of public services to the administrative control or ownership of private corporations [p. 445].

In this climate, employers paying higher insurance rates increasingly began to distinguish their economic interests from those of the healthcare industry. In the absence of public control and in the face of rising costs, employers and insurance companies set about to establish a system to manage costs.

If Starr is correct in his pronouncement that medical planning has now become the discipline of medical marketing, then it is imperative that corporate marketing personnel understand the product they are selling. In the case of group therapy—the hands-down winner of cost containment in the mental health industry—the marketing people need to understand the essential conditions that must prevail in order for the group therapy program they have sold to deliver the services promised.

Another impetus for the corporate health service industry to comprehend the art of group therapy is the need to be accountable to the public. The recent disciplinary action by the Rhode Island Department of Health underscored the failure of one managed mental healthcare company to address the complaints of patients and their families about delays and denials of treatment for seriously mentally ill patients.

With the rise of a more sophisticated mental health consumer, corporate entities must be better prepared to meet the real needs of their patients, lest subscribers seek to redress their grievances in court or by the sanctions of state regulatory commissions. State-of-the-art group therapy programs and competently trained group therapists have the technology to provide the treatment necessary for these patients and to avoid costly legal battles and disciplinary actions.

ABOUT THIS BOOK

I wrote this book for mental health professionals who find themselves in the current managed care marketplace working for staff model HMOs or professional groups organized to serve individuals under capitated contracts. These workers include the following:

- Clinicians with little or no training and preparation who are required by their employer to conduct groups

- Supervisors of group therapists who are asked to supervise without sufficient training or mastery of the subject

- Mental health clinic managers who are instructed to increase the percentage of group therapy visits without prior knowledge of systems theory or organization development as applied to mental health delivery

- Students of group therapy who want to learn the systematic progress of a group through the various phases of development that parallel the individual's growth in group

• Group therapists who want to integrate into their practice the notions of object relations, systems theory, Redecision Therapy, the emergent leadership roles of Ariadne P. Beck, and the stages of a group therapist's personal and professional development

Many of these readers will feel the rush to fill the demand created by a new industry and will want to know answers to the following questions: What are the possibilities and limitations of group therapy? Given the context of strictly limited benefits, what people can be served by this method? What patients will require systems that offer more comprehensive and time-consuming treatment plans? How can we make the introduction to group therapy positive for people who generally express a culturally determined bias for individual treatment and no small amount of trepidation for group treatment? How can the group therapist build from the start an expectation of help within the patient? How must the group therapist be trained in order to shoulder such responsibility? How must the organization create a context that will allow the group therapist to be successful?

ORGANIZATION OF THE BOOK

The first eight chapters of *The Promise of Group Therapy* formulate in detail the support the group therapist must receive from the organization in which the groups develop. Special assistance from each level of the managed care system is essential for the success of the group therapists and the program they create together. The organization must be willing to experiment with new ways of conducting groups and at the same time be respectful of patient rights and cognizant of the responsibilities borne by the clinicians who treat them. The final five chapters address the issue of competence and illustrate what the clinician must know in order to lead well. This second part of the book is a companion volume to six hours of videotape that clearly illustrate the theoretical considerations outlined in the text. This video has been edited from sixteen and a half hours of live group therapy sessions led by Vivian Nelson and me. We are a married co-therapy team that has collaborated professionally for over twenty-one years. Viewers of the videotape will see us model leadership in a time-limited group and demonstrate therapeutic interventions appropriate to the level of the group's maturity.

Mastery in the field always implies a large degree of first-hand learning. Through observation of the interaction of group members, the viewer can see the development of group phases and the emergence of leadership roles predicted by Ariadne P. Beck of the Chicago Group Development Research Team. Specifically, the video shows the behavioral markers that define her phases of group development and illustrate how leaders with specific roles emerge from the group's membership to assist in the transition from one phase to the next. The viewer will be able to familiarize herself with these and other theoretical considerations crucial to the practice of group psychotherapy. I have made references in Chapters Eleven and Twelve of the text to certain parts of the video, which we have created especially for our readers. We trust the dialectic between theory and action, description and visual image, method and *in vivo* modeling will prove useful in training both the eye and ear of the clinician to the many phenomena of group therapy. (Videotape ordering information appears following Chapter Thirteen.)

PROSPECTS FOR GROUP THERAPISTS

Group therapists, as mavericks in the mental health community—never quite accepted nor fully appreciated—stand in amazement at the threshold of prodigious growth in their profession. Will their skills at last be used by the millions who are appropriate for group treatment? Will they be welcomed to train a new generation of practitioners in the subtleties of the art they so love? It would be unfortunate and highly ironic if the new corporate management of mental health overlooks or underestimates—as once did the psychiatric, psychological, and medical communities—the profound power of group therapy to influence behavior and heal.

I have written this book based on the premise that a specific course of organizational preparation and professional training will lead to a high-quality product. I present these ideas both as a prescription of what we can do in the short term and as a general outline of how we must proceed in the long term, if we are going to take advantage of the opportunities that await us.

The promise of group therapy lies yet before us. My hope is that consumers, providers, and corporate managers, for a variety of political, regulatory, and economic reasons, will cooperate to inaugurate a golden age of group therapy teaching and practice that will stimulate innovative methods and action research and build a strong foundation for our profession as we enter a new century.

Berkeley, California   BILL ROLLER
January 1997

—ᴧᴧ— Acknowledgments

I wish to gratefully acknowledge the help of the following persons in the conceptualization, editing, and consummation of this book: my former colleagues at the Mental Health Service of the Group Health Cooperative of Puget Sound; Jim Durkin, for suggesting I call Jossey-Bass to produce a videotape; Alan Rinzler, for his shepherding the project forward; and Vivian Nelson, my wife, for giving up so much of her own time to participate in her husband's dream.

Many thanks are due to the people I have worked with in groups over the past twenty-six years; much of what I say in this book I have learned from them.

I would like to thank Oliver Kerner of Chicago, who long ago introduced me to the idea that I would learn the most by listening to my patients; I also want to express deep appreciation and affection for Ariadne P. Beck, whose theory has opened so many doors to my understanding of group behavior.

Thanks to Avis Rumney for her generous contribution.

Thanks are due also to the members of our video production team for their supportive presence: Rich Kambak, Don Scully, Cheryle Stanley, Gary Norris, Richard Dailey, John Clark, Renee Kremer, and Todd Schindler.

Final thanks are due to those special individuals—Victoria Stievater, John Hanvy, and their fellow group participants—who demonstrated remarkable trust and waived their confidentiality to explore spontaneously with Vivian and me a short-term group—a process that resulted in our video, *The Promise of Group Therapy: A Live to Tape Demonstration of a Time-Limited Group.*

B.R.

The Promise of Group Therapy

PART ONE

Necessary Conditions

CHAPTER ONE

Organization Development and Group Therapy

W hen I began my tenure as the first group psychotherapy coordinator for the Group Health Cooperative of Puget Sound in 1980, the first task I set for myself was to learn the structure of the organization and meet the decision makers. At the time, I was criticized by some of my peers for meddling in the affairs of management, which clinical professionals were supposed to ignore in order to focus on clinical responsibilities. Yet to practice group therapy in a cost-managed system, group clinicians must be aware of how the entire system works, because our success depends directly on how well the system refers people to groups.

PROMOTING GROUP THERAPY

Three factors are key to the rise of an organizational culture in which group therapy flourishes: (1) educating the consumer, (2) training the clinician, and (3) educating the organization.

Educating the Consumer

The organization must educate consumers to take an active role in their healthcare. In the field of group therapy, this begins by teaching the purposes of group and by giving a sense of what is possible to accomplish. Providing sufficient and realistic knowledge allows the consumer to choose group therapy—an important factor in helping a person become motivated to take part in a group therapeutic experience. This education includes information on the benefits that can be derived and the financial incentives that can be gained by participating in the group program.

For example, the prospective group candidate who has presented with symptoms of depression will want to know that her condition can be treated in a group, and a little about how that treatment proceeds. The candidate will also want to know that the group therapists are well trained and experienced in the treatment of the condition that afflicts her, and that the organization believes enough in this form of treatment not only to develop a special program for its delivery but also to provide a benefit package that makes it advantageous for the consumer to be treated in group. Providing information of this sort helps the potential group patient begin thinking of herself as a member of a therapy group prior to her entry.

Financial incentives to enter group can also be designed in a number of creative ways. At Puget Sound, we structured the patient benefit such that a group session "cost" one-half to one-third of a standard individual session. In that way, a person could receive two to three times as many treatment sessions under the same benefit package by choosing to enter group treatment. In systems that require co-payments, the co-payments for group can be reduced by one-half to one-third as an additional incentive for patients to use group therapy.

Training the Clinician

The clinical professional must be trained for competence in the treatment of patients in group psychotherapy. This training consists not just of instruction, in order to gain theoretical understanding of the complex processes of group, but also of emotional preparation for group leadership, which always involves a considerable amount of time devoted to learning about group as a participating member.

The goal of training for competency is to allow the group therapist to gain a dual perspective: that of an objectively trained eye for the abstract processes that underlie the content of group interaction, and a subjectively trained sensibility for empathizing with the pain and suffering of the individuals who seek help. In addition, the group therapist must possess excellent psychological boundaries that prevent the loss of self in the often bewildering array of projections and projective identifications that bombard an individual who enters a group; paradoxically, these boundaries also permit psychological intimacy with colleagues and people in treatment.

The group therapist must also be skilled at introducing the public to group therapy and educating the public as to the benefits and limitations of group treatment. This aspect of marketing or "selling" group therapy to consumers is a necessary component of group therapy practice, because only one in one hundred persons will seek group therapy on their own. We know from our experience in the HMO industry that forty in one hundred persons are both suitable and appropriate for group therapy treatment. Therefore, it falls to the group therapist to educate the other thirty-nine. Such education involves the sale of an intangible product that must be convincingly presented by therapists who truly believe that groups can improve people's lives.

Educating the Organization

The managers and decision makers of the organization must understand the product they are promoting, because group therapy is a complex human *service* that matches skilled professionals with subscribers to the health plan who have specific, often pressing needs. For group therapy to be effective, the organization must clear the way so that clinicians can offer treatment and patients can choose treatment in group. Organization managers must learn how to create a context in which mental health services, and specifically group therapy programs, can be effectively used by patients.

First, the marketing division of the organization must bear fiscal responsibility not to sell more employer contracts than its clinical professionals can serve—nor to promise potential consumers services that the organization cannot deliver. To do so would undermine the morale of the treatment team and send a message to the consumer that the organization is not to be trusted—a chilling start for a service like group therapy, which for its successful completion requires basic trust, from initial contacts and clinical interventions to follow-up procedures.

Second, the organization must learn to appreciate the complexity of the tasks of starting and maintaining treatment groups. It must not pressure providers to assume the leadership of groups before the providers have received adequate preparation and resources to accomplish the task. The organization must allocate the necessary and sufficient resources for providers to do their jobs well. These resources—in addition to in-service training—include meeting rooms, lighting fixtures, and comfortable chairs that create a positive and healing ambience for group members. I once consulted with a manager who seriously considered cutting back on tissue boxes, not realizing their importance in the therapeutic environment. Such false economizing sends a negative message to both patients and clinicians and should be avoided. Suitable co-therapists will also be required for certain high-stress groups involving people suffering from deep and acute traumas and losses.

Third, the performance goals that management sets for group therapists must reflect a realistic understanding of what is possible. For example, to establish an arbitrary goal that each clinician lead four groups each week—or that the percentage of group visits relative to overall patient visits be increased to 30 percent within one year—will have a demoralizing effect for staff who may truly believe they are not working hard enough. A wise manager will not want to induce resentment among staff for failing to meet unattainable production goals, but rather will set up rewards for incremental growth that fit both the sophistication of the providers and the needs of the patients. Some rewards and incentives for providers include paid time off for professional enrichment and a reduction of clinical hours relative to time in the office.

CONSUMER TRUST IN THE ORGANIZATION

How the consumer views the organization as a whole reinforces either positively or negatively the outcomes of mental health treatment. This fact was brought home to me quite clearly when I completed a medical utilization review of selected group psychotherapy patients at the Group Health Cooperative of Puget Sound. We cover the study in detail as I consider the offset effect in Chapter Seven, but here I want to cite the relevant statistics that show the similarity in response between this experimental group of 115 group psychotherapy patients and a randomly selected sample of 5,664 consumers in two satisfaction surveys given independently during the same month by the Mental Health Service and the Administration of Puget Sound.

Overall Satisfaction with Treatment in Group Therapy

$N = 115$

Completely satisfied: 47 percent

Somewhat satisfied: 43 percent

Somewhat unsatisfied: 8.7 percent

Completely unsatisfied: 1 percent

Overall Satisfaction with Services at the Medical Center

$N = 5,664$

Completely satisfied: 48 percent

Moderately satisfied: 46 percent

Slightly unsatisfied: 4 percent

Not satisfied: 2 percent

After studying the striking similarity between the cooperative-wide consumer survey and our own group therapy consumer survey, we concluded that we had tapped into the expression of a larger phenomenon. Satisfaction or dissatisfaction was being reported for the medical and health services at the Group Health Cooperative of Puget Sound at large, including the mental health services provided by the group therapy program. This finding seems to correlate with Saul Feldman's observation: "More in mental health than in any other field, the way people feel about the organization in which they are receiving help has a major effect on the outcome of that help. In effect, the organization is an important part of the treatment."

The side-by-side comparison of these two studies is worthwhile because it portrays an operational definition of trust as expressed by healthcare consumers. Trust in the operation of the larger organization transfers to the trust subscribers feel for the quality of treatment they have received and expect to receive from their group therapists. The trust the organization demonstrates in training their clinicians translates into the trust and willingness that subscribers show by entering a therapy group. Building this context of trust is essential because of the dynamic connection between the individual and the organization.

In terms of general systems theory, this connection is an example of *isomorphy,* a term derived from the joining of two Greek words, meaning "the same form." Isomorphy means that in a complex system there are similar organizing structures that operate beneath the diverse contents of any system. The notion of isomorphy expresses the reciprocal relationships that exist between the organization and the individual within a specific context, the proper consideration of which is the work of organization development.

THE ROLE OF ORGANIZATION DEVELOPMENT

As we are beginning to see, the success of group therapy depends on organization development, which can be defined as the effort to understand and enhance the relationship between the individual and the organization in which he works or is a member. The individual always interacts with the organization within a specific context that includes historical, economic, sociological, political, philosophical, and psychological factors. Both the individual and the organization are embedded in the specific context, which becomes the matrix for all their interactions. The individual and the organization are influenced reciprocally by the context in which they interact. That context includes beliefs and values that are held by individuals personally, by the specific corporate culture as a whole, and by the nation, with its multifaceted and often contradictory social and cultural mores. A chief assumption of organization development is that attempts by the individual or the organization to change will always be facilitated or limited by the specific context in which they find themselves. Those who practice organization development help individuals and organizations make changes by analyzing the interactions between the organization and the individual to see what adaptations are possible given a specific context. Once a change is implemented, there must be a further effort to create a social and organizational context that supports and maintains that change over time.

One of the factors that has impeded the growth of group therapy in the mental health industry to this point has been the failure to grasp and employ the concepts of organization development. Too often, mental health managers have assumed incorrectly that clinical providers alone are responsible for the effective delivery of care to patients, forgetting that the values and policies of the organization and the needs and expectations of subscribers play equally powerful parts. When managers conceive of group therapy in terms of organization development, they pay greater attention to the context in which the patient receives help.

Of Bagels and Mental Health

Just the other day I saw two newspaper headlines in rough juxtaposition. The first read, "Noah's Bagels, Local Success Story, in Line for Corporate Buy Out." The second read, "Regional Mental Health Care Provider Considers Merger with the Largest Insurance Company in the Industry."

In both cases, the consumer has some reason to worry. She may wonder, Will my bagel taste as good as before? Will my neighbor who makes bagels lose his job? Will my healthcare dollar buy as much as it did before? Will my needs for mental healthcare be lost in the pursuit of bigness and efficiency?

These kinds of questions arise when changes occur that affect the context in which individuals and organizations interact. This is the meaning of organization development for me as an individual: How should I negotiate a path to getting what I want from an organization, given a particular set of opportunities and constraints?

Change

It is ironic that mental health professionals, many of whom consider themselves "agents of change," have been slow to embrace the notion that change is primarily a social phenomenon. Socially oriented change theorists have long perceived the group as a powerful instrument to effect change. For many years these theorists have found a home in the world of business and commerce, but not mental health. The joke has been: "If you want to study group interactions at the university level, enter the school of business, not psychology. Business knows that if you want to make money, you must learn how to function with people in groups." That statement is no less true now than in the past.

Even the best-trained group therapists will fail to prosper in an organization that does not allow them to succeed. The most carefully structured organization will not sustain group practices over time unless it provides group therapists ongoing training and supervision that focuses on forming personal boundaries, exploring projective identification, and the working through of countertransference.

In the absence of training in such preventive measures, group therapists face professional burnout and loss of productivity. Group therapists are highly exposed because they cannot hide their mistakes in the privacy of individual treatment. Group therapists are visible and vulnerable. It is imperative that the corporate culture establish and maintain organizational boundaries that conserve and nurture group therapists. Training and the positive incentives of appropriate organizational structure are inextricably linked, and together they create a practical alliance for success that must be thoughtfully crafted.

At both the level of the therapy group and the level of the corporation, the group is the social unit of change because in the group setting I can comprehend the context in which I as an individual interact with the organization. In a group, I will display the full range of my coping and defensive strategies in relation to others. I will obtain feedback from others about my own behavior and may quite often be surprised to learn that not all people experience me the same way. I may also be astonished to find that others perceive me in very similar ways. It becomes difficult for me to dismiss the characteristic ways that a number of observers see me, even if I am resistant to seeing myself that way. Their perceptions—whether positive or negative—reinforce the way I perceive myself. In the social unit of the group, I can also experience my own resistance to change and discover the organization's limitations, traditions, and customs that circumscribe my efforts to change.

I believe that as educators we have done a good job changing the attitude of the public toward mental health treatment as a force for positive change in the quality of people's lives. There is now a growing expectation that mental health coverage will be provided as part of the return for our healthcare dollar. Health planners and providers must come up with new ideas in the delivery of mental health services to meet the growing consumer demand. As part of this process, the organization must explore and adopt special strategies to champion group therapy.

NINE WAYS TO ENCOURAGE GROUP THERAPY

It might be helpful at this point to compare two organizations and how they constructed their group therapy programs. I intend this to be an object lesson in what to avoid and what actions to take in order to improve and expand group treatment delivery.

While employed as group psychotherapy coordinator at Puget Sound, in my capacity as an external consultant I had the opportunity to study the department of psychiatry for a large health maintenance organization in northern California, hereafter called Northern California. This gave me the unique opportunity to examine the Northern California system and compare it with the system at Puget Sound on the dimension of group therapy delivery. At the time of my comparative study, 40 percent of all patient visits at Puget Sound were group therapy visits, whereas fewer than 10 percent of all patient visits were group therapy visits at Northern California. My study is now dated, but the principles of sound organizational structure that promote group therapy apply as much today as they did then.

Let's consider nine aspects of organizational structure and decision making that have a direct impact on the operation of a group therapy program.

1.   The first aspect is *differential pricing*. In my study, Northern California allowed no differential pricing between the two modes of treatment—group therapy and individual therapy. One patient visit equaled one patient visit regardless of modality or length of time consumed by the provider. In contrast, Puget Sound allowed for pricing differences between modes of treatment. This became one of the cornerstones of the group program because it gave consumers an incentive to consider and consent to referrals to a therapy group.

We found differential pricing both ethical and consumer-conscious, because it passes along to the consumer savings that the provider enjoys. It conforms to the community standard of practice that has long recognized the cost savings of group compared to individual treatment. The practice also conveys a subtle and powerful message to the consumer: "Your wise choice of group therapy is acknowledged and appreciated."

2.   The second aspect is the *inclusion of master's level clinicians and nurses* as practitioners of group therapy. The Northern California program at that time excluded master's level clinicians (Marriage, Family, and Child Counselors and master's degree in nursing) from conducting groups. Such a policy is misguided: it excludes some of the better trained and most-experienced group therapists, group therapy supervisors, and group therapy program managers from participating. In the absence of a doctorate in group psychotherapy, which has

never been conferred by any university or college in the United States, the possession of a doctorate itself does not qualify a professional in the clinical practice of group psychotherapy.

As indicated earlier, a degree in business may in some respects better prepare group professionals than a degree in a mental health discipline. Only recently has an attempt been made by the American Group Psychotherapy Association to codify what constitutes a trained group therapist, and then only at a minimal standard of competence. The attempt is laudable: it embraces master's level clinicians and cites the kind of training, experience, and supervision necessary to meet the minimum standard. In contrast to Northern California, Puget Sound welcomed master's level nurses and family counselors, who brought diversity and breadth of experience, training, and organizational expertise to the group program.

3. The Northern California system adopted a strict hierarchical (vertical) organization that followed the medical model. In such a structure, psychiatric physicians dominated the organization's decision making and resource allocation, such as utilization of space and support staff time, with psychologists and social workers bringing up the rear in descending order. Unfortunately, such hierarchies among clinicians stifle the free flow of referrals between therapists that is so necessary for the sustenance and replenishment of psychotherapy groups. *Functional equivalence among the various clinical disciplines* for most kinds of therapeutic care must be respected; this alone permits clinicians to refer with confidence to appropriate groups conducted by a variety of qualified clinicians. At Puget Sound, this meant that psychiatrists, psychologists, social workers, nurses, and other master's level clinicians were considered equivalent for general treatment responsibility.

Such a practice does not deny the variety of expertise on staff or among members of a treatment team (knowledge of psychotropic medication and psychological testing being two examples). However, it does permit a collegial atmosphere in which group referrals can be made across the lines of the various professional disciplines without the prohibitions that exist in a hierarchical system. A doctor can refer in confidence to a master's level clinician with the sure knowledge that competent care will be given. An organization can thereby avoid unnecessary division and conflict within the group program. Patients are sensitive to the attitudes and beliefs of their referring therapists to such an extent that patients' expectations of help and positive outcomes can be built in or sabotaged depending on the degree of enthusiasm with which the referral is made.

4. Puget Sound adopted functional equivalence among clinicians because of its early dedication to democratic principles as a consumer cooperative. As a fourth aspect of organizational structure, it cannot be overstated that *equality is one of the most important underlying values that permit the establishment of group therapy programs and the treatment of patients therein.* We must always remember that at some level, the members of every viable therapy group seek to create a kind of fairness among themselves even in the face of severe pathology. In a system that keeps this principle at the forefront, the consumer remains the focus for satisfaction, not the provider nor the clinic manager.

In the Northern California plan at that time, physicians became the "customers" to be satisfied rather than the mental health consumers who came seeking relief of their sorrows and suffering. This is a hazard that cost management people can easily fall into when they think of mental health services *only* as a product. It is essential for them to remember that what is being delivered is a *service* and that the judgment of what is effective and satisfying treatment ultimately rests with the consumers themselves. In the corporate management of mental health, I believe cost managers have taken the place of physicians in many respects, creating a new kind of hierarchy that can also compromise group therapy programs if these managers refuse to recognize the people who receive the care as the first priority.

When I say that the dynamics of one system (functional equivalence of clinical staff at the provider level) influence the dynamics of another system (the capacity of clinical staff to communicate enthusiasm to a patient about a therapy group) and also influence the dynamics of a third system (the ability of therapy group members to form a group and relate to each other as peers), I am again speaking from the perspective of isomorphy, the concept of general systems theory and organization development introduced earlier. Isomorphy, often called parallel process, exists at many levels of the complex systems that make up a comprehensive group psychotherapy delivery program. I discuss this concept at greater length in Chapter Eleven, Phases of Group Therapy Development.

5.   In the Puget Sound system, *highly skilled and trained entry personnel effected a triage of patients, discussed the treatment options—including group therapy when appropriate—and generally prepared the patient with the expectation that group therapy may be offered, and if it is, will probably be successful.* The group therapy coordinator and other clinical professionals devoted many hours to the selection and training of entry staff so that they could carry out their mandate to introduce the first-time consumer to the Mental Health Service, reduce delays in service, facilitate the entry of some patients into immediate-access groups, and build in an expectation of help at the initial point of contact with the patient.

Instruction in triage procedure allows entry personnel to separate callers into three categories: emerging crisis, manageable anxiety or conflict, and potential long-term care. Persons assigned to each of these categories are given an appointment with a therapist, with the exception of some patients in crisis who can be referred directly to a crisis-type group. As I have stated previously, trust is a behavior that finds isomorphic resonance at various levels of the complex systems that make up the group therapy program. Management and professional staff must trust the special training program for entry personnel and their ability to make skillful judgments in order to accept the entry staff's referrals to psychotherapy groups. The group psychotherapists must trust the patients to follow through with the commitments and contracts they make in groups. And patients must trust that their clinicians have the skills needed to help them.

In contrast, the Northern California system provided no trained entry personnel to triage patients on the phone or in person. The expectation that group therapy might be offered was never discussed by the secretary who fielded all calls and set up individual appointments. Secretaries were untrained in the most basic of interview skills.

In order to reach the thirty-nine out of one hundred people who are appropriate for group but do not request it, those staffing the entry positions must have specific training. The training should be limited in scope but broad enough to encompass predictable situations that require a high degree of confidence to execute. A wise clinic manager will want some of her best and most adept people at the front desk to interface with the consumers as they enter the system.

6.   Puget Sound *embraced the co-therapy model* for over 50 percent of its groups. The success of the group therapy program can be

demonstrated by the successful collaboration and communication among staff members. The existence of highly competent co-therapy teams is an indication that this kind of cooperation is widespread within the entire mental health service and is further evidence of positive isomorphy at work.

Although seemingly paradoxical in a program that wants to be less labor intensive, co-therapy sets in motion a powerful reciprocal incentive for conducting psychotherapy groups. Co-therapists who like to work together look for opportunities to do so, and start more groups. The more groups the co-therapists do together, the more they learn to like each other and the more effective and productive they become as a team. This definition of productivity includes the variable of work environment, which includes facilities, climate for effective communication, and employee opportunities to find satisfaction and professional growth in collaboration with each other.

For example, if two therapists can manage only two groups each week on their own but can conduct six groups each week working together, the goal of higher output is served. This illustrates the way co-therapy allows synergy to flourish in the group therapy program. *Synergy* is here defined as a synthesis of the skills and knowledge of two persons and can be expressed as "one plus one equals more than two." The combination of two therapists augments and expands the capabilities of both. A mature co-therapy team brings higher energy into group formation and new life to the leadership function.

As I indicated previously, therapists' behavior and the possibility for change as they interact with their environment and each other are the most crucial factors in the enhancement of productivity. By comparison, the Northern California system generally eschewed the co-therapy model—either because it might threaten the vertical hierarchy of clinical disciplines, or, lacking a deeper understanding of the meaning of productivity, Northern California perceived co-therapy as wasteful, expending two therapists when only one would do. One of my most productive group experiments came about when I shared the leadership of a crisis group with an entry-level person who was in training with me. Although this is not co-therapy as we define it because the two persons are not equal in experience or knowledge, the formation of such teams, called *nequipo teams,* facilitated the training of staff in group therapy. In this particular case, my entry-level assistant helped us streamline the direct referral of patients from entry to a treatment group by efficiently bridging the two.

7.   At Puget Sound, *group psychotherapy was perceived as a primary form of psychotherapeutic treatment and the treatment of choice for many conditions.* This perception was communicated both directly and indirectly to consumers, making referral to group highly desirable. The practices of clinical professionals and the attitude conveyed by the managers at the highest level of the healthcare system must embody this perception.

At Northern California, group psychotherapy was institutionalized as a secondary or "inferior" form of treatment. Once this notion is communicated to consumers, referral to group therapy becomes almost impossible once individual therapy has commenced.

Mental health delivery systems that adopt group therapy for economic reasons alone and continue to believe that group therapy is the inferior alternative to individual treatment will inevitably communicate that message to their patients, and the group therapy program will suffer as a result. I want to emphasize that differential pricing of individual and group modalities, as I recommended previously, does not convey unequal respect or regard for the cheaper mode of treatment. In other words, because group therapy costs less does not mean it is worth less. If the primacy of group therapy for many conditions becomes a value of the institution, consumers will believe they are getting as much or more quality service for less money when they are offered group therapy.

8.   At Northern California, the group therapy program was structurally weakened by an unwillingness to put centralized decision making authority in the hands of a coordinator who had specialized in group treatment and was dedicated to teaching the principles of group process. In my experience, whenever I observed group therapy flowering either moderately or extravagantly in whatever setting, there was always one person committed on a daily basis to the organization, operation, and development of groups. *A group therapy coordinator, who has the authority to allocate resources, train and supervise professionals, and organize and develop groups, is an essential component in the development of a group therapy program.* A group therapy coordinator must organize the program with an eye to the entire system of delivery, being cognizant of how the system affects the formation of groups at every level. At Puget Sound, the group therapy coordinator not only assumed management responsibility for group development but became chief training officer for sixty clinicians in the field

of group therapy. In that capacity, I organized seminars and training opportunities for my colleagues and made myself available to them as a supervisor.

9.   Related to the functional role of the group therapy coordinator, *a viable group program must provide for ongoing training and supervision in the area of group psychotherapy.* Quite simply, Northern California did not provide those learning opportunities in a comprehensive or systematic way, and Puget Sound did. The presence of ongoing training in group therapy for staff produced a salutary effect on the morale of my colleagues. A greater esprit de corps was in evidence. Training of this sort gave to therapists a powerful message of their importance to the system. Therapists were being told that their work was valued enough that resources were set aside for the enrichment of their skills, and this became a potent antidote against demoralization and burnout.

I have enumerated these nine aspects of organizational structure and decision making in order to demonstrate the scope of the comprehensive planning that must go into the creation of groups in any institution or system of referral that presumes to offer group psychotherapy to its subscribers. In subsequent chapters, I will return to these aspects to further elaborate their significance. Just as they establish a context for a group therapy delivery system, so other factors create a historical context that must be considered as well.

Why does it take so much time to put these aspects in place? Can the start-up time for a group program be condensed by skillful management, focused training, and external consultation? What are the forces that resist change in a system of mental health delivery? How do changes become a part of the culture of an organization? These subjects will be addressed next.

CHAPTER TWO

Resistances to Group Therapy

Why does it take so much time and effort to create a group psychotherapy program? An interesting conflict of values emerges from the rise of group therapy practice. That conflict is the face-off between the profit motive on one hand and the belief in rugged individualism on the other. This larger context must not be undervalued as a cause for much of the ambivalence about implementing group therapy delivery to appropriate populations.

Economic good sense shows group therapy a winner. However, when the desire to lower costs of delivery and increase profits is matched against the powerful mythology of the rugged individualist, and the equally strong desire to find individual solutions to personal problems, there is a collision of values that confounds the patient, the caregiver, and the system in which the care is given. Let's look at some of the ideas behind this conflict.

THE INDIVIDUAL AND THE GROUP

A central human paradox is confronted each time a person affiliates with a group: "Only I can truly know myself—and yet I feel terribly alienated and alone unless I am known by others." Existentially, a man or woman in group *is* different than when alone. The shattering power of this experience calls into question many of our cherished assumptions about human nature, such as the enduring nature of identity and personality over time and place. Such unsettling experiences in group, where the defenses of individuals are laid open and the vulnerability of the individual exposed, become a terrifying prospect for the individual who rigidly holds to the belief that he is somehow immune to such influences.

Both Jacksonian and Jeffersonian democracy, as it is espoused and practiced in the United States, presuppose a self-reliant individual who only gives up his or her rights, and then only provisionally, for the common good. The idea of giving up one's right to privacy for one's *own* good is alien to the free-thinking individualist.

The guiding light for rationalism in the eighteenth-century Enlightenment, when ideas about democracy were reawakening, was René Descartes. The Cartesian world was a world in which individuals endeavored to understand reality based on each individual's perceptions, like little islands of consciousness working independently to perceive the whole. Communication between these individuals was possible for practical purposes but not necessary to the understanding of the self, which could be divined through reflection and introspection.

The idea that the self was an *intersubjective* construction fashioned out of the necessity to communicate with others and dependent to a large degree on the perception of others, took hold in the late nineteenth and early twentieth centuries. There is now a large body of clinical data from social psychology, including group therapy, supporting this notion. However, Americans for the most part remain Cartesian in their thinking and assumptions about themselves.

I believe these forces of philosophy, myth, and national and cultural identity shape the historical context of our lives and quite unconsciously undermine our honest efforts to forge group therapy programs in the United States. Thus, despite strong economic incentives to provide group treatment, there are for many people equally strong sociological, cultural, and personal reasons to oppose entering group psychotherapy, and their reasons for opposition find considerable support in what Americans believe about themselves and tell each other they believe.

THE POWER OF HISTORICAL CONTEXTS

Alexis de Tocqueville, that astute observer of nineteenth-century American habits and customs, noted one of the defining characteristics of United States' culture that distinguished it from the monarchies of Europe. "Americans," he said, "are born free, not made so." It was apparent to the Frenchman that, with the exception of blacks who were brought to America as slaves, Americans enjoyed an atmosphere of freedom that was their birthright—not something hard won by struggle or rivalry with others. This single characteristic, invisible and unconsciously experienced, set Americans apart and endowed them with certain traits and predictable kinds of behavior. For de Tocqueville, this was the historical context of liberty in which the American character was shaped.

In similar fashion, and on a smaller scale, we can expect historical contexts of various kinds to shape the behavior of organizations that manage mental health delivery. Within a specific historical context, the chief assumptions may go unchallenged because they are invisible to the people who hold them. Managed mental health organizations have radically changed the financing, management, and utilization review of individual treatment as practiced by the fee-for-service mental health professionals; ironically, they have also, without exception, adopted the prejudices and practices of the fee-for-service community in their neglect of group psychotherapy delivery. U.S. Behavioral Health, a major managed mental healthcare organization, will serve as an example.

U.S. Behavioral Health was founded by individuals who had deep roots in the community mental health movement, a movement that endeavored to make mental health services more readily available to the public and sought to employ methods of intervention appropriate to the populations served. The goals of community mental health were immediate access, timely intervention, early diagnosis, and short-term treatment—referring patients to the private sector of providers within the community when more in-depth, long-term psychotherapy was needed or requested by the patients themselves. Group therapy was a part of the community mental health movement from the beginning, and yet it is important to recall that community mental health, even at its height, never utilized group psychotherapy to anywhere approaching its full potential. Similarly, U.S. Behavioral Health has never realized its potential as a provider of group therapy services.

In 1994, the chairman of the board of U.S. Behavioral Health did a survey of its exclusive network of providers organized in group practices at specific geographic locations throughout the United States. The survey revealed that only one site used group psychotherapy for 40 percent of all patient visits. Most sites reported group therapy utilization rates of 10 percent or less. In light of this organization's avowedly friendly posture toward group therapy, how can we explain this outcome?

In the case of U.S. Behavioral Health, the structuring of the benefit package such that the patient's co-payment for group therapy is the same as for individual therapy is certainly not an incentive for patients to enter groups. Also, in the absence of capitation, the fact that providers—especially psychiatrists—can make more money treating a patient individually for fifty minutes than in a small group for ninety minutes, without the trouble of organizing a group, is another impediment. Yet these two factors account for only a part of this phenomenon. The larger issue is the historical context in which group therapy is perceived.

COMMON MISPERCEPTIONS OF GROUP THERAPY

In behavioral psychology, it is axiomatic that it's easier to change behavior than to change attitudes and beliefs. Yet if our attitudes and beliefs prevent us from being effective as psychotherapists, it behooves us ethically to change as much as we can. This is particularly true when our beliefs and prejudices match those of our patients—and we reinforce their own fears and superstitions consciously or unconsciously by our avoidance of group therapy. In this complex process, therapists may project their own fears onto their patients, then watch the patients identify with the fears and act them out accordingly by avoiding group treatment. The attitude and beliefs of providers and managers for managed mental health, whether staff model HMOs or point-of-service, independent practitioner networks, are crucial to the functioning or nonfunctioning of psychotherapy groups. When their attitudes and beliefs are influenced by the historical context—as they must be—the effect can be prejudicial in the extreme.

Some commonly held beliefs about groups that derive directly from the historical context of the United States are elucidated here. I will address six common beliefs that adhere to our culture and language; for each of these beliefs I will also offer an alternative interpretation of group therapy that significantly shifts the frame in which it is usually perceived.

Fewer Choices for the Individual

In one of the earliest documents of the nation, *The Federalist Papers*, James Madison expressed the suspicion that groups, or as he called them, factions, might become a threat to the liberty of the individual by invoking the "tyranny of the majority." This belief persists in the fear that I will have fewer choices in a group than I have as an individual, because I will be forced to do as others want. A corollary to that fear is that I will have to listen to others and never be heard myself.

Many people experience the loss of choice in their families of origin because they had to compete with siblings or, in some cases, with parents for what they wanted. They bring that perception to group, where they expect their wishes to be severely limited by the demands of others more powerful or deserving than they. The notion that participation in group can actually expand a person's range of choices is novel, and is met with disbelief by more skeptical group members. Yet groups constantly strive for fairness among their members, and "Let's take turns choosing," is a commonly articulated sentiment.

It simply is not true that I have more choices as an individual than as a member of a group. I realize that this fact would not be so readily apparent to me had I never been a member of a group. There are three continua of choice that encompass the experience of people both in groups and alone. Whether I stand as an individual or with others, my experience of these continua is essentially the same.

The first continuum ranges from "No Choice" to "Too Many Choices." The one side of this continuum expresses the sadness and rage of being a victim, as in "I would not have done it, but I had no choice." The other side of this continuum expresses the overwhelming omnipresence of freedom, as in "I can't escape being free even if I want to."

The second continuum ranges from "Refusing Choice" to "Embracing Choice." The one end of this continuum voices the wish to remain in doubt, as if by doing so I could entertain the illusion of endless possibility. The other end of the continuum voices my belief in finitude and the painful, exquisite loss and exhilaration I experience by choosing one direction and not the other.

The third continuum ranges from "Making the Wrong Choice" to "Making the Right Choice." Both positions firmly fix me in the realm of judgment, which determines my emotional responses. If I choose wrongly, I can be hopeful that I'll choose more wisely in the future; or, feeling irreverent, I can claim that it doesn't really matter how I choose.

If I choose rightly, I can be fearful that I won't be so lucky next time; or, feeling reverent, I can aspire even more fervently to choose wisely in the future.

Groups Are Inherently Fearful

Fear is the emotion most commonly reported by people entering therapy groups of any kind or size, and this phenomenon becomes the thesis around which I develop criteria for the readiness of a clinician to conduct groups (see Chapter Nine). People want to avoid groups because groups are perceived as scary: unpredictable things happen, people become angry and unruly, and as the process becomes chaotic, people resort to violence. I can project my fantasies of violence on others and then become frightened by my own projections.

Group leaders themselves are not immune to fear. To learn to understand and manage one's own fear in group is one of the central goals of training and supervision in group therapy. Normalization of fear as a defining experience in group becomes a goal for both patients and leaders. Providing information about the groups to patients before entry can diminish their anxiety somewhat, yet the existential impact of fear remains—and emerges for most people in our culture in any social setting or group where they are called upon to speak about themselves. Focal group psychotherapy lessens the fear of the patient (and the therapist) by establishing highly structured group interactions that focus on the achievement of goals that are stated and defined in operational terms.

However, people gather in groups not to frighten themselves but to garner courage from their association and exchange with others. If fear is the most commonly expressed emotion early in a group's formation, courage is the quality most frequently admired by group members in the later stages of development. Perseverance, tenacity, and even stubbornness come to be appreciated as valuable assets by a group that has faced its anxieties, stayed committed to each other, and, through struggle, increased the self-esteem of its members.

The Individual Gets Lost in the Crowd

Another belief is that I will become lost in the group. My wish to be seen is primary, and my belief that I will not be seen can be a torment. "No one will see me. I'll be invisible. If I am seen, it will not be for who I am but simply how another person wants me to be. I'll be manipulated into being someone I am not." People often say these phrases to themselves as they anticipate joining a therapy group.

The truth is that groups have the capability to acknowledge the existence and value of members in a way that is quite unlike any other. Group members act as mirrors for each other, and in those mirrors we can see ourselves very close to the way others see us. In this regard, groups are most efficient in reducing the deleterious effects of the "Don't Be Important" injunction that so many people with low self-esteem carry around inside them. Group members are witnesses to each other's lives. People learn how much they matter because they are listened to and their stories are remembered and retold in the group. Far from being lost, the standard operating procedure of cohesive groups is to make sure that all of their members are seen and heard, that all have roles to play in the work of the group.

Group Interaction Kills Introspection

There is a belief that my intense involvement with a group reduces my capacity for introspection. In fact, the opposite is the case. There is no opposition between group relations and probing deeply into the self. Group therapy stimulates deeper reflections on the self because individuals see so many parts of themselves in others, and this perception awakens the individual to an inner life to which she may have been oblivious.

The Individual Lacks Privacy in Groups

The group violates the privacy of the individual. The curiosity of others is corrosive and will not help me attain knowledge of myself but will cause shame and embarrassment as I expose myself to other people's eyes.

It is true that group members will probe each other for information and personal details, yet this curiosity can also be viewed as a sign of caring and interest by fellow human beings. One of the key boundaries that individuals must establish in group therapy is the capacity at any point to say no to interrogations. This is a fundamental assertion of the sovereignty of the individual, which paradoxically must exist if the group is to develop a true sense of intimacy among members. From the very beginning, the group therapist must strengthen this value as a cornerstone of group construction. One of the most powerful learning experiences possible in group is the discovery that the sharing of private thoughts and memories, in the proper context, will serve to deepen their meaning in our lives.

Patients Don't Want Conflict

This belief seems intimately tied up with the projections of therapists who, as a class, tend to be placaters and conflict wary. The eighteenth-century thinkers, including the authors of *The Federalist Papers,* knew that the central political significance of groups was conflict—a fact that modern clinicians often want to ignore. But what are the clinical consequences of conflict?

For many group members, conflict in their families of origin implied the possible loss of love or loss of control such that acts of abandonment or violence might occur. Conflict inevitably brings group members into emotional engagement with each other. Such engagement can prove to be quite positive, although at the time it may seem to the group that the opposite is true. The feeling of universalization and oneness is exploded by the comprehension of real differences in personalities and interests. Idealization collapses also, if the therapist herself is the object of attack. Group therapists must be willing and able to keep the focus on the conflict, lest the attention of the group be diverted in other directions.

The positive outcome for persons who can tolerate anger in their treatment group is the insight they can obtain when they see the resolution or cessation of the conflict without physical damage or loss of self-esteem.

A NEW WAY TO PERCEIVE GROUPS

An innovative program must create a new paradigm as a substitute for the ways in which groups have been perceived historically. Sometimes the paradigm created may seem counterintuitive or paradoxical, as expressed in the statements "Groups of strangers are often easier to talk to than a single friend," or "The distance group members perceive between themselves and their leader can sometimes be more helpful than the closeness they perceive in individual therapy." The former is a statement often made by group members in clinical settings; the latter is a construct derived from experiments in social psychology that has practical utility in the treatment of borderline personality disorders. The effort to embrace a positive paradigm for the individual's experience in the group must continue, not to "sell" the prospective group candidates on the modality but to realign the thinking of clinicians who buy into the chief assumptions of the historical context in which groups have been perceived. Such backward thinking stifles the creativity needed to experiment with new approaches to treatment.

I recall the trepidation with which many clinicians viewed our first homogeneous group for depressed outpatients at Puget Sound. The superstition of group contagion filled the air. Images of patients dragging each other lower and lower into the depths of melancholic oblivion fraught the minds of my colleagues. In fact, as we continued the experiment and started more of these groups, we discovered the tremendous potential for fun that was released in such groups. Patients who had developed exquisitely attuned senses of humor began to reveal themselves after they first tested if we in the group would accept them in their most depressed states. (I report in detail on this group in Chapter Three, where I describe it as an example of a group structured in response to an assessment of patient needs.)

An even greater fear of contagion swept the clinic when we began groups for parasuicidal patients, that is, people who had all tried to kill themselves at least once. Legal counsel for our malpractice insurance was put on alert. Tiresome jokes of "Jim Jones and his Kool-Aid club" abounded. Despite the research data of Rosen, Motto, Asimos, and Billings, which demonstrated the success of such groups, fear and prejudice reigned supreme in the minds of many of our colleagues.

Ultimately, we found in practice that the patients in this homogeneous, open-ended group strongly bonded to each other, and their cohesion served to prevent repeated attempts at suicide. This one group was able to offset the medical costs of repeated emergency care and hospitalizations that amounted to thousands of dollars.

Other paradigm shifts include further paradoxes, such as the following:

- An individual can discover more about himself in a group of strangers than he can talking with a gathering of those he knows well.

- A good deal of what is usually called external or social in human life is at the same time deeply internal and of powerful dynamic influence as the individual develops. Groups allow an individual to explore relations with others and at the same time probe deeper into the self.

- The better my personal boundaries, the closer I can allow myself to be with others in a group.

In the effort to establish an historical context in which group therapy can thrive, the role of group therapy coordinator takes on great significance because it is that person's job to call into question the commonly held beliefs about groups and to symbolize the realization of a different paradigm for understanding groups.

THE ROLE OF THE GROUP THERAPY COORDINATOR

As I indicated in Chapter One, a group therapy coordinator is an essential component in the development of a group therapy program. By outlining the salient features of the job description, I'll show how the group therapy coordinator, when given the proper authority, can redefine the historical context in which group therapy is provided and create new models for perceiving groups. The following five points summarize the duties the coordinator must perform in order to make this transformation possible.

Program and Organization Development

A program begins with ideas, and the group therapy coordinator must become a source of ideas. These ideas may be new approaches to a familiar patient population, or familiar approaches to a newly identified patient population, or innovative ways to facilitate the referral of people to groups. Not all ideas are workable, so the coordinator must have the daring to test new ideas that, if proven viable, can be adopted as standard of practice by the entire HMO staff or the whole network of independent providers. Clinicians in either setting will be slow to experiment because they lack the authority to initiate or they allow their negative perceptions of groups to dissuade them. The wish to look good to their peers is a very understandable motivation for maintaining the status quo. By contrast, the group therapy coordinator is being paid to bend if not break the status quo in relation to how groups come into being.

As group therapy coordinator at Puget Sound, I sought the advice and consent of the Group Therapy Committee, composed of fellow group colleagues, in order to set program goals and arrange priorities for the kinds of groups needed, the duration of groups, and the physical space required. I implemented program decisions through cooperation with the clinic manager, clinic chief, and fellow clinicians. Together, we selected therapists to initiate and develop needed groups at the Mental Health Service. In addition, the group therapy coordinator must create a context in which group decision making is possible, one that focuses the attention on process issues as they affect the everyday operation of the staff or network of providers at large. Such issues include the anticipation of conflict, and its prevention and resolution among clinicians, between clinicians and management, and between clinicians and nonclinical support personnel. Attention to process in the organization becomes the work of the coordinator because she cannot perform her primary task of group expansion and coordination if conflict or confusion blocks the communication process in the larger organization. The group therapy coordinator must have the authority to initiate, when appropriate, the skillful application of her knowledge of group dynamics to the organization as a whole.

Program Management

The group therapy coordinator must become a highly visible, readily accessible manager of the group program. She must be the first to explain the position and defend the priorities of the group program to decision makers in the organization. Group therapists must feel that the group therapy coordinator is their advocate with both clinical and top management in the organization. The group therapists' perception of the coordinator as their advocate is central to their willingness to take risks in the interest of providing group services. Without strong leadership as exhibited by highly vocal and vigorous advocacy of groups in the system, group therapists will lose confidence in their own ability to sustain groups over time.

The group therapy coordinator must be focused on both expansion and coordination in the discharge of her duties. In the area of expansion, she must build incentives for consumers to utilize groups and for therapists to lead them. She must also plan and anticipate for greater program capacity to accommodate increased patient demand for groups, as a result of improved systems of referral.

In the area of coordination, the coordinator must design, with the help of the Group Therapy Committee, an equitable system to spread existing and potential referrals among the several groups available. At the same time, she must streamline the referral system, keeping in mind sound clinical judgment, to help group therapists find appropriate people for their groups and prevent a backlog of patients waiting for groups. In this capacity, she will organize the task of making group referrals from entry personnel to group screening interviews by clinicians, or when suitable, directly into treatment groups. In all aspects of coordination, the group therapy coordinator should work in close collaboration with the group therapy program assistant, who carries out decisions and whose vital tasks are outlined in Chapter Three.

Direct Clinical Practice

The group therapy coordinator models the very essence of a group therapist, conducting as many or more groups than any person on staff or within the provider network. By example, this person leads other clinicians into thinking, "If she can do it, maybe I can too." The coordinator need not be an outstanding group clinician, only a very competent one. In fact, a clinician that is *too* good at groups— and too willing to let everyone know about it—can prove a detriment to a group program. Hubris is not a leadership quality that endears colleagues nor does it bode well for teaching others a complicated skill.

While at Puget Sound, I would take the opportunity to work with any clinician as a co-therapist in a group they were beginning in order to help provide momentum during the start-up period. Often, these pairings were nequipo teams, because the clinician with whom I shared the group leadership was neither equal in experience nor equal in knowledge with me. The task in these teams was to supervise and assist the clinician in becoming more of a peer in the field of group therapy. I stress the importance of these teams to the overall vitality of the organization in Chapter Five.

Consulting and Teaching

The group therapy coordinator is in a unique position to reinforce positive beliefs about group process among clinic staff or network providers. He can disseminate information pertinent to developments in group psychotherapy and group process and act as a resource person in these fields. In this capacity, he can act as a resource person to consult with providers and management concerning issues of group process in general.

At Puget Sound, I conducted regular weekly seminars on topics essential to the practice of group therapy. These seminars were scheduled at times most convenient for therapists to attend. My job description called for me to visit various point-of-service sites in order to facilitate advanced learning in group therapy. Most of these teaching opportunities took place in group supervision or seminar formats, although I was available to consult with therapists requesting supervision about their treatment groups. These supervision sessions were face to face when possible, but I found that once I established initial rapport with a colleague, I was able to supervise successfully by telephone. In this way, I was able to encourage professionals within our organization to develop their skills as group therapists.

Evaluation and Research

The group therapy coordinator, with the advice and consent of the Group Therapy Committee, plans and organizes ways to define and evaluate the success of treatment groups in terms of meeting patient goals, clinician goals, and management goals. This is always an ongoing process. Instruments to evaluate and provide feedback to clinicians and administrators should be developed in collaboration with committee members. The group therapy coordinator must have the authority to seek help outside the organization, when necessary, to find the expertise he needs to create meaningful evaluation procedures.

The group therapy coordinator should also design and implement simplified research studies concerning the effectiveness of groups in treating patients, as well as studies that reveal the effect of increased group utilization on the morale and esprit de corps of the organization as a whole. Of particular interest to managed care mental health organizations are studies that attempt to measure the degree to which timely and appropriate mental health intervention offsets the cost of medical expenditures for the same set of patients. In Chapter Seven, I report on one patient study we designed at Puget Sound that looked at the dimensions of both consumer satisfaction and the offset effect.

After the many resistances to group have been at least confronted, if not surmounted, managers and clinicians can begin to consider the various processes of group formation. The next chapter addresses this subject and gives examples of how to proceed in creating groups.

CHAPTER THREE

Forming Groups

—◁◁◁▷—

Group formation begins with an idea of how people ought to be assembled and a theory of how, in that context, they might improve their chances for health and happiness. Most ideas for assembling patients spring from perceived similarities based on what people have experienced and how they think and act, with the assumption that the closer the match between the people gathered, the better the outlook for progress. Most theories for improvement share the assumption that people must interact in some way in order for personal changes to come about. Both of these concepts have generally proven quite useful in the practice of group psychotherapy, and have alleviated suffering and enhanced the quality of lives. Let's take a closer look at the manifold and intricate ways that groups can form.

It has been customary for comprehensive group therapy programs to organize treatment groups on the basis of two criteria: (1) the presenting symptoms or underlying pathology of the patients and (2) the theoretical approach of the therapists conducting the groups—cognitive-behavioral, psycho-educational, psychodynamic, interpersonal, Transactional Analysis, object relations, and systems theories, among others. In practice, this means that treatment groups are formed around the way patients' needs are perceived by entry personnel and diagnosing clinicians and the way group therapists believe the treatment should proceed. In forming groups, three questions are salient for group therapists: Who shall attend? How will they get there? What will we do once they have arrived? In theory, these three steps should flow as a seamless whole. In practice, their integration is far from seamless, and the details of how each step is accomplished is well worth examining. In this chapter, we look at the complexity of both patient selection and therapist theoretical approach as they combine in the formation of treatment groups. How patients get to the right groups is the focus of Chapter Four.

PATIENT SELECTION: THE COMPLEXITY OF A HOMOGENEOUS GROUP STRUCTURE

Most therapy groups provided by managed mental healthcare systems will be labeled according to the presenting problems of the participating patients (crisis groups, male battering groups, coping-with-loss groups) or their symptoms and illnesses (depression groups, eating disorder groups, posttraumatic stress groups). Entry units or referring clinicians will then send patients to these groups in an attempt more or less to match the homogeneity presupposed by the group names. Various theoretical methods are then applied to the people assembled. It's important to examine the structure of these homogeneous groups.

Leo Tolstoy commented that "All happy families resemble one another, but each unhappy family is unhappy in its own way." It seems compelling, then, for group therapists to find out how each of the members in their homogeneous groups suffer in their own characteristic fashion.

Homogeneity is stressed in the literature of short-term or time-limited group therapy as a factor in allowing rapid cohesion to occur. The unifying themes around which groups have traditionally been organized have been age related (mastering an adult developmental task, such as retirement or parenthood), symptom related (managing depression), crisis related (coping with the stress of divorce or job loss), related to chronic illness or death (coping with the loss of a loved one or the pain and anxiety associated with chronic illness), or trauma or violence related (groups for battering males or survivors of abuse). It is important to note that even with the best intentions of clinicians in selecting patients for their groups, in practice the so-called homogeneous groups will have a good number of each of these themes present at any one time. Thus, the person who finds herself referred to a depressed group may discover people in crisis, suffering from a chronic illness, or facing the death of an aging parent. The label given a particular group is most useful to clinicians in organizing people into convenient units for treatment, but the label can never completely define the treatment process that evolves for the individuals in a specific group. As the systems thinker Ludwig von Bertalanffy has said, "The map is not the territory." We should not mistake useful theoretical constructs, such as homogeneous groups, for the actual groups in which people struggle to affiliate and differentiate from others.

In a certain sense, all people who enter group therapy belong to a homogeneous group, that is, that set of people who have chosen to join a group for whatever reason. We know that people who do, represent a minority—although a significant one—of all the people who seek mental healthcare. We know there are factors, such as access to information about group therapy, the availability of groups, and the general appropriateness of patients, that strongly influence who joins. If there are self-selecting factors at work in the process of why a person chooses to enter group therapy, we know virtually nothing about them. Given that all people who enter group have at least one thing in common by virtue of their membership in a group, it seems important to investigate both what brought them to group and the similarities and differences among them.

Undoubtedly, patients can identify best with others experiencing similar problems—and this is often stated by patients when asked how their group treatment has been helpful or meaningful to them. The phenomenon is known as universalization, and is one of the curative factors in brief group psychotherapy. Yet the identification with similarities in others can prove to be a pseudo-mutuality that, if not confronted or at least acknowledged, can lead to serious misconceptions about what an individual must do in order to make changes in his behavior and better adapt to the social environment in which he lives and works.

This is one of the critical elements that distinguish psychotherapy groups from support groups. Therapy groups can be supportive and often are, but support groups are rarely therapeutic unless they challenge the maladaptive behavior of the individual. To rest in the safety zone of "homogeneity" and never see the very real differences that exist between individuals in a group setting is to retreat from the hard therapeutic work that is possible in short-term group therapy. That work entails perceiving differences within obvious similarities and working through the inevitable conflicts that ensue. This is one of the significant factors in Phase 2 of Ariadne P. Beck's theory of group therapy development, which I discuss in Chapter Eleven.

PROBLEMS IN FORMING GROUPS

Planning what to do in a particular group will relieve much of the group therapist's anxiety and is recommended for the clinician, especially in the early stages of his professional development, as I outline in Chapter Nine. But the best efforts at planning are often undone by three phenomena that occur regularly in group therapy: (1) the inevitable uncertainty and imperfections of our criteria for patient selection, (2) the disheartening paradox of unintended consequences, and (3) the surprising tendency for different patients to need different approaches in the same group. The first frustrates our attempts to assess the needs of our patients and classify them as a group in the hope that they will respond positively to our methods. The second undermines our belief that we can be in control of what happens in our group. The third awakens us to the fact of individual difference, which requires us as therapists to be flexible in the application of any of our theories to our groups. These three phenomena are contingency factors, and together they exert considerable power in the functioning of a group. I will give examples of how they affect our ability to assess and treat patients.

Uncertainty in Patient Selection

This contingency does not have to be a major obstacle in organizing a group of patients unless the group therapist is driven to adhere to rigid criteria for selection. Flexibility is the key to negotiating this difficulty.

Some patients who do not meet the exact criteria for admission to your group may in fact work out quite well. For example, borderline personalities who somehow manage to make it into your homogeneous depressed group may prove to be a cathartic stimulus to otherwise inert and withdrawn group members. The schizoid person may become deeply loved by fellow group members who are coping with the drama of multiple crises, because they admire how well she contains her emotions. What if a patient presents with dysthymia and yet has a significant anxiety component that complicates the picture? Is she a candidate for a depression group or an anxiety group or another group entirely? Henry Spitz, in his text *Group Psychotherapy and Managed Mental Health Care,* takes note of dilemmas of this sort and addresses them from the point of view of diagnosis as it relates to treatment protocols for group therapy.

Professional modesty dictates that we recognize our mistakes in patient selection for groups. How we as clinicians respond to our mistakes and how we protect our patients from damage are essential features of our skill as group therapists.

Unintended Consequences

When a group therapist plans a group, he is most often responding to a need perceived among the patients entering the managed mental health system by whatever means. He intends to provide the patients he selects (or who are selected for him by entry personnel or by a group therapy case manager thoroughly acquainted with the criteria for inclusion) with a group experience that addresses their most salient mental health issue. The group therapist believes he can anticipate what that most salient issue will be for the individuals coming to his group. However, as the following incident demonstrates, that is not always the case.

I once designed, after lengthy pre-group interviews, a group of men and women whom I perceived as "depressed outpatients" with no other defining characteristics in common. They became the core group members for an ongoing group, one open to referral with an ever-changing constellation of patients.

After several weeks, I watched the men drop out for various reasons, and I could only come up with women to replace them. One night in group, my female assistant therapist commented on the discrepancy between what we had intended and what was actually happening. We were surprised to learn that the group was pleased with an all-female membership. With that in the open, each woman spontaneously began to uncover for the first time her history of sexual abuse. I was deeply moved when my co-therapist revealed that she herself had been abused as a child. Although I had organized this group, I was the last to discover the purpose for its organization.

In another instance, my co-therapist and I planned to exclude suicidal patients from our ongoing group for people coping with loss. All patients had lost a family member or friend to death and were suffering various degrees of inconsolable bereavement—in some cases complicated by the patients' own loss of physical health or vitality. Although suicidal ideation was a topic of discussion in the group, we had carefully referred to other groups all persons who had a history of suicide attempts or threats. We were not prepared for the suicide of two of our members within the first year—even though we were quite aware that this population was at risk to do so. We had somehow believed that planning would insulate our group from such traumas.

The group task became coping with the loss of group members and discovering personal reasons for living. Seeking a purpose in life had very practical implications for these people and was not in the least an idle philosophical pursuit.

Different Patients Need Different Approaches

Group therapists must always be cautious of a "one size fits all" approach to the treatment of their patients. One example is the limitations of the "here and now" orientation—a method widely recommended for time-limited group therapy. This orientation confines the interaction of the group members and leaders to what is happening among the people in the room during the meeting. Such a practice seeks to avoid time-consuming digressions into the past or patients' telling stories about what happened "then and there"; this approach, in the presence of a skillful therapist who acts as guide, seeks instead to maximize the potential for patients to work through some of their problems relating with peers and their distortions about how they perceive themselves. For example, when a patient reacts strongly in conflict with others in the group, the group therapist does not respond with the question, "Have these kinds of conflicts happened before at other times in your life?" but rather with the question, "What can you do now to resolve this issue for yourself?" The therapist strives to keep the focus of the work on the members present in the treatment room. In this way, the group concentrates on the stages of its own development, being cognizant of approaching termination and looking for ways to apply outside of group what each member has learned through the group. This can be an excellent process to follow, if all the individuals who compose the group can benefit from staying so narrowly focused.

However, stringent adherence to this method may severely limit what some individuals could accomplish in group, because patients work differently to accomplish their goals. For example, a man whose remembrance of a forgotten, traumatic scene from his past is stimulated by his participation in group will need to return to that scene in a powerful way that will help resolve the issue that feeds his current anxiety. To back away from that work because it does not fit the format of the group is a disservice to the patient, who did not ask to have his memory activated in that way and could not have predicted that it would be recalled with such force. Part of the knowledge and preparation needed to be a group psychotherapist includes a deep appreciation for the distinctive ways in which our patients suffer. In this respect, there is no substitute for the art of listening and responding to the special needs of human beings as they sit together in a group. This skill always demands great flexibility on the part of the clinician and demonstrates the high art of group therapy practice.

Exclusive focus on here-and-now interactions among group members without reference to the historical antecedents that give the interactions deeper meaning can be, in some instances, an abdication of responsibility by the group therapist, who may be missing an opportunity to teach her patients something revealing about themselves. Group therapists must embrace both a here-and-now focus and historical analysis. A high level of skill is required to make interventions of this order in short-term work, yet group therapists must not be discouraged from doing so. (In Chapter Six, I give an example of how this can be done.)

PLANNING FOR A STAFF MODEL HMO

At the Mental Health Service of the Group Health Cooperative of Puget Sound, the goals of treatment were the reduction of presenting symptoms and an increase in the ability to function at work, in family relationships, and in personal friendships. The goal was not personality change.

Treatment Groups

We organized three tiers of treatment groups. The first consisted of crisis-oriented, immediate-access groups that treated relatively homogeneous populations in ongoing groups of ever-changing constellations, ranging from five to twelve persons in each group. Patients averaged eight sessions of group attendance, with a range of one to thirty sessions over the course of a year. Each session was ninety minutes long. Eighteen percent of patients attended just a single session. A patient's leaving after one session of group was not necessarily considered premature termination for this group. Sometimes, one session was sufficient to address the needs of a particular individual: some wanted simply to know they were not crazy; some decided they did not want to work in the group format. Those dissatisfied with the treatment offered could return to entry personnel for assignment to another mode of treatment.

The second tier consisted of time-limited groups, usually lasting ten to twelve weeks, that focused on a particular topic relevant to the concerns of the individuals selected for the group. Eight to twelve patients were screened for inclusion in these groups by entry personnel and by individual clinicians who referred them directly to the groups. Some groups were psycho-educational in nature, and other groups allowed patients the option of renewing membership for another twelve-week course of treatment, depending on the goals of treatment. Patients committed themselves to coming for the time-limited periods, and changes in the constellation of the groups were not permitted during each twelve-week period. Personality disorders were not excluded from these groups, unless object relations were severely disturbed and precluded the ability to listen and communicate minimally in a group setting. The maximum duration of these groups was three to six months. These first two tiers defined short-term group therapy as we practiced it.

We did experiment with a third tier of longer-term groups for less than 10 percent of our treatment population. Roy MacKenzie estimates that 15 percent of the population will be highly disturbed and require ongoing maintenance therapy in groups to prevent hospitalization or decompensation or both. This 15 percent may include a sizeable number of high medical utilizers, depending on their diagnoses. It is therefore in the interest of the organization to develop special groups to give these people a sense of belonging that is denied them in the larger social sphere. Veterans Administration Mental Hygiene Clinics successfully conducted groups of this nature for many years; my mentor Donald Shaskan was one of the clinicians who pioneered their implementation. These patients need a substantial organizational commitment and may require years of maintenance doses of group treatment in order to facilitate their adaptation to life.

Time of Group Meetings

In assessing the needs of outpatients, the practitioner of group therapy clearly understands that most people work during the day and are therefore available to meet together only in the evenings. This means that group therapists must plan to meet with their groups at 5 P.M. or after. At Puget Sound, groups were scheduled regularly at 5:30 P.M., and a second round of groups was scheduled at 7:30 P.M.

Group Therapists and Co-Therapists

All crisis-type groups were organized to be led by co-therapy teams. This plan was adopted for two reasons: (1) so that groups could meet every week without interruptions caused by therapist sickness or vacations, and (2) as a provision of therapist self-care. Our Group Therapy Committee judged that it was clinically too challenging, and therefore unwise, for a therapist to contain the trauma of patients week after week without the comfort and collaboration of a co-therapist. In addition, because it takes time to learn how to become a co-therapy team, co-therapists who had worked together before in a number of groups were given priority status to lead crisis-type groups. The group therapy coordinator's role as consultant and supervisor to crisis teams proved to be invaluable in maintaining the professional equilibrium and personal equanimity of teams exposed to such high levels of stress.

Time-limited groups of a noncrisis nature were usually conducted by a solo therapist. Couples groups were an exception: male-female co-therapy teams were preferred because the patients benefited from seeing a man and woman model equal communication and respect for each other. Weekend groups that met once or twice to address such special topics as Redecision Therapy (see Chapter Six) or assertiveness training were also co-led when the group ranged in number from twelve to twenty-four persons.

A TALE OF TWO GROUPS

In the following section, I will examine two examples of homogeneous groups that were created by two separate mental health clinics to serve the needs of two discrete populations of depressed outpatients. It is instructive to see how both mental health clinics assessed their patients similarly and yet structured group services on theoretically different premises.

I will compare a homogeneous group for depressed outpatients treated at the Central Mental Health Service of Puget Sound with a cognitive psychotherapy group of depressed individuals at the Gundry Hospital of Baltimore, Maryland. Both groups functioned in an open-ended manner, that is, accepted patients into ongoing groups whose constellations were always changing. Both embraced the objectives of helping patients achieve relatively rapid and long-lasting alleviation of depression. Both clinics preferred the open-ended format because it allowed greater flexibility in recognizing the differences among patients regarding the time they required to meet the stated treatment objectives. Co-therapy was a standard of practice in both formats.

It is ironic and therefore important to note that both group approaches reported similar levels of success in the treatment of depressed patients, despite the widely differing theoretical orientations of the respective group leaders. This outcome lends support to one of the more infuriating paradoxes that emerge in groups: "Group members get better in spite of our theories, not because of them." There are factors inherent in group process itself, some more definable than others, that contribute to the positive outcome of meeting in groups. Those clinicians and managers who assess patient needs and structure group services must keep this idea in mind: it may be the group itself and not our beliefs about how to conduct the group that is most decisive in producing results.

Depressed Group at Puget Sound

This depressed group was called into being in order to meet the needs of depressed outpatients who were referred directly to the group by clinicians or trained entry personnel. The leaders did not interview candidates before they entered group, but trusted the judgments of their colleagues and entry staff. The co-therapists defined their method as analytic-expressive with a touch of behavioral conditioning tossed in.

Although we called the group a homogeneous group, that term must be qualified in light of the people who actually came to the sessions. It might be helpful to refer to the assessment chain that we used to further differentiate the patients who were appropriate referrals to our group. The people who were judged suitable for a homogeneous depressed group were at the same time judged suitable for a heterogeneous group with regard to the presence of the following characteristics:

Assessment Chain for Referrals

Emerging crisis that produces depression	Chronic or organic depression without identifiable crisis
Medical illness that causes reactive depression	No medical illness
Agoraphobic and socially isolated depression	Sociability complicated by anxious depression
History of trauma	No history of trauma

This list of the chain of possibilities that must be considered in the assessment of a patient before entering group illustrates the complexity in structuring a "homogeneous" group for depressed outpatients.

The majority of the patients who attended our group were in their thirties and forties, with an age range of twenty-two to fifty-five years. The majority conformed to the *DSM-III* diagnosis of Dysthymic Disorder and reported suffering depressive episodes of various duration of two years or longer. In all, 25 percent of group members were prescribed medication, mostly tricyclic antidepressants or lithium carbonate. A total of 20 percent were without jobs upon entry into group, and over half stated they lacked a stable love or friend relationship.

Three criteria emerged as indicators of success in overcoming depression for this group of people: (1) the patient discontinued medication upon mutual agreement of therapists and patient that it was no longer needed to maintain control of mood; (2) the patient obtained a job, or found a new position that was more satisfactory from the patient's point of view; (3) the patient established a relationship or friendship that met some of his needs. On the basis of these criteria, we discovered that a majority of the group members who stayed beyond one session experienced a modicum of success on one or more dimensions. The group met for ninety minutes each week; the average course of treatment was eight sessions.

As co-therapists, we did not avoid using the word *depressed* to designate our group. It was posted prominently on the group therapy roster board visible as people entered the Mental Health Service. We produced a two-page, five-by-eight-inch salmon-colored flier entitled "Depressed Group," which was given to each patient referred to the group. The flier stated the following:

Being depressed is a dead-end position. We may feel dead inside and have no energy to be involved with others. We may feel worthless inside with nothing to give. People often isolate themselves during periods of depression. We feel sorry for ourselves and show a lack of interest in other people and things. When depressed, the world becomes a narrow place—and we can see very little that seems exciting, challenging, or pleasurable to us. We may also feel helpless—that whatever could be enjoyable to us is unattainable.

WHY A GROUP?

A group helps you switch focus from the self-absorption of being depressed to re-entry into the world of the living. We will practice using our sense of humor to activate ourselves—but not in a way that group members will feel put down or made fun of. Group leaders will be there to assist and will attempt to help each member. The group will discuss how we often become depressed to avoid taking an action or making a decision. As trust grows and a safe feeling develops, the group will encourage you to take the risk of being undepressed, which may be a new and unfamiliar experience for you.

Characteristically, patients in this group held fast to their depression as a possession—yet spoke as if it controlled them. For these patients, inclinations to rescue others in the group competed with equally strong urges to become withdrawn and self-absorbed in melancholy. Gradually, the members' distorted beliefs about the experience of anger were challenged through the expression of resentments in the group setting. As co-therapists, we found that being taken seriously was associated with the patients' ability to accept recognition from self and others. It was not uncommon that patients could state precisely what they needed to do to feel better and yet would categorically avoid doing these things.

In response to the patients' behavior, the co-therapists employed specific therapeutic strategies and attitudes. Our chief rule was never to make an attempt to cheer up anyone in group. Such an effort invariably proved negative because it repeated what the patients heard on a daily basis from friends and family in their well-intentioned attempts to change the patient. Efforts by patients to cheer up each other were rare and usually met by contempt and bitter resentment. We allowed the patients to be as depressed as they wanted to be in group. Patients reported that they experienced much relief because of this attitude.

We found that deepening trust was not as critical a condition for patient sharing as the common and immediate identification process. To our surprise, veteran members said things to new arrivals that they had not revealed to the therapists, and these testimonies became the chief source of our learning what was helpful in group.

As members improved, we acknowledged the change but were careful to restrain our enthusiasm. Cheerleading and pep talking were strictly forbidden. We stated that we were pleased for them but made it clear nonverbally that we did not expect them to please us by being less depressed. Our attitude was that we would accept them depressed or otherwise. We openly encouraged members to support and befriend each other outside the group setting.

We laughed a lot in this group. There was among the patients a finely developed sense of humor—a dry delivery and exquisite timing of punchlines that guaranteed hilarity. Much of the humor seemed unintentional and came about quite spontaneously. It was characteristic of the group that humor was used to expand the perception of a problem to include other people. Humor also served the social function of making contact with others at a different emotional level. Examples of humor included the patient who with genuine admiration stated, "I don't see anyone here trying very hard to act happy."

Much laughter accompanied his statement, signifying relief that a facade was not necessary here.

One woman stated her fear that she might be "drummed out of the depressed group" owing to her belief that she was no longer depressed enough to qualify for membership. Pursuing the metaphor, another person said, "I'd like to make a ritual of the defrocking." A third stated, "We'll strip off her brass buttons and take away her Kleenex box!" Paradoxical intent was used to convey the sense of fun and excitement that was possible in a depressed group.

Depressed Group at the Gundry Hospital

The treatment philosophy that informed the leaders of this depressed group was succinctly stated by David Roth and Lino Covi: "Our clinical approach involves the utilization of both accepted cognitive procedures and group process to alter depressogenic beliefs." The group was effectively used to challenge the cognitive distortions that depressed individuals make in the way they perceive events in their lives. Cognitive theory holds that once these distortions are corrected by the individual, the negative and depressive affects associated with the distortions will diminish. Treatment proceeded along the lines of both long-term and short-term goals for the patients. Long-term goals included the lessening of depressive affect and the learning of skills that allow patients to work cognitive therapy on themselves apart from the group. Short-term goals involved the concrete steps necessary to reach the long-term goals.

At each session, patients reported their score on the Beck Depression Inventory and told what they wanted to accomplish that week. The group therapist was active in helping each patient maintain continuity from week to week, seeing that issues were not just dropped or avoided. Homework assignments were a regular part of the group norms, and members helped each other in formulating individualized assignments that would have a good chance of being achieved, thereby positively reinforcing the individual's efforts to change. Patients closed each session with a recap of what was important for each person at that meeting.

A rather careful preparation was designed for patients prior to their entry to group, consisting of four to eight meetings with one of the leaders in order to familiarize the new member with the operational procedures and language of the treatment. Patients learned cognitive-behavioral skills and were encouraged to ask questions of their leaders to seek clarification if they found themselves confused.

The group was also carefully prepared to receive a new member, in the belief that many premature terminations could thereby be averted. Members were invited to discuss their thoughts and beliefs about the entry of a new person. Members were also asked to plan a strategy of how to help the new person become a part of the group. Once the person joined the group, the veteran members provided models of how to use the cognitive therapeutic tools by explicitly stating what had been helpful for them. Core group members proved their utility at this juncture because they could assist the new member in questioning the accuracy of her cognitions and expectations about the group. Typical new member cognitions included the following:

"I'm always going to remain an outsider."

"I'm going to come across as stupid."

"I will hold the group back."

"My problems are worse than everybody else's."

Once the new member had a sense of belonging to the group, the focus of the group returned to the incremental experiments or homework that group members devised for themselves to test their ability to adapt in the world. Insight attained from exploring member-to-member or member-to-leader interactions was not emphasized or encouraged as in more analytically oriented groups.How did the therapists know that the process was working? Positive signs of the group's success included patients learning the following: (1) how to nondefensively listen to constructive critical feedback, (2) how to disclose intimate experiences, and (3) how to form stable relationships.

As a patient approached graduation from group, he asked himself, "Have I changed my depressogenic belief system? Can I continue to function as my own cognitive therapist?" The entire group participated in this process, which inevitably led to the question of whether he could manage future episodes of affective disorder. This allowed the patient to develop a strategy for coping with future depressions. Such a strategy must incorporate the belief that reexperiencing depression is not a failure but an opportunity to apply the skills learned in group to further personal growth.

As we can see from the Puget Sound and Gundry Hospital examples, there is considerable latitude in the way short-term psychotherapy groups can be structured to meet the needs of patients. This fact carries important implications for group therapy case managers or group therapy coordinators who will structure group services in their respective managed mental healthcare settings. The key is to remain flexible and willing to experiment in the interests of better serving patients.

Once groups are set up, the question of how people find their way to them becomes crucial. The next chapter shows how to make that happen.

CHAPTER FOUR

Establishment of a Referral System

One of the great anxieties that grips group therapists will be recognized by all practicing group clinicians. It is the sinking feeling that comes from seeing a group gradually lose its members through attrition and termination. Even the successful completion of a course of treatment by a patient in group can be met with apprehension, if no new members are foreseen on the horizon. The diminution of the central cast of active group members, or the "core" group, as it is called, is perceived by remaining group members and their leaders as a threat to the survival of the group. Beginning group therapists in particular suffer anxiety when they see their carefully crafted handiwork withering away.

This consternation is felt acutely in ongoing groups in which the existence of a group culture and history, however brief, in the form of certain group members who have committed to the process and who have a stake in the outcome, allows for the rapid advancement of the group's development when new members are added. Even time-limited groups endure this anxiety, especially in the early phases when the majority can desert a group en masse, leaving behind bewildered patients and shocked leaders. Considering that these terminations and discontinuations are a regular and expected part of group psychotherapy, it is important to prepare group therapists for this eventuality and to allay the fears of members who stay.

Group therapists take heart and do not become discouraged in their efforts to start new groups and maintain ongoing ones—if and only if they can depend on a viable, operative referral system that can guarantee a supply of appropriate patients for their groups. Designing such a referral system and training both clinical and nonclinical personnel in the mechanics and dynamics of its successful operation is the number one priority for any group psychotherapy program, whether it exists within a staff model HMO or within the context of an independent practitioner association or network that is contracted as an exclusive panel for a managed care organization and receives referrals from the organization's computer-linked case management staff. Group therapists within any comprehensive mental health delivery system of any size will always depend on the referrals of others to make their groups happen. It is only the solo practitioner who leads at most one or two groups each week who has any chance of supplying himself with an adequate number of referrals. As I stated in the Introduction, a competently trained and skilled group therapist, working at her full capacity to treat in short-term group therapy, will require 250 referrals to her groups each year. This level of group referrals requires organization, planning, specific entry strategies, and training. I will elaborate on each of these essential factors in the following sections.

ORGANIZATION

The organization of a referral system must take precedence over other corporate priorities if group therapy is to become a primary mode of mental health delivery. Once patient needs have been accurately assessed or anticipated and the appropriate services have been structured, it is mandatory to find ways to get the patients into the groups. The organization of such a referral system demands resourcefulness and flexibility from all parties: entry or intake personnel, case manager or program assistant, group clinicians, the group therapy coordinator, and of course the people who will become group members.

In a staff model HMO like Puget Sound, the position of group therapy program assistant is pivotal. She acts as a repository for referrals to groups not immediately open or not currently in progress, and she functions as a way station for groups in formation. Such a service is indispensable to the group clinician, who is relieved of the anxiety associated with not having a sufficient number of people to begin a group. As referrals collect, the group therapy program assistant informs the group therapy coordinator and the Group Therapy Committee, which consists of clinical professionals dedicated to the delivery of group therapy, who then take the responsibility of finding or selecting leaders for the needed groups. The recruitment of appropriate leaders for groups is a major duty of the Group Therapy Committee and the group therapy coordinator, and they must be prepared to assume the responsibility of leading a group themselves if they are unable to find a suitable group therapist. This is the commitment that the coordinator and the committee members make as part of their job description.

Predominance of Self-Referrals

At Puget Sound, the majority of the patients entering the mental health system were self-referred; that is, they initiated the contact with our entry personnel based on their knowledge or belief that they were entitled to a mental health benefit. Sometimes patients would be encouraged to use mental health benefits based on a variety of educational materials published by the HMO and made available to plan members in the interest of public health and prevention.

Those patients not self-referred came to the Mental Health Service through referrals from their primary care physicians or, in cases involving courts of law, judges or family mediators. In contrast, managed care mental health systems that consist exclusively of networks of mental health providers and contain no primary care physicians working in close coordination with them receive almost all their calls from self-referred plan members. Their calls are taken by trained case managers who check for eligibility and often determine medical necessity based on established criteria. These case managers then become the referral source for mental health providers under contract with the managed care plan.

In the case of the exclusive provider panel that serves patients referred by a case management operation, it is imperative that the case manager—or the group therapy case manager, if that useful position has been created—assess the need for new groups based on the data from intake personnel on patients appropriate for group therapy. The case manager then canvasses the provider panel for suitable group therapists to lead the desired group. The group therapy case manager may have to recommend the expansion of the provider panel to include certain group specialists if clinicians on the panel are unable to serve as group clinicians and begin the necessary groups.

In the staff model HMO, the group therapy program assistant calls patients, informs them of their acceptance to the various groups, and gives them the starting dates and places of meeting. This service is again an extraordinary help to the group clinician, who is spared the time-consuming activity of contacting by phone each of the patients who will be entering her group. This assistance is one more incentive for clinicians to serve as group therapists.

The group therapy program assistant also assigns rooms appropriate to the size and kind of group specified, and keeps track of the group space available to achieve the optimal use of space. The size of the group meeting space should not be minimized as an important psychological factor in the treatment of specific conditions. At Puget Sound, we discovered that the crisis-type groups and groups that treated depression, parasuicidal behavior, bereavement, and life-threatening medical conditions required much larger rooms than did time-limited groups that treated persons suffering from bulimia and survivors of sexual abuse.

Group Therapy Program Assistant

The nonclinical position of group therapy program assistant was crucial to the success of our referral system at Puget Sound. In a staff model HMO, in conjunction with the group therapy coordinator and the Group Therapy Committee, the group therapy program assistant was responsible for the operation of the group therapy program. She was the resource person for the program and provided information to all concerned. She was the liaison for the program with the clinic manager, the office manager, the intake unit, the clerical support staff, the group therapists and the referring therapists, and the patients referred to groups. Careful attention to the responsibilities of this position is germane in order to understand the intricacies and success of the Puget Sound group therapy referral system.

The group therapy program assistant attended weekly Group Therapy Committee meetings as a resource person to update the committee on referrals waiting for groups, the need for specific groups, clinicians wanting to start or experiment with new groups, and the current requirements for space that must be allocated for group treatment. As secretary for the Group Therapy Committee, she recorded minutes and kept track of decisions by the committee regarding announcements and memoranda to clinical staff about groups needed based on the flow of referrals. She also publicized the need for specific groups and the existing groups available for referral in regular group therapy newsletters circulated to all clinical staff in the five mental health centers that operated under the Puget Sound umbrella in the state of Washington. In this way, all parts of the mental health system remained informed of decisions and activities that affected the group psychotherapy program.

In effect, this person was responsible for the daily operation of the group program; the group therapy coordinator was responsible for the clinical decisions of what groups to have and who would lead the groups. As repository for group referrals, the group therapy program assistant was the person who physically organized the groups and contacted potential members by phone with information about the time and place of groups as well as about the therapist or therapists who would be conducting them. From this data, she assembled the group folders containing the names of and billing information about each patient entering groups, and made these folders available to the group therapists. These folders were then returned to her for an accurate tally of group attendance.

The group therapy program assistant completed all billing for group therapists, which proved to be another perquisite for therapists conducting groups. She also kept track of the group referrals who did not show for group. This data was useful to the Group Therapy Committee in planning for those individuals who did not follow through on the referrals to groups and the reasons for their absence, if these were possible to know. We found that a certain percentage of referrals could be expected not to show up—and this had implications for the care and preparation we gave or failed to give to patients prior to their referral to a group.

In conversations with potential group patients with regard to their invitation to join particular groups, the group therapy program assistant served at an extremely high level of competency. She would first inform herself about the group by consulting with the group therapy coordinator and the group therapist or co-therapists on the type of group, the logistical details, and the appropriate referrals. Once the referrals were made, she would call the potential group members, answer their questions, and reassure them about group process and the therapists leading their group. This step in the referral process is most efficiently carried out by a nonclinical person, but must be executed with great sophistication and gracious demeanor. The person calling must be sufficiently knowledgeable about groups to answer inquiries and yet be so congruent as to know when to say, "I believe you'll have to ask your therapist about that when you come to the group." Once calls were made, she would then inform the group therapists about the progress of the group in formation and the patients who responded affirmatively to her invitations.

The presence of the group therapy program assistant in the clinic, like that of the group therapy coordinator, was a constant reminder to therapists that group therapy was wholly consistent with the standard of practice in the operation of the clinic. She was responsible for a group therapy bulletin board that was prominently placed near the mailboxes of all clinicians and kept current with groups open for referral. In addition, when clinicians picked up their group folders, she discussed informally with them the emerging picture of group needs, based on the latest referral information, including the need for co-therapists.

PLANNING

The planning of specific groups is an ongoing process that proceeds from a careful and constantly updated needs analysis. Planning includes both the number and the kind of groups that the group program will offer at any point. Planning which groups to form necessarily overlaps with the functions of the referral system, because the success of patients referred to existing groups determines whether those groups will be continued or replaced by more effective formats. In addition, shifting patterns in the nature of the problems presented by people coming in the door strongly influence both management and clinician perception of which groups are needed.

The scheduling of group leaders to conduct groups may require envisioning groups one year in advance, especially if there is a high demand for a group at a time when many group therapists will be on vacation or otherwise unavailable. The concept of maintaining capacity for consumer use of groups is imperative. This means that some groups with a low patient census will be allowed to maintain operation in order to have the capacity to absorb sudden influxes of patients suitable for referral. Extended benefits may be given to appropriate patients to enhance the life of these groups. This kind of long-range planning involves the study of referral patterns for a year or more. The group therapy case manager or the group therapy coordinator (depending on the model of provider affiliation) must become familiar with and keep abreast of these referral patterns in order to anticipate future trends in utilization.

Certain groups can be planned with alternating group leadership in "cascade" fashion. For example, one pair of co-therapists may take a twelve-week term conducting a "couples in crisis" group. At the completion of the twelve-week term, one leader will be replaced by a new therapist who will serve another twelve-week stint, after which the remaining original therapist, having served twenty-four weeks, will retire to be succeeded by a new therapist, and so forth. In this manner, group leaders are always available for the high-demand group and a continuity is established by rotating the use of co-therapists that significantly enhances the quality of the treatment offered.

Ongoing psychotherapy groups with an ever-changing constellation of patients became a major point of entry for up to 50 percent of our group therapy referrals at Puget Sound. As I noted in Chapter Three, the average stay for patients who remained beyond one session was eight group meetings—so the aim of short-term therapy was effectively achieved despite the existence of a group that seemingly never ended. There is, however, a lingering suspicion that ongoing groups mean long-term therapy, despite the statistical evidence to the contrary. The utility of such groups is proven, and yet it requires special care to keep them afloat. The biggest challenge is supplying a referral base that will provide sixty to eighty appropriate referrals each year, the amount necessary to sustain one ongoing group with an ever-changing constellation. This may involve top management decisions to alter benefit packages in a way that favors the proliferation of therapy groups. For management to make these changes requires strong advocacy of group therapy by a group therapy coordinator or group therapy case manager who understands the somewhat counterintuitive fact that expanding group therapy incentives and opportunities actually lessens the overall costs of therapy utilization.

Organizational Incentives

Organizations that do not have a full-time staff on salary, but instead authorize exclusive panels or networks of providers to serve patients referred by a case management operation, present a somewhat different set of circumstances than staff model HMOs. Network provider organizations, such as U.S. Behavioral Health, must by several means encourage their network providers to specialize in group therapy. First, the appointment of a group therapy intake coordinator or case manager as part of the entry process for patients would allow appropriate individuals to be funneled to providers who had devoted time and energy to forming therapy groups. Because network providers are not expected to deny treatment to any plan member who is referred, the group therapy intake coordinator can make sure that providers specializing as group therapists can receive a high number of patients suitable for group. In this way the group therapist can be assured that his practice will not be dedicated primarily to individual treatment but will leave room for the treatment of appropriate group candidates.

Therapists in fee-for-service private practice will often refer appropriate patients to their private practice group therapy colleagues with the assurance that they also will receive referrals in return. These referrals are based on a working knowledge of their colleagues' practices, the kind of groups they offer, and the patient dysfunction in which they specialize. Some of these patients referred to group will choose to continue individual treatment, so the referring therapist does not experience a loss of income. However, the network provider is not inclined to refer patients sent to him to other network providers no matter how appropriate the person is for group, because it would mean a loss of income for the referring therapist. The patient cannot remain in individual treatment with the referring therapist, and because all referrals originate from the case manager and case management operation, the system does not have in place the institutional norm of network providers referring to each other. The managed care organization must create incentives for network providers to refer to those clinicians specializing in group therapy such that the referring providers are not penalized by diminished earnings. A referral fee might be paid directly to referring providers, or additional referrals could be sent to them as a bonus for their cooperation in building the group therapy program throughout the network.

Capitation is another incentive for specializing in group therapy. As the highest level of risk for providers to assume, capitated contracts spur network providers to develop groups in order to keep the cost of treatment within the bounds of the money allocated for each individual covered under the plan.

For example, if I am a network provider for a managed care organization and I agree to be compensated on a capitated basis, I and my network of fellow providers may be allocated a maximum of $600 per year for each patient that enters treatment. This means that however ill this patient is, we have agreed to supply the necessary care for $600. This arrangement works in my favor if the patient requires only six to ten sessions of individual therapy. But if the patient requires greater attention and more comprehensive care, perhaps thirty to forty sessions, I will be working at a loss unless I have a group that can meet the patient's needs. In that case, I would benefit from having in place a coordinated system by which I could refer to group therapists among my network of fellow providers. In effect, the existence of group therapists in the provider network helps spread the risk and furnishes a safety valve for the accommodation of high-utilizing patients. Under capitation, all providers have a stake in the expeditious treatment of each patient because they all share in the financial risk. Capitation by its very nature requires greater coordination and cooperation among the members of a provider network; coordination and cooperation are the very processes essential to the sustenance of a group therapy referral system.

Some staff model managed mental health programs that offer direct access to mental health on a capitated basis (such as Pacific Applied Psychology Associates) have offered special incentives to their full-time clinical employees. Such incentives include cash bonuses and time off for the successful activation of therapy groups, so that group therapists can work less for more money.

In the absence of capitated contracts, network providers will not be inclined to start groups, because they may earn more money treating a patient individually for fifty minutes than in a small group for ninety minutes, without expending the effort to create a group. They will not be inclined to refer to group therapist colleagues because they do not have a stake in reducing the overall cost of treatment for patients referred to their panel.

Both staff model HMOs and network provider organizations can stimulate the use of group therapy by devising favorable benefit packages for plan members. For example, a plan member might be charged a co-payment for individual sessions and charged no co-payment or a significantly reduced co-payment for group therapy sessions. Another benefit package might be a graduated scale of co-payments: zero payment for the first ten group sessions, $10 for the next ten sessions, and $20 or more thereafter.

Private Fee-for-Service and Network Providers

The case for private fee-for-service therapists is very different than for network providers. Whereas private therapists must go to the public and market aggressively for patients to enter their treatment groups, marketing a group to the public is not effective or efficient for network providers. That is because many individuals will not be covered by the plan or will belong to other plans with their own exclusive provider panels. Network providers who want to lead groups must depend on their intake coordinator or case managers to provide them appropriate referrals drawn from persons covered under the plan. If the managed care organization has built incentives for network providers to refer to other network providers, the group specialist must depend on referrals from that source as well. The network provider does not solicit the public but rather his own colleagues and intake managers to foster his practice as a group therapist.

In contrast to the scarcity of referrals for private practitioners, there is an ample supply of patients seeking help from any managed mental healthcare network of providers. In 1996, managed care operations claimed 67 million plan members, or "covered lives," to use the argot of the industry. The existence of an intake coordinator or case manager testifies to the need to control patients' access to services. Yet the appropriate patients must be identified, informed, prepared, and sent to the providers specializing in group therapy. That is the goal of an effective system of referral.

Without capitation, the network providers may see group therapy as a threat to their livelihood, because groups require fewer providers to treat the same number of patients at a lower cost. The advent of group therapy might mean that fewer providers would be retained on managed care provider networks. With capitation, the intake coordinator is not constrained to rely so heavily on "medical necessity" as a criterion to control access to treatment and can identify suitable people to enter an expanding group therapy program, which can accommodate a larger number of people at a lower cost.

Space

Although some therapists experimented with "leaderless" groups during the height of the Human Potential Movement in the 1970s, the concept of a "spaceless" group is absurd. All groups need sufficient space in which all members can meet at the same time. One of the chief duties of a Group Therapy Committee in a staff model HMO is to anticipate the space requirements for groups. Because group therapy is practiced most often in the evening hours, group therapists are essentially clinicians practicing at night. The allotment of adequate space for groups in the evening—and the provision of security for that space, including the opening and closing of treatment rooms—is a major concern for group therapy planners.

One of the first studies I carried out with my mentor was a comparison of patients' perception of psychological distance from the therapist in group therapy as opposed to the same therapist in individual treatment. It was demonstrated that patients in group perceived greater distance from their therapist, a conclusion with important implications for how distance creates a necessary psychological condition that permits certain group processes to occur. I believe that patients referred to groups that do not permit adequate psychological distance will be prone to premature termination or will obtain less than optimal results in their tenure as group members. This is an intuitively obvious but little-understood phenomenon of group dynamics.

SPECIFIC ENTRY STRATEGIES

Those responsible for mental healthcare delivery should encourage experimentation with various ways to bring patients into the group therapy program. As discussed in Chapter Two, the managers of the group program and the group therapy coordinator must risk breaking or at least bending some of the cultural conventions that handicap the full use of group therapy by those who can benefit from it. Therefore, intake coordinators or group therapy case managers should consider using such entry procedures as immediate referral to specific crisis-type groups with group clinicians skilled at introducing group methods to new patients. The judicious use of direct referrals of this kind should be augmented with considerable phone contact or face to face contact time during which specially trained intake personnel give detailed information on the purpose and values of the group that is being recommended.

Simon Budman of Harvard Community Health Plan has found a single one-and-a-half-hour workshop useful to prepare patients for group therapy and to assist them in choosing group therapy as their mode of treatment. He also employs a single follow-up meeting six to twelve months after termination of a fifteen-session time-limited group to assess the effectiveness of the group experience.

Some experiments, such as using large intake groups to introduce mental health options to consumers new to the health plan, must be used advisedly, if at all, because the gathering of people in groups of any kind in the field of mental health, even for purposes of educating them about their mental health benefits, implies the start of a therapeutic process. The use of group in such formats could prove more frustrating than satisfying to patients, as they may come to the group with expectations for treatment, despite admonitions to the contrary.

TRAINING

The position of group therapy coordinator, or its equivalent, is the cornerstone of any training program in both staff model or network provider systems of delivery. Every successful group therapy program I have ever known has incorporated a clinician authorized to stimulate group development by training personnel.

Entry and Nonclinical Personnel

The most efficient training I carried out in my tenure at Puget Sound was the many weeks I spent going over intake protocols with entry personnel. We focused on identifying and informing plan members who called for assistance about the options available to them in our group therapy program. The initial contact with patients is important because it prepares the patient for his experience. Pamphlets describing the purpose and goals of the various groups available can be placed in the waiting room and distributed to the referring clinicians, who then dispense them to patients. This procedure establishes an expectation of assistance and allows time for patients to identify with the stated rationale for the group. (An example of one such pamphlet is given in Chapter Three, where I describe the depressed group.)

Attitudes of success and anticipation of help can be built in from the first discussions with entry and intake personnel. At Puget Sound, intake workers were familiar with all the groups open for referral and had at their fingertips up-to-date information about the general purpose and selection criteria for each group. With careful training and supervision from the group therapy coordinator, the intake workers had the authority to refer patients directly to crisis groups focusing on depression, suicide, emerging crises or psychological trauma, and chronic medical illness.

In some cases, nonclinical intake workers were invited to share the leadership of these groups with a clinical group specialist so that the intake worker who had made phone contact with the patient would also be present when the patient entered the group. These shared leadership arrangements, called nequipo teams, or unequal teams of clinical and nonclinical personnel, were created with training in mind but proved very efficient as a method to introduce new members, who are naturally wary and anxious, to a group. The education of consumers in the purposes and values of group psychotherapy is a priority, and it usually takes at least one positive group experience to fully accomplish it. The patient may trust her referring clinician or group therapy intake coordinator and come to group, but she will not stay or return unless she finds some value in being there.

As group therapy coordinator, I would give feedback to intake personnel on the outcomes of the people they referred to the various groups. In this way, intake workers became more skillful in the judgments they made and more aware of their mistakes in judgment. I would also arrange for referring clinicians to receive feedback on the outcome of group referrals they made. The group therapy program assistant would gather information from the group therapists in the form of brief evaluations that would then be reviewed by the referring therapists. In a very large program, this review was not always possible, but the majority of referring therapists learned about the outcome of patients they sent to groups.

Group Therapists

In order to flourish in a system that provides a large number of referrals, the group therapist must grasp the essential theory that allows him to operate effectively either in a time-limited format with a set number of group sessions and fixed membership, or in an ongoing format with new membership every session. Ariadne P. Beck's phases of group therapy development and Yvonne Agazarian's analysis of subgroups, both systems approaches to understanding group process, have proven to be reliable predictors of small-group behavior and therefore are useful tools for helping group therapists maximize the value of group as an instrument to heal the individual. I have devoted Chapters Eleven and Twelve exclusively to the theory of Ariadne Beck. Of particular import is the trust the clinician must exhibit in the ability of a particular group to find the most effective methods to communicate with its members. One of the enduring paradoxes of group structure is that despite a certain tendency for groups to go through the same specific phases of development, there appears to be an extremely wide variety in the ways groups actually move through these phases. The group therapist who cannot exude confidence that the group members will find their own way to evolve as a group will prove to be a weak link in the referral chain. The issue of trust and its relation to training is addressed in Chapter Five.

With respect to trust, once again the concept of isomorphy has meaningful application, this time in the context of a referral system. The underlying existence of trust at each level makes the work of a referral system possible. Group therapists must trust the assessment of the Group Therapy Committee or the group therapy intake coordinator that certain treatment groups are needed. They must also trust the judgment of intake personnel or the group therapy intake coordinator that the individuals referred to their groups are appropriate. The group therapy coordinator must trust the good faith of management in providing the necessary incentives and benefit packages that make the referral of patients to groups both economically sensible for the consumer and rewarding for the provider. The patients themselves must trust that the managed mental healthcare operation knows what it is doing by referring them to group psychotherapy and trust that the therapists possess the skills to help them in the context of the group. A breakdown of trust at any level of this system produces an impasse in the effectiveness of the referral system.

THE ROLE OF THE GROUP THERAPY COORDINATOR

The group therapy coordinator has central responsibility to see that all operations of referral run smoothly. She acts as liaison between entry staff, the group therapy program assistant, and group clinicians so that each step of the referral process meets the needs of the patients by moving them swiftly to the groups especially designed for them. In a managed care corporation that contracts with a panel of independent practitioners, she acts as liaison between intake coordinator, case manager, and group clinicians in order to serve the needs of the patients by connecting them with the proper group therapist. She must wear a number of hats in this capacity.

Sometimes, she will have to educate the intake coordinator as to the purposes of the group that the clinician is providing. At other times, she will have to streamline the process of getting the referral through entry staff or the intake coordinator and into the treatment group. Often she may need to structure groups so as to maintain their capacity to receive new patients. That might mean discussion with the group therapy program assistant and the group clinicians about the need for ongoing groups in certain critical areas, such as crisis and immediate-access groups. For patients receiving care in case-managed, exclusive provider panel environments, the group therapy coordinator might recommend the restructuring of case management and the creation of a group therapy case manager with responsibility to keep an eye on essential groups that must remain open for referral to meet the needs of patients coming in the door. The question of maintaining group capacity to meet expected need and to adjust rapidly for unexpected need must always be kept in mind by the group therapy case manager because the members of the exclusive provider panel must be informed to create the needed groups.

In a network of exclusive provider panels, the responsibilities of a position like that of group therapy case manager would include adjusting group therapy benefits for patients in ongoing crisis-type groups so that a core group of patients would be in place when new patients are ready to be referred. The group therapy case manager would also be able to extend group benefits for certain patients in order for selected time-limited groups (eating disorders, agoraphobia, assertiveness) to have a sufficient number of members in order to start. Extended group benefits would be an incentive for patient participation in the group therapy program and would fit well with the need for flexibility in maintaining the group's capacity to take in new patients rapidly.

The role of the group therapy coordinator in establishing trust as an operating principle for the group program has special implications for the referral system. First and foremost, he must deliver on his promises. If he says that the group program can accommodate 20 percent of all patients coming in the door by the end of the year, he must be able to make that happen. He must resist pressure to make unrealistic goals. Stating overly ambitious goals to please clinic managers or directors will fail as an organizational strategy because intake personnel and referring clinicians will become discouraged and lose confidence in the referral process when the patients they send are not placed in suitable groups. If the group therapy coordinator promises group therapists more resources, such as advanced training or clerical support for their groups, he had better be able to supply them. Demoralization of group clinicians through lack of resources will stymie the development of the most needed groups. If he promises intake personnel expanded benefits for patients selecting group therapy as a means to facilitate the patients' entry into group, he had better be prepared to negotiate that kind of deal with the lawyers who write the managed care contracts. The group therapy coordinator must be the vital connection between the referral system and the corporate decision makers who allocate resources to the program.

Competition

Competitiveness arises in the realm of referrals. Who "owns" the patient? Who controls the referral process? Will I lose prestige as a clinician if I am not selected by my colleagues? Will I lose power or income by referring my patient to group?

The intense competitiveness among professionals who work for some staff model HMOs and independent provider networks has led one of my colleagues, who worked in the slums of Los Angeles, to portray these organizations' structure as having "all the cohesiveness and cooperative spirit of a loosely formed teenage gang." Again, the concept of isomorphy operates here: competition among clinicians and how it is addressed and worked through will be mirrored in the intense competition that arises early in every psychotherapy group. Competition is predicted by Ariadne Beck in the evolution of a therapy group and will be the focus of much attention in Chapter Eleven.

The group therapy coordinator for independent provider networks must have the authority to channel suitable and appropriate patients to the groups that match their therapeutic needs even though certain providers want to bring the same patients into individual treatment. The group therapy coordinator finds himself in direct conflict with individual therapists who fear they will be left behind in the race for dollars. As stated earlier, this competition for patients is substantially reduced in capitated systems where group treatment produces a favorable economic outcome for providers and does not threaten them with loss of income.

In staff model HMOs, the issue of competition concerns who gets to do particular groups and who gets to work with whom in the context of co-leadership. Both the Group Therapy Committee and the group therapy coordinator must have the authority to initiate specific groups and to select clinicians to conduct them. However, they must be careful to use that authority lightly and consider the feelings that emerge for group therapists who are not selected for the task. A sense of fairness and equality must pervade the selection or appointing process, because a clinician who has felt slighted in the process will not be inclined to refer to groups in the future. It is the specific job of the group therapy coordinator to anticipate these competitive issues and construct procedures that allow equality of opportunity for those therapists wanting to lead groups. The group therapy program assistant can be helpful in this regard, by spreading existing and potential group referrals across the groups that may compete for the same kind of patients. An equitable system for allocating referrals to groups, even if not perfect, can do much to smooth the ruffled feathers of therapists eager to begin their groups. Again, harmony among the providers on this dimension is crucial, as a few disgruntled therapists can create a serious impediment for a system of referral.

Patients

The group therapy coordinator must also be responsible for the content of the "training" whereby potential group members are introduced to the purposes of the groups to which they are referred. As I indicated in Chapter Three, the "why" of the group must be carefully thought out as part of the process of assessing the needs of the patients to be served. The why should be constructed in language free of jargon and communicated in a manner that is clear and concise yet does not oversimplify the task of treatment.

What, then, should intake coordinators or referring clinicians tell the prospective group patients? First, the patients should know that much time has been devoted to planning the groups they will join. The group leaders will be familiar with the kinds of problems that will be discussed, and although the leaders are not there to provide solutions to problems, they will be able to help the patients think through their problems by allowing them to express the emotional as well as cognitive parts of themselves.

Second, they should know that groups involve conflict. The gradual appreciation of differences among individual members is revealed as the group matures and becomes a means by which conflict can be resolved. The experience by which conflict is resolved and individual differences understood is known as group process. When a group member experiences the fear of conflict and the relief of its eventual resolution, there is a noticeable increase in the individual's self-esteem. This is called growth or maturity in the context of group and is one of the central goals of group therapy.

Third, patients should know that groups mean affiliation with others. During the group process, we learn to correct our initial impressions of others and discover, for example, that a person is more similar to us than we thought, and in a way we hadn't suspected. Or we discover that a person is quite different than we thought, and in ways that prove to be astonishingly complex and meaningful to us.

Fourth, they should know that their participation in group will have an end, either by the termination of the group or the completion of their commitment to it. The patient's ability to leave the group and feel OK about himself, while also letting the other group members know how important they were for him and what he has learned from them, is one of the great accomplishments of group process and one that has some of the most lasting positive effects.

The issue of referral, or how patients arrive in therapy groups, is the single most crucial problem that management and clinicians wanting to develop group therapy programs must face. They must pay thoughtful and timely attention to this one issue in order to produce creative and deliberate blueprints for action. This chapter has demonstrated a few examples of how one might proceed toward this goal. Once a referral system has been established, ongoing training in group leadership becomes vital to helping group therapists sustain their practices and nourish themselves both as professionals and as people. Clinicians will refer to colleagues for whom they have high regard and with whom they share a team approach to treatment planning. The next chapter will address the issues of common purpose and collegiality as desirable outcomes of ongoing training.

CHAPTER FIVE

Ongoing Training as an Organizational Strategy

I n the current business environment, training is no longer a prerogative of healthcare organizations but an imperative. Peter Boland has been unequivocal in his support of this philosophy:

> An effective human resources strategy includes on-going training for employees who want to acquire appropriate skills to fit new work responsibilities. . . . One of the most important competencies an organization must demonstrate is helping its employees master new technical and process skills. This forces many healthcare organizations to realize the critical and unavoidable role of continuing education for employees. . . . Without resolving this issue, organizations will undercut a key potential of re-engineering: learning faster than the competition.

In light of Boland's statement, ongoing training in group leadership for professional staff is an essential part of the mental healthcare organization's overall strategy for human resource development. Such a strategy must be supported by top decision makers in the organization. They must realize that if the organization's goals are to be met, training is never expendable. Managers must allocate the necessary resources, including paid time away from job duties for on-site training. Unless they earmark corporate funding for professional education on a regular basis and make ongoing training a priority in the budget, it will never happen. Opportunities for learning ought to become a key factor in the organizational culture.

In Chapter Nine, I enumerate the qualities that make group therapists a distinct class of professionals. In this chapter, I want to underscore the importance of how ongoing training helps these professionals become efficient and effective team players and why this is critical for the organization to meet its goals.

ORGANIZATION GOALS

In a managed mental healthcare organization that offers group therapy as a benefit for its plan members, developing group leaders by means of ongoing training is a prime concern. Ongoing training and professional development achieve five important goals: creating a willingness to lead, developing a common purpose, fostering collegiality, promoting esprit de corps, and reducing the potential for professional burnout. In the absence of these conditions, the group program will not expand, and the group therapists will not sustain their practices. I'll elaborate on each of these factors as they affect the operations of mental health delivery.

Willingness to Lead

In the case of staff model HMOs, you might assume you could organize a group therapy program by simply hiring group therapists; given the proper historical context and set of institutional values, such a plan might have a chance for success. However, most mental health programs have a mix of clinicians with a wide variety of training and backgrounds—some of which may include group dynamics. There will be an assortment of attitudes and beliefs about groups based on personal education and experience, including negative encounters.

I believe that an unwilling group leader can be no more successful than an unwilling group patient. The therapist must experience choosing to lead. Any training component must identify, from a number of highly skilled professionals with little group experience and not a little trepidation, those candidates most willing to make the transition to group therapist. Inviting these candidates to add to their already considerable skills is a diplomatic way of introducing such training.

Common Purpose

A sense of common purpose is a desirable outcome of any training within the context of an organization. Yet training programs should not produce clones who think and act alike, even though certain similarities in philosophy of treatment, theories of intervention, and professional values will be expected among those who spend a good deal of time together studying and consulting on group process and group leadership. Effective training programs should be designed to build on the individual strengths of the professionals who make up the professional staff or network of providers. Differentiation is the key to helping therapists find their highest level of competence and apply their craft in ways that best suit their skills.

For example, when clinicians gather in peer supervision to discuss how to lead a group that is rebelling against its leaders, many therapists are tempted to defend themselves against what they perceive to be challenges of their authority by the patients. How therapists respond to such challenges varies with their personality and history. Unless the leaders see the challenges coming from the group in a larger theoretical context, that is, as an expression of a necessary and predictable phase of group development, they may mistakenly construe what is essentially a group phenomenon to be a personal attack. How each therapist works through the emotions of such common situations is a matter of personal difference. But the process of working it through and the belief that it can be resolved, while keeping both the treatment group and the self-esteem of the leaders intact, are common threads that unite group practitioners.

A sense of common purpose underlies all the efforts of training because it lets therapists function as a treatment team and allows them to refer to each other with confidence. It allows therapists to identify with each other's work and share goals in common, even when there are differences in personal approaches and professional strategies. Group therapists can be instructed in the purposes and values that transcend such individual differences, and I give my perspective on these purposes and values in Chapter Ten.

Collegiality

Collegiality is a measure of the ease of communication among professionals who have occasion to work with each other, either in staff model HMOs or provider networks. It is a product of the trust and good faith that professionals demonstrate toward each other. The evolution of trust and good faith are themselves outgrowths of positive shared training experiences.

For example, when clinicians join an ongoing seminar or peer supervision group, they are expressing a desire to learn about both the field and themselves. To varying degrees, they will share their vulnerability as they discuss the problems they must confront in their work lives as group therapists, and in some instances, how their private lives affect and are affected by the work they do. This capacity to show vulnerability is a positive trait that engenders collegiality, because each clinician can readily identify with the predicaments her fellow workers encounter. The following case is an illustration.

At one staff model HMO, a senior member of the psychiatric staff, who had once been clinic chief, joined an ongoing peer supervision group to discuss the adolescent group he was currently leading.

His participation in the group evoked mixed emotions from the other members. Some of the nonmedical therapists were pleased, as it was not common for psychiatrists to partake in peer supervision sessions. Yet others in the group felt intimidated, as if the former chief's presence would keep them from admitting their weaknesses to one who had not long ago been their boss.

When the man began sharing his difficulties with his group of teenagers, the atmosphere changed. As he drew parallels between the anger he felt toward one particular boy in his group and his own son, the other therapists were quick to identify with his struggle and offer stories of their shortcomings with their own children. In this way, he felt accepted as part of the group and was able to receive good ideas on how to deal with his countertransference reactions to his patient.

The ability to work through the problems that arise depends on and positively reinforces an atmosphere of trust. Colleagues can come to each other with the confidence that their shortcomings will be looked on as difficulties common to the field. In well-constructed training sessions or supervisory meetings, colleagues are encouraged to give feedback to each other in good faith and not as a way to undermine or negatively judge each other's efforts. The nature of the training experiences should be designed to lessen the tendency of colleagues to take competitive advantage of each other.

Competition among staff members during training sessions can be addressed and worked through as part of the naturally evolving phases of the group process, as in this situation:

In one supervisory group organized for network providers of a managed care plan, a very bright and energetic psychologist got into a theoretical battle with a male colleague over how she ought to treat a borderline individual in a group she had just begun. The colleague thought she ought to confront the patient when he made provocative and aggressive remarks in the group, whereas the psychologist believed she must tread lightly lest the patient leave the group prematurely. The leader of the supervisory group was astute enough to notice that the supervisory group itself was rather new, having met just three times with its current membership. The leader suggested that the members of the supervisory group were contending for position and recognition, a situation similar to that of the treatment group in which the borderline patient was striking aggressive postures. This realization helped the psychologist confront her own difficulty in seeing herself as powerful in her treatment group.

Supervisory groups should always have trainers knowledgeable about group dynamics and skillful at assisting members through conflicts involving rivalries. The resolution of such conflicts enlarges the clinicians' trust that their treatment groups also can evolve to more mature levels of functioning. How the trainer leads the group to this understanding is significant. She can model trust by believing that the group members will find their own way to mature as a group without undue direction and control by its leader. Attenuating rivalries among colleagues has obvious positive advantages for the organization.

Esprit de Corps

The concept of esprit de corps defines the quality of the work environment and includes convivial relationships with colleagues and an open spirit of cooperation and collaboration. It involves a willingness to teach others what you know without arrogance and to ask for help without embarrassment. The cultivation of such an atmosphere is a safeguard against mistakes, because fellow clinicians feel secure enough to be congruent and capable of saying what they understand and what they don't.

For example, a work environment that values ongoing training also values learning; clinicians are encouraged to ask questions and to be curious. I don't have to act like I have all the answers and neither do others. If an entry-level person comes to me, puzzled by some aspect of the group referral system that is not working, I won't censure him for "not knowing his job" but instead will listen to how he'd like to make his job better. If my colleague is having difficulty managing a borderline patient in her group, I can suggest that she get some peer supervision. This is possible when group supervision is appreciated by the organization and is already in place for clinicians to use. Those who participate together in training events often form a bond with each other that allows them to spontaneously offer assistance in the future and be open to help in return.

Burnout Prevention

In no field of psychotherapy are the practitioners so vulnerable as in group psychotherapy. This has both personal and professional consequences for group therapists. They must provide themselves with a network of support that helps them maintain equanimity in the face of what can sometimes seem to be withering psychological insults in the form of projection and projective identification by patients. Even the best-trained group therapists will experience distress and anxiety when exposed over time to the intensity of these processes. Professional burnout occurs when clinicians must double and treble their defenses in order to cope at their jobs. Therapists report diminished satisfaction in their work, accompanied by a loss of interest and curiosity in the field and a drop in performance standards.

Ongoing training and supervisory opportunities help stem burnout among group therapists. Sharing work experiences, especially some of the most disturbing ones, with a peer is rejuvenating. Often, a clinician absorbs too much of the pain, sadness, or anger that patients release in their groups as a part of their healing process. The phenomenon of projective identification alone, whereby the group therapist first contains and then identifies with the specific content of a patient's projection, can unnerve a group therapist long after the group session has ended. The following case is an example.

I once treated in group therapy a veteran who suffered from severe posttraumatic stress disorder. He had been in combat, and during group sessions he often experienced intense flashbacks accompanied by memories of physical pain. He usually dissociated during these episodes, leaving the room psychologically without letting on to the group what was happening to him. During these episodes, I became the target of the patient's projective identification. In this rather unconscious process, the patient projected his pain onto me. As group therapist, it was my job to "hold" or sit with his pain and not "act it out," that is, not act as if his pain were my own and express it in some way.

However, during one session, I began saying things like, "The group is experiencing a lot of pain." In other words, I attributed to the group the pain that had taken possession of me. The group members were confused by my statements and could not relate them to what they were feeling. I also began to experience some of the patient's complaints, such as insomnia and agitation.

In this particular case, I had the good fortune to be working with a co-therapist, who perceived my behavior and recognized how peculiar it was compared to how I usually acted in group. Otherwise, I probably would not have noticed how strangely I was behaving and would have continued to identify with the patient's projection. It would have become increasingly stressful for me to lead this therapy group under those conditions, and I might have considered stopping the group, as other patients projected their disavowed emotions for me to contain.

In the absence of a co-therapist, there are other options open to me. If I could attend a supervisory group in which I was able to relate the story of my patient in the previous example, it is likely that one of my colleagues would have grasped the meaning of what was happening to me and helped me understand why I was so beside myself. As groups of colleagues work together over time, they become quite astute in comprehending the dilemmas that necessarily entangle us as we lead therapy groups.

The possibility of burnout for the group therapist increases with the level of pathology and severe crises suffered by her patients. For this reason, at Puget Sound we established co-therapy as the standard of practice for therapy groups that treated these conditions.

OPTIONS FOR ONGOING TRAINING

The training of clinicians to practice group therapy can take the form of theoretical seminars, supervision groups for clinicians who are either leading or wanting to lead treatment groups, and opportunities for an experienced group mentor to share the leadership of a treatment group with a professional in training. All of these options are a part of successful ongoing training programs.

Process groups with clinicians who work together as a team are also very productive, but they require considerable time and emotional commitment from all concerned and should be used only when specific conditions apply. These conditions include full agreement and cooperation from organization decision makers, sufficient cohesion as a work group to withstand the stress of process consultation, and good faith on the part of the team leader who invites the consultant to initiate the process. At the end of this chapter I briefly describe one process consultation I conducted ("Process Groups for Clinicians").

Seminars

The training of the group therapist must always proceed on both abstract and concrete levels, usually simultaneously. The abstract level is critical because group therapy is the most abstract of therapeutic modalities, and therefore the group therapist must become adept at integrating theoretical notions into the treatment of people facing very real and sometimes extraordinary problems in living. It is often daunting for the therapist to encounter the manifold abstractions that constitute a group's process: the symbolic communication, the nonverbal behavior, and the constant projections going in all directions at once among group members.

This degree of abstraction is lacking in other treatment modalities and requires the leader to use his imagination to conceptualize the deeper emotional connections that might exist among strangers who have gathered in a group in part to discover these very connections for themselves. The group leader must be aware of his responses, both cognitive and emotional, and must often contain his responses within himself so as not to act out in ways confusing to the patients, as I did in the earlier example of projective identification.

The concrete level of training is essential because the changes that patients make in their behavior are the tangible results of their participation in groups, where they experiment in both acting and thinking differently in relation to themselves and others.

As a consultant for various clinics, I have conducted seminars covering specific topics, such as "countertransference in group" and "termination in group." The seminars took place once each week for a month; each meeting was one to two hours long. Each subsequent month, I began a new series on a new topic. I usually limited attendance to no more than eight people to make space for a certain degree of group interaction.

Training seminars must strive to help the group therapist integrate theoretical knowledge with her own group experiences. And if her experiences in group both confirm and contradict a theory, she can learn that no one theory encompasses all that occurs in group. Having a theory to hang one's perceptions on, so to speak, is an excellent way to train a group therapist to perceive accurately and to observe and listen closely. It can prove most enlightening to discern when a theory doesn't fit the particular circumstances of the group.

A seasoned group therapy instructor facilitates the learning by clinicians because she is able to point out where a theory applies and where a new theory or idea is needed to account for the phenomena that emerge. This kind of education can be most exciting, because it requires a good deal of active and imaginative participation on the part of the trainees. Videotapes can augment the learning possible in seminars of this kind. For that very purpose, we have produced a special videotape illustrating the ideas of Ariadne Beck presented in Chapters Eleven and Twelve.

Supervision Groups

A regular program of training and peer supervision can be built into the schedules of therapists in both staff model and network provider panels, so that clinicians can act like a college of scholars and researchers dedicated to personal and professional growth. These training groups can be either time-limited or ongoing with new members being added at set intervals. A peer focus is paramount in these groups because it fits with the emphasis placed on patient equality in all group therapy formats. A nonhierarchical approach stimulates formation of the co-therapy teams so necessary to meeting the demands of groups focused on people in crisis or who are severely mentally ill.

A trainer might form a supervision group to stimulate the start of new therapy groups. The clinicians would assemble to discuss the many obstacles that prevent group formation and propose ideas of how to overcome them. Subgroups might develop consisting of those who were discouraged by the prospect of starting a group and those who were more sanguine about it. The existence of the two subgroups would serve to polarize and contain the conflicting emotions experienced by the therapists and help them move from ambivalence to action. During that process, individuals in the group might discover others with whom they'd like to form co-therapy teams, so that the promise of collaborating with another clinician becomes an additional motive for beginning a new group. One positive outcome of such supervision groups is the establishment of co-leadership pairs, showing again that one of the most important results of ongoing training is the increased chance to collaborate with colleagues.

Another kind of supervision group might be formed to uncover the blind spots of group therapists as they work with their most difficult patients in their groups. Such groups could meet for months and go very deep in their exploration of how therapists internalize the psychological world of their patients in group.

Shared Leadership

One aspect of the training I have especially promoted among staff model HMOs is the development of *nequipo teams*, or teams consisting of one master therapist and one assistant therapist who learns from the master by sharing the leadership of a treatment group. The term *nequipo* derives from the fact that the two members of the team are not equally equipped in knowledge or experience to lead groups. Such teams are highly effective both in training group therapists and in treating patients. They affect the morale of the organization positively and stimulate the formation of new treatment groups. The nequipo team becomes an important way to allow experienced group therapists to convey their knowledge to novice and beginning group therapists. This method of training lets the group mentor be in the same room as the protégé, who can experiment in advancing through the various stages of development (enumerated in Chapter Nine) while under the watchful eye of a master. The goal of this training arrangement is for the assistant to advance toward equality with her teacher. The patients do not suffer in this arrangement as long as treatment and training retain equal standing as central purposes.

In my experience, the quality of the group program is always enhanced, because the more experienced clinician is challenged to learn more as she responds to questions that she herself may never have considered. The master must look afresh at key phenomena perhaps long taken for granted. Many innovations in the delivery of group therapy have resulted from serendipitous exchanges between student and teacher. For example, much of what we have learned about the treatment of borderline personalities in group therapy has resulted from the experiments of students of group therapy who challenged the accepted wisdom of their teachers that such patients were unable to benefit from group methods.

Another approach to training is the *co-learner team,* a team consisting of two therapists who are both just beginning to learn about group therapy. Such teams are supervised by an experienced group therapist, who contracts to meet with them on a regular basis not only to discuss the progress of their treatment group but also to provide an ongoing analysis of their evolving co-therapy relationship. Both the organization and the supervisor must be willing to commit the time necessary to train co-learners in this comprehensive way.

Process Groups for Clinicians

I was once invited by a regional manager to consult with his entire mental health service with the goal of stimulating the development of new therapy groups. The consultation began with a discussion of group therapy, but as we examined resistances to beginning groups, a number of problems in how the service functioned as a team began to emerge. It became clear to me that the most salient need was not group therapy consultation but an organizational intervention that involved conflict resolution.

After obtaining agreements from the chain of command, I renegotiated the contract with the team and began consultation with them about their own process as a work group. This proved to be both productive and time consuming, occupying thirty-six hours over the course of a year. Although not originally intended for that purpose, the process group became a means to address and correct a number of dysfunctional patterns in the work team. Such consultations can be fruitful but must be negotiated separately, because the goal is not narrowly defined as group therapy development but broadly defined as organization development. All parties involved must understand the difference.

Once an organization has incorporated ongoing training as a fundamental part of human resource development, managers can explore innovations in the group therapy programs they offer. In the next chapter, I introduce one example of creative group therapy that adapts well to managed mental healthcare.

CHAPTER SIX

Redecision Therapy: An Innovation in Short-Term Group Treatment

~~~⌇∿∿⌇~~~

In previous chapters, I have described the kind of groups that have become the standard of practice for treating patients in most managed care systems that provide comprehensive group therapy. These groups are founded on the basis of several assumptions:

- The patients referred are experiencing a crisis or symptoms with varying degrees of pathology.

- The groups will be convened in relatively homogeneous constellations that reflect these crises and degrees of pathology.

- The groups will operate according to one theory or another of *through the group* treatment, whereby group members help each other, and the group process itself becomes the instrument of healing.

- The group will progress through various stages of development, which the therapist will recognize and use in the service of helping the group mature and assisting group members to meet their goals of greater adaptation and ego strength.

- Group cohesion, considered the counterpart of therapeutic alliance in individual therapy, is fostered as a goal of treatment.

In short, these are the parameters that define group practice in managed care, and they work very well with the population of patients they are intended to serve.

However, there is a large class of plan members in every managed care system that has needs distinct from this population. The satisfaction of this class of individuals ought to be of concern to managed mental health organizations if they intend to sell contracts to employers in an increasingly aggressive sales environment.

For example, a departure from the traditional gathering of patients in standard groups in managed care environments can well be justified in the case of high-functioning individuals seeking to use their mental healthcare benefit. This is a sizeable population, certainly the majority of people who are plan members in managed care systems. They are not mentally ill nor in crisis, and yet they may want to use their mental health benefit to confront some troubling or distressing aspect of their lives. Organizations must begin to offer innovative approaches in short-term group therapy especially designed for these people.

The standard approach to these plan members has been to tell them that their treatment is "not medically necessary," in effect telling them they are not sick enough to enter the system. Although it may be a relief for some to know that they are not crazy, that message fails to affirm the anguish a person may be experiencing, no matter how slight that suffering may appear to an outside observer. It may have the negative effect of discouraging people from making changes in their lives regardless of how unhappy they are. Being told "We have nothing to offer you" does not contribute to the satisfaction of plan members.

A more positive approach would be to say, "We have anticipated someone like you and have developed a short-term group to address ways in which you can change. Are you interested?"

The organization has a stake in the satisfaction of plan members because that information filters back to their employers, who contract for managed care services among bidders in a highly competitive market. The willingness of management to explore new forms of attending to the needs of plan members is a measure of how adaptable the organization will be to changing conditions and how well it can sustain its plan membership over time. Innovations in group treatment must conform with the time constraints of managed care yet break the rules of standard practice so that healthier plan members can participate in short-term group therapy. Redecision Therapy is one example of a new approach.

REDECISION THERAPY

Of the several behavioral, cognitive, and brief interventions that have been cultivated in recent years, one clearly stands out in the way it combines many psychologically astute concepts in a format that is ideally suited to short-term group therapy with highly motivated, high-functioning patients in managed care systems. Its practitioners must possess a depth of knowledge and skill that takes time to acquire, but once mastered, Redecision Therapy can prove most effective for patients who have the capacity to diligently pursue its course.

Redecision Therapy is a creative synthesis of Gestalt and Transactional Analysis pioneered by Robert L. Goulding and Mary McClure Goulding. It allows people to make changes in themselves while engendering a powerful group process that positively reinforces each redecision. The groups are designed for people who want to identify and change their early childhood decisions in order to enhance their professional growth and personal happiness.

Redecision Therapy is, in my opinion, the treatment of choice for short-term group therapy with high-functioning individuals in managed care settings. This is true for ten reasons.

1. It allows the formation of heterogeneous groups, because the organization with respect to pathology is not important.

2. As an example of *in the group* treatment, where the therapists conduct individual therapy with each patient in a group setting, it is less time consuming than Transactional Analysis, which concentrates deeply on family-of-origin information, and it is more cognitively focused than Gestalt, which places so much emphasis on emotional release.

3. It is more efficient compared to most of the other methods of short-term group therapy that rely on *through the group* treat-

ment, because the phases of group therapy development become less important to the treatment.

4. Group cohesion, so critical in other methods of short-term group therapy, is not needed to bring about change for individual members.

5. It effectively bypasses as much as possible the dynamics of transference (both libidinal and sibling) that become so arduous to work through in psychodynamic and interpersonal methods.

6. Bonding with the leader and fellow group members, although it occurs, is less important than with other therapy methods.

7. Because cohesion and group development are not emphasized, groups can be larger, in the range of twelve to twenty-four individuals.

8. The amount of time devoted to each individual's therapy is limited (twenty minutes per session).

9. Groups can meet one time and schedule one follow-up session, for a total time commitment of four to twelve hours, depending on the length of sessions.

10. Greater significance is given to positive reinforcement, by which the group can support each individual's redecision and determination to behave differently in the world.

Focus on the Individual

Most of the short-term group therapy methods implemented under managed care systems treat patients *through the group*, meaning that the group process, including stages or phases of development, is the primary method for assisting the individual member. The group leader or leaders focus on group objectives and tasks to be accomplished, and this is a significant rationale for organizing homogeneous groups according to specific themes or patient symptoms. In this context, group therapists generally would not focus twenty minutes of undivided attention to a single member while the rest of the group observes. Such individual attention is not warranted in this method because it hinders the growth of group cohesion. Group cohesion is achieved by a series of interactions among members that are guided by the leader and become progressively more complex as termination draws near.

Redecision Therapy, however, is an example of *in the group* treatment, meaning that the interaction between the therapist or therapists and each group member becomes the focus for brief, intense therapeutic work. This is an especially attractive feature for managed care mental health, because it permits the option of forming a heterogeneous group that includes persons with a wide variety of issues. The group therapist forms a therapeutic alliance with each individual based on an explicit therapeutic contract—involving what that individual wants to change about herself—that is stated openly to the group. The group leaders are the authorities and facilitators who direct the individual member through a series of steps that lead to a moment of insight and understanding, called the redecision, that is deeply felt emotionally and leads to behavioral changes the patient will immediately begin putting into practice.

The group is explicitly left out of the steps leading up to the redecision because its comments can interrupt the flow of the dialogue between the group therapist and the individual as well as interrupt the individual's internal dialogue between Parent and Child ego states. Group feedback and sharing of meaning always follow the redecision work as a means of positive reinforcement. Such sharing by observers leads to a group cohesion of a kind, based on familiarity with each other's stories.

Historically, Redecision Therapy has been applied in group settings, but the technique may be skillfully applied in individual and couple therapy as well.

Appropriate Referrals

Highly motivated individuals with good ego strength and without personality or thought disorders are selected for a brief, intense group therapy experience. Four sessions of two hours each are often adequate to let each person work through one piece or more of redecision work. More or less time can be contracted for depending on the time constraints on the group therapists. Patients must be able to tolerate a high level of emotional intensity and ambiguity and to contain their anxiety while focusing very intently.

At Puget Sound, we offered weekend programs so that a group of individuals could meet for six hours on two successive Saturdays and thereby complete a full course of treatment. Flexibility of this kind in the organization and the group therapist is essential in inaugurating a group of this nature.

Michael Hoyt has commented that HMOs provide "fertile contexts for the development of innovative short-term group therapies" (1995, p. 61) and has experimented using the redecision model with patients at Kaiser Permanente in Hayward, California.

Theoretical Considerations

Redecision Therapy takes place in the here and now but draws on the power of decisions that a person made at critical points in her development, decisions that may have worked for her at the time but are now more a nuisance or obstacle to her health and happiness. The technique does not presume a deep or personal knowledge of the patient or the patient's history. Group members hardly need to introduce themselves, and a typical group might begin with the simple question by the leader, "Who wants to change something about themselves?" The phrase "work on something" is avoided because it supports the belief that an indefinite period of time is necessary in order for people to change.

Redecision Therapy explicitly avoids transference—although even in brief encounters it is amazing how rapidly transference can occur. There are specific things a therapist can do to discourage transference. One is to avoid saying things like "Tell me" or encouraging patients to please the therapist. Staying focused on what the patient wants is the key to success in Redecision Therapy, because in most cases the patient had to give up what he wanted in order to please parent figures.

Redecision Therapy instills hope by reinforcing the personal beliefs that (1) "It's possible for me to change," and (2) "I can change relatively quickly," given the proper conditions—including my willingness to practice new behavior as a result of my redecision.

With a motivated population, the resistances to work are actually lessened by the presence of group members. Their silent witness to the work that unfolds serves to lower defenses and allow the therapy to proceed swiftly and deeply.

Injunctions

The Gouldings spoke of certain pathological messages from parents to their children, which if taken up can lead to chronic life problems for the person as an adult. They called these messages injunctions and described them as follows: "Injunctions are messages from the Child ego state of the parents, given out of the circumstances of the parents' own pains: unhappiness, anxiety, disappointment, anger, frustration, secret desires. While these messages are irrational in terms of the child, they may seem perfectly rational to the parent who gives them" (1979, p. 35).

Injunctions are mostly passed on nonverbally, and they remain out of the consciousness of the parent who transmits them. Understanding the injunctions and how they impede the choices of patients in the here and now is a vital part of the training of a Redecision therapist. Although usually not spoken of directly to the patient, they become a point of reference for the therapist as the patient enters the steps to a redecision. The injunctions condense the thousands of possible messages into an elegant list the therapist can remember and around which she can design intervention strategies. The injunctions are as follows:

Don't.	Don't make it.
Don't be close.	Don't be a child.
Don't be important.	Don't be well.
Don't belong.	Don't grow up.
Don't be.	Don't feel.
Don't be you.	Don't think.
Don't trust.	Don't be sane.

Steps to Redecision

The four steps in Redecision Therapy are as follows:

1. "What do you want to change?"
2. "Is there a scene from your past or a memory of how your aspirations have been thwarted?" Experimentation with the patient of various creative ways to access the decision made as a child.
3. Redecision.
4. Positive reinforcement of redecision by group and therapist(s).

I shall follow the steps of redecision work and show what is possible through the intensely focused application of its methods. The follow-

ing transcript is taken from a group of outpatient volunteers organized for the purpose of demonstrating Redecision Therapy. I co-led
the group with Vivian Nelson. The time elapsed for this segment of
the group, its first and only meeting, was seventeen minutes. I have
added comments (bracketed, in italics) to illustrate how the theory is
applied and how the therapist can move the therapy along as rapidly
and efficiently as possible without loss of meaning for the patient.

ANNOTATED TRANSCRIPT
OF A REDECISION GROUP

VIVIAN: Who wants to change something about themselves? *[Co-therapists call for contracts.]*

ALISON: I want to change something.

BILL: Move over here.

ALISON: I want to change a feeling about myself of being unimpor-
tant, invisible—it's been there a long time. I have a sense of where it
came from in my family—a narcissistic mother, an alcoholic father,
two brothers—that boys were more important, smarter than girls.
I was third born in the family.

BILL: How are you feeling? *[Co-therapist does not ask for more history
because that takes Alison away from the feelings just emerging in her after
stating her contract of what she wants to change.]*

ALISON: Mostly anxiety.

VIVIAN: Is there ever a time when you do feel important? *[Co-therapist
responds to the issue Alison wants to change, keeps focus.]*

ALISON: Usually a time when I'm all alone and doing something just
for me: gardening, artwork.

VIVIAN: When you're alone and doing something creative you feel
important?

ALISON: In the context of being with other people I fade. I have a hard
time saying anything. I pull back. What they have to say is more
important.

BILL: Do you have a memory of a scene in your past that will demonstrate the anxiety you feel? *[Co-therapist returns to the affect and asks*

about the scene associated with the affect that Alison may be reliving at that moment.] (Silence—four seconds)

ALISON: There's a memory just a few weeks ago when I was with my mother in San Diego. She said to me, "You don't want to go to the beach to swim today, do you?" It wasn't "Do you want to go to the beach today?" There were at least five other times she said "you don't want" such and such.

BILL: Applying things to you that belong to her.

VIVIAN: I hear "Don't want" *[Co-therapist names the injunction.]*

ALISON: (*Nods head yes*) "Don't want" was pretty strong.

VIVIAN: It's important to want . . . *[Co-therapist adds "important" because in her contract Alison said she wanted to be important.]*

BILL: Will you begin with a dialogue with Mother? *[Co-therapist requests that Alison externalize her internal dialogue with Mother.]* Let's start by having Mother here. Turn your chair to face this chair. So this is Mother. Can you picture her there? Describe her for us? *[A call for descriptions helps Alison to visualize Mother in the room.]*

ALISON: An old grey-haired lady—seventy-six years old, with glasses—stooped over from osteoporosis; she's timid and scared all the time.

BILL: How are you feeling looking at her?

ALISON: A little anxious . . . just looking at her I remember the competition—will I get what I want or what she wants?

BILL: Go over there and be Mother. Start with "You don't want . . ." *[Co-therapist feeds back to Alison the very language she used when she described the earlier scene.]*

ALISON: "You don't want to go to the beach today."

BILL: Tell her more. *[Co-therapist coaches Alison to improvise.]*

ALISON: "You don't want to go and get sand in your shoes—and possibly get red—get sunburned. . . ." (*Pause*)

BILL: "I want to interrupt you. I'm Alison's therapist—are you trying to help her by telling her this?" *[Co-therapist interrupts to get inside Mother's head.]*

ALISON: "No . . . no."

BILL: "Are you trying to communicate something to her?"

ALISON: "I'm trying to communicate to her that it would be easier for us to skip the ocean."

BILL: "But you're not phrasing it that way. Phrase it, 'It will be easier for us—for us. . . .'" *[Therapist stresses that Mother is speaking for herself.]*

ALISON: "It will be easier for us . . . if we didn't go to the ocean today . . . if we stayed by the swimming pool I'd like that better. I don't want sand and sun and salt water. . . ."

BILL: That's the memory. So go back over there. *[Co-therapist reinforces Alison's memory of how she had to let go of what she wanted in favor of Mother.]*

ALISON: "So you don't want to go yourself to the beach today? I'd kind of like to go. . . ." *[Alison begins to differentiate herself from Mother.]*

BILL: How are you feeling at this point?

ALISON: When she says it as I statements, I feel compassion for her. She's got needs and feelings—as opposed to when she states "you don't want." When she states it as I statements, there's less competition.

BILL: Don't be you—be like me. *[The co-therapists name another injunction.]*

VIVIAN: Don't want what you want—want what I want. How do you feel when I say that?

ALISON: My stomach does a little bit of a flip flop. *(To mother)* "Wait a minute—how come it's always what you want?" *[Alison experiences the cognitive dissonance that accompanies the emotional state leading up to a redecision.]*

VIVIAN: Say it *(indicating chair)*. *[Co-therapist invites Alison to externalize her inner dialogue, this time at a new emotional level, confronting her mother.]*

ALISON: "How come it's always what you want? Half the time I don't even know what I want. Never permission to consider it. Can't I ever figure out what I want?"

VIVIAN: Tell her the answers to those questions. *[Co-therapist invites Alison to take responsibility for herself and take the power away from Mother.]*

ALISON: Questions about how I'm going to figure it out?

VIVIAN: Yeah.

ALISON: The only way I'll figure out what I want is to have the freedom to think about possibilities—and try them or maybe even do something without quite knowing—to experiment. I can't do it from the position of not being allowed to want anything. *[Alison starts to feel her own power.]*

VIVIAN: Tell her what you want.

ALISON: "Ummm . . . my wants are pretty vague and undefined. Sometimes I get a clear signal, but most of the time I don't. I feel vaguely confused. This is what I should want—what I think you would want for me. Is it OK to want this? Do I just think I want it because it's easiest. . . ." *[Alison gets lost in an impasse of self-doubts.]*

BILL: Can you go to that scene in your life when you decided to be like her? Before you became aware of— *[Co-therapist asks Alison to move through her impasse by picturing another memory of childhood.]*

ALISON: I think it was pretty young—I think it was more intuiting what she wanted.

BILL: How old is this mother?

ALISON: That mother would probably be thirty something—

BILL: Is she young, vibrant, pretty?

ALISON: Yeah.

BILL: Tell your mother how much you want to be like her—you're pretty small.

ALISON: I'm a year and one-half. I can't say much. (*Laughs*)

BILL: OK.

ALISON: But it profoundly happened. Several times . . .

BILL: Talk to her. *[Co-therapist gives no precise instructions on what to say, unlike in the first scene, for two reasons. First, the language used in the contract will not fit this young memory, and second, Alison must be able to empower herself and not adapt again, as she did with Mother, to what someone else wants her to do.]*

ALISON: "Mommy I love you. I want you to be happy—I want you to love me."

BILL: Tell her what you're willing so that—

ALISON: "I'll do most anything you want."

BILL: Tell her what that means for you. *[A call for the early "decision" Alison made in response to her dilemma of craving Mother's love at any cost]*

ALISON: "It means I'm going to give up knowing who I am—and giving up the opportunity to know who I am . . . and give up being able to make decisions—not being able to decide what's right and what's wrong for me."

BILL: How are you feeling now? *[A call for the emotions Alison feels now in response to seeing how she sacrificed herself in the bargain with Mother]*

ALISON: Umm . . . a little more anxious.

BILL: Go inside and look at the anxiety.

ALISON: (*Pause*)

BILL: Does this all feel real to you? *[Co-therapist keeps Alison focused and checks to see if she is able to contain the contradictory feelings and parts of herself that she is revealing. This is where the ego strength of the patient must be adequate, as persons with fragmented egos will simply dissociate or deny what is happening at this point in the therapy.]*

ALISON: Pretty much.

BILL: Look at the anxiety—it's important what you feel . . . not what she says.

ALISON: I'm scared because I don't quite know what this means . . . I don't know where this is going to lead.

BILL: Verbalize your fears. *[Co-therapist stays with Alison's emotions.]*

ALISON: (*Strong affect, tears*) I'm afraid I'll never know who I am or be happy with who I am—and I'll pretty much always wonder why I'm alive—and pretty much struggle to stay alive *[Alison lets herself feel the despair she usually represses in order to keep her "agreement" with Mother intact.]*

BILL: What's Mother doing? *[Co-therapist evokes Alison's feeling for Mother.]*

ALISON: She's looking sad. She doesn't quite want this for me—and doesn't know what to do. *[Alison experiences Mother's powerlessness, a step toward taking her own power and making a redecision.]*

BILL: She really didn't know what to do—you're a much better mother to yourself than she was. Are you willing to take another chair and be the mother you needed?

ALISON: OK.

BILL: That's your child over there. *[A different chair is used to symbolize another part of Alison.]*

ALISON: OK. (*To child*) "You get to choose what you want. It's OK for you to do—to know what you want. You can find some kind of sustaining meaning in life . . . some kind of joy." *[Alison begins her redecision by offering her little girl the permission to want things for herself.]*

BILL: Is she hearing you? Is she listening?

ALISON: I think so.

BILL: You can ask her what she wants—she always wanted a mother that would ask her.

ALISON: (*To child*) "What do you want?"

BILL: What is she doing? *[Co-therapist reinforces Alison's implicit promise to pay attention to her little girl and what she wants.]*

ALISON: She's looking kind of confused.

BILL: It's a new question, isn't it?

ALISON: (*Nods her head yes.*)

BILL: You can ask her every day. *[Co-therapist introduces the possibility that Alison can put into practice every day the redecision she has made.]*

ALISON: That's a novel idea.

BILL: Wouldn't that be different?

ALISON: (*Nods*) Um humm.

BILL: Are you willing to make that promise to her?

ALISON: Yes.

BILL: Tell her what you promise. *[Co-therapist directs Alison to make the promise to herself, not to the therapists.]*

ALISON: "I promise every day I'll ask you every day what you want. You don't necessarily have to answer—but it will be an opportunity for you to think about it." *[This is the behavior change that will break the "Don't be important" injunction that Alison indicated in her contract.]*

BILL: Anything else you want to tell her? *[In this vulnerable state, a call for Alison to state other injunctions she may be avoiding is appropriate, if the therapist keeps to the original contract and does not expand the time boundaries to do more work.]*

ALISON: "It's OK for you to want to live." *[A surprise. The "Don't be" or suicide injunction surfaced, and Alison faced it without the help of the co-therapist.]*

BILL: Does she hear you?

ALISON: Yes.

BILL: Do you love her?

ALISON: "I love you. . . ." *[Nurturing statements in very soft voice]*

BILL: How are you feeling?

ALISON: Sad, relieved, and a little angry.

VIVIAN: Come back in this chair and see how it feels to receive those new messages. Can you hear them inside? Do you remember? *[Co-therapist emphasizes remembering what happened, as a redecision is a cognitive shift that must be reinforced and anchored in the strong emotions that are evoked.]*

ALISON: Um humm. I think because it's so new I feel sad—also I feel cared about. (*Tears*)

VIVIAN: Sometimes when we long for something—and finally get it—it seems to touch that sadness that is a deep feeling—so it seems likes sadness.

ALISON: I suspect you're right.

VIVIAN: Do you want to tell the group about anything? *[A call for closure]*

ALISON: I lost the fact there was a group here—now I feel embarrassed about it. It feels neat to know I can each day renew that commitment to myself.

VIVIAN: Do you want to hear from people? How it related to them?

ALISON: Sure. *[The group can positively reinforce her redecision and at the same time build an atmosphere of trust so that the next individual can begin.]*

As this demonstration shows, Redecision Therapy is a tightly structured, spare, and highly directive kind of individual therapy practiced in a group setting.

In this context, the group serves not only to lower defenses but to mobilize the energy of its members to make changes in their lives. It is particularly suitable for plan members on the healthy end of the mental health spectrum. The next chapter focuses on the people at the other end of that spectrum, patients who need ongoing, long-term care, and discusses the idea that appropriate group treatment can reduce the cost of overall medical services for these individuals.

CHAPTER SEVEN

The Offset Effect

T he offset effect is the assumption that timely and appropriate mental healthcare of patients can reduce significantly their use of medical services. This phenomenon has been of great interest to HMOs and managed care operations, and has been the subject of valuable research, including studies by William Follette and Nicholas Cummings of Kaiser Permanente Medical Group in San Francisco and William Kogan of Group Health Cooperative of Puget Sound.

Based on my own clinical observation and research, I believe that a substantial number of those individuals who use medical services at elevated rates will both need and respond well to mental health treatment. Early identification and provision of group therapy to these people, where appropriate, is the subject of this chapter.

AN OFFSET STUDY OF
GROUP THERAPY OUTPATIENTS

My particular interest at Puget Sound was to investigate how group therapy might reduce the visits to physicians by patients identified as high utilizers of medical services.

As group therapy coordinator for the Mental Health Service at Puget Sound, I initiated a study of 115 outpatients then in group therapy treatment at our clinic. Our goal was to conduct one of the first offset investigations to consider as factors both the mode of psychotherapy and the patients' perception of the treatment.

We administered a satisfaction questionnaire to our subjects (the results of which are reported in Chapter One) and received consent from 109 patients to contact them by mail six months later for follow-up measures. Our task was to examine their medical use patterns over a seven-year period. Although our study lacked a control or comparison group, which limits how much we can generalize to other populations, we believe the responses we obtained from our experimental group were highly descriptive of the population we served during those years.

The Patients

Nearly one-half of all patients responding reported they had been in group therapy before their current group therapy experience. From this we may assume that these individuals had an awareness that group therapy might be offered to them and a sense of what they might expect from their treatment. Nearly one-half of the patients were interviewed for the first time by our mental health service within one year of the administration of the questionnaire, indicating the acute nature of the population we served.

Initial diagnoses were distributed as follows: depression, both acute and chronic, 23 percent; life crises, including marital dysfunction, 19 percent; family abuse and battering, 13 percent; personality disorders, 6 percent; loss associated with physical disabilities and disease, 9 percent; and chronic psychoses, 3 percent.

Of the seventy-eight patients who were still plan members in 1983 and whose medical charts we reviewed, 70 percent of all their mental health visits were for group therapy. Group therapy was clearly the primary mode of treatment for this sample of patients.

Results

Contrary to the belief that mental health consumers are generally high medical utilizers, we found that nearly 70 percent of our sample were in fact low to moderate medical utilizers based on a scale devised by

William Kogan. This scale described yearly mean patient visits by categories and defined them as follows: zero to 3 visits, low utilization; 4 to 13 visits, moderate utilization; and 14 or more visits, high utilization. Our most interesting finding had to do with the category of high medical utilizers. High medical utilization often accompanied increased mental health visits, regardless of whether the one form of utilization preceded or followed the other. In these cases, both could be viewed as part of the same utilization curve. It was not possible to presume from our data that mental health treatment influenced medical utilization or that medical treatment influenced mental health utilization. In some cases, outside the scope of our study, mental health utilization could be considered a logical extension of medical treatment, and physician referrals to the mental health service would be evidence of that fact.

Implications

One generalization about high medical utilizers did appear justified by our data: these patients' increase in mental health utilization seemed linked to their overall utilization of medical services. However, such a pattern did not characterize the majority of patients in our sample.

This supports two important conclusions. First, to study a population of mental health patients without looking closely at the high medical utilizers among them could distort the meaning of the information obtained. One distorted conclusion might be that mental health consumers are high medical utilizers.

Second, to study high medical utilizers in isolation from the more general cases could mislead researchers to make inferences about the mental health population as a whole. One misleading inference could be the presumption of an offset effect, rather than the statistical interpretation of regression to the mean following high utilization.

The offset effect remains an interesting and possibly valid hypothesis, but for more complicated reasons than the simple "mental health provision reduces medical care consumption" formula. Our study yielded some pertinent data that shifted the discussion from the reduction of medical utilization to the recognition of mental health as primary care in its own right. Our study recommended further and more complete integration of mental health and medical care delivery, especially for patients on the high end of the spectrum of medical utilization. For that category of patients, we saw a tendency for increased medical utilization and increased mental health utilization to follow a similar pattern during the same approximate time period. This phenomenon supports my belief that mental healthcare, and specifically group therapy treatment, is fundamental and necessarily goes hand in hand with the primary medical care of these patients.

THE ROLE OF GROUP THERAPY IN MEDICAL CARE

Various research studies report that from 60 to 70 percent of all physician visits have no diagnosable organic etiology, meaning that patients came to their internists and primary care physicians with complaints related to psychosocial aspects of their lives. It is also estimated that 80 percent of all psychotropic medication is prescribed by primary care physicians, a tacit admission by doctors that they are confronted with mental illness on a regular basis in the general practice of medicine. The offset effect assumes that many of these problems could be more efficiently addressed by behavioral or mental healthcare interventions. The idea is that greater savings could be realized if the emotional distress of the patients were attended to directly.

There is strong evidence that group interventions are just as effective as individual therapy in addressing psychosocial problems. Once medical managers become cognizant that group therapy carries equal effectiveness, the efficiency of the method makes groups an even more desirable treatment option.

To that end, it is important to switch the focus from simply reducing the use of medical services to making possible the appropriate use of group therapy. Given the many psychosocial reasons that motivate people to make appointments with their physicians, comprehensive managed care organizations must become aware of the ways in which joining a therapy group can improve the general health of their plan subscribers and lessen the need for physician visits. In fact, there are cases for which the managed care organization should consider encouraging the use of appropriate group interventions in order to prevent high utilization of medical facilities and costly medical testing procedures. This conceptual shift by an organization is not only cost-effective but also ethically sound as a way to enhance healthy outcomes for plan members, because it helps them improve their ability to take care of themselves.

Behavioral healthcare is not the same as mental healthcare. The former involves education of the public, changes in lifestyle patterns, programs in exercise and nutrition, and overall increased awareness of health-promoting activities that lie within the control of plan members. It also deals with questions of compliance with healthcare recommendations and patient motivation for self-care.

Where there is a definable mental illness, however, mental healthcare is indicated and should be initiated to prevent decompensation, hospitalization, and the conversion of psychological symptoms to somatic ailments and complaints.

Seriously Mentally Ill Patients

There are very good ethical and practical reasons to identify and treat mentally ill plan members in group therapy in a timely fashion. Mentally ill patients who remain undiagnosed can often become high utilizers of medical care. This is especially true with patients who complain of multiple somatic problems, or those people who express their emotional distress in bodily symptoms. Patients suffering from depression and general anxiety disorders often fit this description and can be adequately treated by group therapy, as I indicated in Chapter Three.

Specialized groups for other patients with identifiable conditions should also be considered—in particular, those patients who are likely to accelerate the pace of their medical utilization as their mental illnesses progress. Patients experiencing somatic symptoms and suffering from borderline personality disorders are an example of this kind of patient.

For example, at Puget Sound I treated an adolescent who repeatedly attempted suicide, consuming many emergency room and inpatient days recovering from her self-inflicted injuries. Her course of treatment—at first, in our group for parasuicidal patients, and later, in a group for seriously ill young people—was turbulent and her attendance sporadic, but it did succeed in interrupting her cycle of physical mutilation. We provided group therapy (and a few sessions of individual treatment) as an alternative to her inpatient hospitalizations, at decreased cost for the health plan and for the patient in terms of physical pain.

We found that it paid off to substitute less costly group therapy interventions for exceedingly more expensive emergency room care in the cases of high-utilizing patients who suffered from borderline disorders, extreme histrionic disorders, and, in some cases, narcissistic personality disorders. Early identification of these individuals by primary care physicians helped us plan their treatment in appropriate groups. These treatment groups were able to discourage the patients' "acting out" in ways that involved injuring themselves and thereby requiring costly medical attention.

The training of primary care physicians to identify these individuals and refer them for appropriate group therapy interventions is one goal that can be achieved through a greater integration between mental health and primary care. The group therapy coordinator can cooperate with clinic managers in providing physicians with the necessary information by means of personal contacts, group meetings, brochures that describe services, and frequent telephone exchanges.

In another case, prior to the court's mandating treatment in group therapy for this patient, a battering male had inflicted injuries on his spouse requiring lengthy hospitalizations. His identification as an abuser was the result of astute observation by the emergency room physician, in coordination with the co-therapists of the group for male batterers. This cooperation between services, and the good communication skills such cooperation implies, prevented further pain and suffering for the spouse and medical expenditures by the health plan.

In yet another case, a woman suffering from a severe personality disorder acted out her anxiety and ego deficits by behaving in sexually promiscuous ways and refusing to employ methods of birth control. Her frequent abortions put her at risk medically and further eroded her self-esteem. She resisted any suggestion of mental health treatment until her primary care physician agreed to co-lead a therapy group for individuals who lacked ego development. His co-therapist, a mental health professional, had suggested the time-limited group as a way of introducing group therapy to patients who would otherwise be too threatened to participate. The bond the woman had formed with her primary care physician was quite strong and allowed her to enter the group despite her misgivings. On completion of the time-limited group, the woman had matured sufficiently to contemplate joining an ongoing group for disturbed individuals.

Management of Chronic Mental Illness

Roy MacKenzie has pointed out that long-term therapy groups can prove useful in preventing the decompensation of patients who suffer from chronic mental disorders. Within certain categories of mentally ill individuals, ongoing therapy groups that are maintained over years can clearly reduce the excessive costs of hospitalization and emergency room utilization.

Managed mental health delivery systems are based on the acute care delivery model. This model works well for that segment of the plan membership that will respond to acute care. However, it does not work well for those who suffer chronic illnesses whose conditions are protracted and in some cases highly resistant or unresponsive to cure. The goals are different for this population: they are to relieve some symptoms and to forestall further dysfunction. The goals of group therapy with these individuals emphasize improvement in the quality of their lives and as much adaptation to their surroundings as possible, given the level of their dysfunction. Groups organized for these purposes can be highly effective in ongoing formats. This approach means restructuring existing mental health management practices so that the long-term needs of the patients or health plan members take precedence over the short-term focus of the healthcare organization.

William Follette and Nicholas Cummings, in their classic article written thirty years ago on the offset effect, alluded to a certain percentage of long-term patients who needed to continue with mental health visits without diminution over time. They appeared to be lifelong mental health utilizers who had exchanged medical appointments for psychiatric appointments. Anticipating the advent of group therapy in managed care, Follette and Cummings suggested the development of "alternatives to either traditional medical or traditional psychiatric treatment in favor of some attempt to promote beneficial social changes in the environments of these chronically disturbed people" (1967, pp. 33–34).

More recently, Nicholas Cummings has published a journal article entitled "The Successful Application of Medical Offset in Program Planning and Clinical Delivery" and a book chapter entitled "Does Managed Health Care Offset Costs Related to Medical Treatment?" both of which provide the reader with the most up-to-date information in the field of offset studies.

In summary, group therapy has a role in helping certain individuals address their psychosocial needs in a therapeutic setting that allows more time for empathic understanding than do traditional medical interviews. Primary care physicians can serve a pivotal function by identifying potential high-utilizing patients and referring them to appropriate groups. By this process, the managed care system avoids wasting valuable resources on repetitive and costly medical procedures that prove ineffective in the long-term treatment of these patients. The individual plan members will benefit from the smooth coordination between the two panels of medical and mental health providers.

In the next chapter, I shall concentrate on the rights of the individuals who receive care in managed care health plans, and the responsibility that providers have to fully inform them of the implications of their treatment in such a system.

CHAPTER EIGHT

Patient Rights and Therapist Responsibilities

Recent proposals by state legislators have stressed the importance of patients' rights within the sphere of managed healthcare. Specifically, calls have been issued to rescind all so-called gag laws that might prevent providers working in managed care settings from giving full assessments and suitable recommendations to their patients, regardless of the restrictions placed on the care the patients can receive under their benefit. The legislation assumes that it is the patient's prerogative to know the frank opinion of his healthcare provider. Other calls for action emphasize the need for greater protection of confidential material concerning the lives of individuals covered under managed care policies. Given the public's awareness of these developments, it is pertinent and timely to focus attention on the rights of the individuals who participate in these health plans.

After reading many books on the subject of managed care, I was reminded of the scene from Marcel Camus' classic film, *Orfeo Negro*, or Black Orpheus, in which Orfeo is looking for his Euridice. He comes to the Bureau of Missing Persons, where the wind blows through empty halls, scattering papers and documents. He asks the janitor where he might find his lover. The janitor is quite astonished by the question and responds, "There's no people here, Mister."

In the literature of managed mental healthcare that has burgeoned of late, the absence of the individual patient who uses the care that is managed is quite extraordinary. The individual has rights and needs that deserve attention beyond the simple categorizing of people under *DSM-IV* labels—and the necessarily truncated treatment plans that are offered.

We must begin with the questions, What does the individual want for herself, when it comes to mental health? Does her benefit start her on the road to what she wants? What happens if she wants more than her benefit provides? Must she leave the road entirely? Or might she continue on privately—regardless of medical necessity or other gatekeeping criteria—in order to discover new things about herself and deepen the meaning in her life?

RIGHTS AND RESPONSIBILITIES

Patients who enter treatment with a therapist have a right to know the conditions under which they will be receiving treatment. I give the following written statement to all my patients covered under managed care contracts who enter group psychotherapy with me:

Welcome to group therapy. I'm glad you've chosen to work with me in this way because I believe it will be helpful to you, solving problems in living, deepening your capacity to relate to others, and perhaps setting you on a path toward a new sense of yourself.

You have informed me that you want to receive benefits from the managed care company that monitors your mental health benefits so that the cost of your treatment with me will be partially paid for. This means I will be sharing privileged information with a third party payer at your specific request. However, be advised that release of information does not imply nor require that I reveal everything that I am told.

Your managed care company will stop paying for psychotherapy sessions with me after a certain time to be determined by the company. It is possible that once you have embarked on group treatment, you will want to pursue treatment beyond what your benefit covers. In the event that the benefit provided you falls short of your goals as you have stated them to me, I want you to know that I will remain committed to the goals you have set for yourself and that I am prepared to continue providing treatment, should you desire to work with me beyond the managed care limitation. I am willing to negotiate a fee with you so that you can pay me directly and the continuity of your care can be maintained without interruption.

It may be that you will want to continue your work in the group you entered initially. Or, as a result of what you discover in your group, you may want another referral from me for another kind of group—or another group therapist—who will help you delve more deeply into yourself.

You may also find that you use therapy very well—and although stopping your treatment now—you will want to return from time to time to address issues as they arise. You may choose to use therapy as a means of preventive care, confronting problems as they emerge, before they amplify into crises. There are other options that do not appear on the menu of your insurance benefit that you can consider as well. They include couples' groups, multiple family groups, same gender groups, and groups with a particular focus on personal growth.

If you have further questions or want elaboration of my dedication to the therapeutic process you have initiated, please speak with me directly.

As this letter indicates, we must leave room for individual variation and choice in the process of seeking and using psychotherapy. A certain number of individuals will be appropriate and choose group psychotherapy; another set will choose further treatment in other modalities. As providers and managers of treatment, we must allow for these possibilities. As psychotherapists, our responsibility to our patients does not end with their insurance benefit. This must become a cardinal rule for clinicians who work in managed care.

The duty to treat and advise transcends the financial arrangements a patient makes with her employer's representative in the form of managed care. My commitment as a clinician is with my patient and is in the interest of my patient's welfare and volition. For example, I might very well say to a patient whose entitlement is exhausted, "I believe it would be in the interest of your health and happiness to pursue treatment in an ongoing group for individuals who have been sexually abused." Once I have discharged my responsibility in saying this, it becomes the patient's responsibility to act or not act on my recommendation.

The Person Who Wants Personal Growth or Characterological Change

Before your managed care patient is admitted to group, let him know that his benefit circumscribes the treatment that is offered and be clear that long-term therapy is not a part of the benefit. Do not apologize for the brevity of the group experience. The experience can be both positive and curative. Let your patient know that you have confidence in his ability to obtain something for himself. On the other hand, do not disparage long-term treatment. If he gains something and responds well to group, tell him so.

If he expresses a desire to obtain further insights into himself, suggest that he could profit from long-term group treatment in the private sector, if he is so inclined. Those of us who practice in the managed care arena must realize that a number of people we treat effectively in our short-term groups will want to go deeper in their group work and will turn to the private fee-for-service sector to address their comprehensive needs.

Confidentiality

There is no issue more fraught with controversy and conflict than the topic of how to protect the traditional patient privilege to conduct confidential communication with the therapists of her choice. This idea of patient privilege was first pronounced by Hippocrates in the oath he believed each physician ought to avow: "Whatever, in connection with my professional practice, or not in connection with it, I may see or hear in the lives of men which ought not to be spoken abroad I will not divulge, as reckoning that all such should be kept secret" (Clapp, 1974, pp. 565–566).

The traditional contract with the patient has been changed to admit the presence of a third party, namely the case manager or other representative of the organization hired by the employer to manage its employees' mental health expenditures. The rules of engagement must be spelled out to patients, who may not understand the consequences of signing a consent for release of information form. Once personal information about an individual is stored in computers, there is the possibility of it reaching persons who have no compelling need or right to know, including employers and other companies that might insure the patient in the future.

In some instances, individuals have been denied disability or health insurance based on the fact that they had received psychotherapy in the past. The denial of insurance because of such "pre-existing conditions," as they are called in the industry, has been challenged recently by lawmakers intent on amending the unfairness of the practice. But the threat of refusal for insurance coverage has been real and has been an example of the negative consequences that stem from breaches of confidentiality in the past.

Harvard Community Health Plan, for one, acknowledged that until recently it had routinely entered detailed psychotherapy notes into computer records that were then accessible to employees who had no reason to know about the patient's mental health treatment. The HMO has now modified its procedures, separating mental health notes from those pertaining to general medical care, and restricting accessibility. This case shows how pervasive such practices have been, even among some of the best organizations.

What the Patient Should Know

Unfortunately, not all HMOs and managed mental health plans have been so conscientious in preserving the privacy of their plan members by changing policy on the storage of confidential material. It is the duty of providers to inform patients about their policies so that patients will have the choice of paying for psychotherapy privately rather than risk disclosure of personal data. Patients should be informed of the following:

• Insurance companies and their managed mental health plans will request "treatment plans" from your provider. These plans require information on your history, symptoms, diagnosis of mental disorder, and the content of treatment sessions. If you are in group therapy, this could mean that your provider would supply details about the nature of your group and the goals of treatment.

• Your signing of a release of information form releases the provider from any legal obligation to hold in trust what you have revealed to him. The provider renders your personal data and confidences as part of the treatment plan submitted to the managed care company for review and monitoring.

• Once your treatment plan is dispatched, you and the provider no longer control the fate of its contents. As Jennifer Katze says to her patients: "Each company has its own procedures for handling and storing such sensitive and confidential paperwork, and there is no assurance that I can make that it will be handled with utmost discretion" (1996).

• If you have been denied disability insurance in the past, it is possible that the disability company will transfer your history to the Medical Information Bureau, a coalition of insurers that keeps a database taken from insurance applications. Such transferral could have long-range implications for your insurability in the future.

Group therapists are particularly sensitive to the issue of confidentiality because it is one of the central issues of trust that bind a group together. Not only the therapist but each of the group members must hold the sacredness of each other's lives in their hands. Patients in group are concerned about their own privacy and are highly invested in keeping the confidence of their fellow members, as a betrayal of one represents a betrayal of all.

Part of being an effective and trustworthy group therapist means raising this issue of confidentiality with patients in group. Often, how a patient pays for group therapy sessions becomes a focal point for important work in group, whether it is a parent or a spouse who is paying the bill. How much is that person entitled to know about the treatment process and the progress of the patient? This is no less a concern when the partial payer is an insurance company or a managed care operation.

The role of the patient in group therapy and the autonomy she exercises in making the choices she does must always be in the mind of the group therapist. One of the goals of group therapy is to expand the realm of personal autonomy in the patient's internal and external worlds. The astute and ethical clinician must assist the patient by providing her the best information available regarding her health plan, on which she can base her decisions. To do less is to abrogate the contract the group therapist makes with his patient.

PATIENT RESPONSIBILITY

We must realize that the patient is ultimately responsible for his own mental health, whether he values therapy or not, whether he uses therapy or not, and to what degree he uses it. Of course, the resources needed in order to use mental health services in the private sector vary from person to person and are limited for many people. For some, the resources are nonexistent. Yet I have been continually impressed by the motivation of patients to sacrifice considerable amounts of time and money in the pursuit of changes to improve the quality of their lives through group therapy. These people are willing to devote their resources to achieve goals they have set for themselves—goals that have an experiential base and, when accomplished, are often quite visible to others. The patients know when they have accomplished their goals. This is a basic tenet of their autonomy and their core identity as being responsible for themselves.

Choosing a Mental Health Plan

Before selecting a plan to cover their mental health treatment, potential consumers of the services should ask the following questions:

- How will my therapist be chosen? If I can choose my own therapist and she is not a member of the exclusive provider panel, can she become eligible to treat me?
- What are the limits of the care? Are there suitable therapy groups I can enter now, and is there a fixed number of sessions you generally offer to people with my mental health benefit?
- How will the course of treatment be determined? How much say do I have in the process? What are my options if I am dissatisfied with my treatment?
- Will my mental health records be filed with my general medical records? Who will have access to them?
- Can I contract to continue working with my therapist and my group beyond the benefit provided? If I can do so, what will be the cost to me?
- Is my choice to use my mental health benefit as supplied through my employer or health plan worth the compromises and trade-offs I must make?

The Highly Disturbed Individual

The degree of individual psychopathology will definitely limit what a person can accomplish in group therapy—and in some cases determine if he is an appropriate candidate for short-term group treatment.

Sometimes an extremely disturbed person suffering from a personality disorder will benefit from short-term intervention, if she can become aware through her group experience that further treatment is indicated. Although the brief group exposure will not significantly alleviate the patient's mental illness, the clinician can learn from observing the patient in her group and can use that information in order to assess and refer the patient to the appropriate services. The clinician can recommend that the patient or her family expend the assets necessary for the treatment of her mental illness and point her in the direction of therapists who offer long-term individual and group therapy.

THE CHALLENGE POSED BY INDIVIDUALS WHO JOIN GROUPS

In the *Declaration of Independence,* Thomas Jefferson included the pursuit of happiness as one of the "inalienable rights" that governments were to secure for their citizens. It is most telling that Jefferson substituted the phrase "pursuit of happiness" for the word *property* or *possessions* as he developed his ideas from John Locke's seminal text of the Enlightenment, *On Civil Government,* written in 1690. The new American government was not to guarantee happiness but its pursuit—and Jefferson elevated that concept to the status of a self-evident truth.

As mental health clinicians, we are in the business of healing, but at a deeply serious level we are also in the business of assisting citizens in their pursuit of happiness. For Jefferson and other thinkers of the Enlightenment, happiness implied quality of life and meaning in one's life, and these ideas have significance above and beyond the diagnostic categories of pathology and mental illness. Clinicians from Viktor Frankl to Abraham Maslow have reiterated this point in our own time. This emphasis on the individual and her happiness must not be lost in our consideration of mental health delivery.

Thomas Jefferson also understood how the strength of the individual was magnified by membership in a group. He knew that tyrants feared groups because of their tendency to question authority and empower individuals to effect change. For this reason, "the right to peaceably assemble" became a cardinal principle of the First Amendment to the Constitution. Groups also have a natural proclivity toward raising issues of equality and justice because of struggles among members to be seen, to be heard, and to be special—all normative conflicts in predictable phases of psychosocial development. Groups become the natural enemies of forces that restrict the freedom of their members. They encourage individual members to fight for their rights, and in this sense each group always has the potential to become a political force, that is, a group concerned with the equitable allocation and distribution of resources. Even a group organized for the purpose of healing mental illness can arouse its members to take action to protect their rights, secure their liberties, and to pursue their self-interest.

What are the implications of group formation for the corporate management of mental health? Could groups become forces to lobby for more extensive or comprehensive forms of healthcare? Or might they challenge by litigation the system by which resources are allocated to mental health treatment? These possibilities remain remote at present, but they do have historical precedents in other realms of public affairs. Perhaps such thoughts give pause to corporate managers and find expression in unconscious resistance to group solutions in mental health.

In the first part of this book, I have emphasized the relationships that exist among the organization, the provider, and the plan member in the arena of managed mental healthcare. In the second part, I will stress the commitment to training that group therapists must make in order to serve their patients and fulfill the promise of group therapy.

PART TWO

Essential Theory and Training

CHAPTER NINE

The Personal and Professional Development of the Group Therapist

ack in the early seventies, Bay Area Rapid Transit (BART) was ready to start up its commuter trains to serve the greater metropolitan area of San Francisco, when a startling fact became apparent to the many technicians and administrators who had labored so hard on the project. Although the corporate executives of BART had assembled an impressive array of skilled electrical engineers, electronic and computer savants, experienced financial and business people, and other technical folk schooled in urban transit planning, they had neglected one vital thing. They didn't have anyone on their technical or management team who knew about railroads.

This oversight was not immediately recognized by management. Yet it became increasingly obvious to observers that there was something amiss as the new transit facility swung into operation and began to experience more and more problems relating to rolling stock, that is, the transit cars that actually pulled passengers from place to place. Scheduling difficulties surfaced that had not been foreseen on planners' computer screens. Irritating events occurred, such as doors getting stuck and not letting people out at their stops. Various approaches to solving these problems were attempted, such as bringing in more managers and procuring external consultants to help the employees follow the operational design that had been so carefully laid out, all to no avail.

As customer dissatisfaction mounted, the managers got the message that they needed another kind of expertise—an expertise they had overlooked in all their intricate strategies and operational designs: *they needed people who knew how to operate a railroad.* In the rush to put together a complex system, they had forgotten the central purpose for their organization: to move passengers back and forth on rails.

Once decision makers perceived the error in their approach, they set about hiring the best and most experienced railroad workers they could find. Many who were brought out of retirement did not miss the irony that they had been judged obsolete in an age that celebrated managing information rather than managing the task (in this case) of taking people where they wanted to go. With their wealth of knowledge, based on years of observation and practice, the railroad workers were able to anticipate problems before they interrupted service and to predict where new troubles might arise in the future.

THE PURPOSE OF GROUP THERAPY INTERVENTION

This example is instructive when we look at the intensive planning that goes into the structuring of managed care mental health—particularly with regard to group therapy delivery. With all the elaborate procedures for orchestrating a patient's passage through a mental health system, we must not forget the central purpose for the entire operation: to provide the patient with a chance to address her confusion and suffering in a setting that can increase her self-esteem, contribute to her ability to make decisions, allow her to face conflict, and augment her capacity to feel and express emotions. In order to provide such a setting, group therapists, like the old railroadmen, must be prepared both personally and professionally. There really is no substitute for this kind of preparation—and employees who are handed group protocols to follow as one might follow a recipe in a cookbook will invariably fail to fulfill the promise of group therapy to heal their patients. Patients do not come to group to be "cooked" but to be informed and enlightened. Group therapists who merely observe protocols, no matter how orderly those protocols seem on paper or how goal directed, will never grasp the power of the group to influence the behavior of the individual, nor will they understand their own key roles as leaders in the process of change.

Another misplaced metaphor often applied to group therapy is that of "running a group." When I hear the phrase, it brings to mind my own experience as a boy in Illinois "running" my hunting dogs. Now, in fact my hunting dogs were a wily and willful lot, and tended to *run me* wherever they wanted to go. In my quarter century of sitting with groups of individuals I have found the same to be true. My groups are more likely to run me than the opposite. This phenomenon supports my belief in the following paradox: in order to lead a group well, a group therapist must learn to follow. My capacity to follow, to have the patience to watch a group closely, and to anticipate its moves and adapt my approach to ever-changing conditions, even as I remain a step or two behind, is the hallmark of my skill as a group therapist.

It is significant that in his book *Managed Mental Health Services,* Saul Feldman noted the total absence of training as a topic of discussion in a major text on managed care. Unfortunately, the training of providers and managers of mental healthcare systems has been relegated to the lowest level of consideration. This fact has especially negative effects for group therapy, a field in which many professionals act as if no additional training were necessary. As a neurosurgeon friend in Seattle (known for his sarcasm) once told me, "Group therapy is like brain surgery—anyone can do it."

The remainder of this chapter outlines what I believe constitutes the preparation of a group therapist. To say that the group therapist must be prepared for unexpected consequences is too simplistic, yet does convey the paradox that the group leader must be trained very well in order to be open enough to learn from the group.

In his masterwork *Process and Reality,* philosopher and mathematician Alfred North Whitehead stated that "how an entity becomes constitutes its being." The following stages show one conception of how a group therapist is constituted.

NINE STAGES OF DEVELOPMENT

These stages in a group therapist's development have been phenomenologically derived as a subjective attempt to describe the process of a person's growth as he or she makes a career of conducting groups.

My observations are based on a relatively small sample of several hundred individuals of whose efforts I have personal knowledge. Many of my ideas were stimulated in their gestation by work with my mentor, Donald A. Shaskan, as well as by scrutiny of other group therapists with whom I have consulted or trained. The stages I set forth have the status of a working theory and as such require both clinical and empirical validation. It should be noted that there is no set time schedule for progression through these stages. Therapists may regress to earlier stages at certain times of stress or perhaps as a means to integrate some new knowledge into their repertoire of clinical judgment and choices. The stages are descriptive; they are not intended to be prescriptive of how training should proceed. I believe the training of the individual clinician must fit the special needs of each person in training. A "cookie cutter" approach will not suffice.

Two assumptions inform the observations I have made. First, learning group therapy leadership is akin to learning a craft: it is an education in skills, attitudes, the application of theoretical abstractions, judgment, timing, and purposes. As with any craft, a person's aptitude and confidence build with diligent execution under the watchful eye of a mentor or supervisor who upholds a standard of practice and shapes behavior with feedback and positive reinforcement. The learning of the craft implies the transmission of *values,* as well as specific knowledge, to the trainee.

Second, the "how" of group therapy leadership will vary with the developmental phase of a particular group. In other words, groups need different kinds of leadership at different phases of development. The more advanced the leaders are in the stages I describe, the better able they are to choose behavior appropriate to a specific group's phase of development. Part of the art of group practice is the capacity to discern the emerging needs of a group and act accordingly with leadership that addresses those emerging needs. As the group therapist gains experience, more options for leadership become available.

Stage 1: Novice

The novice can be detected by the rigid behavior he usually displays, making inflexible demands (mostly unspoken) of both himself and group members. The novice will unwittingly make the group as a whole into a parent figure, most often the mother in his family of origin. Because of this distortion—and his obliviousness to it—the novice will be least open to influence by the group and to the learning opportunities that appear, as his self-absorption does not permit his focused attention or listening.

This stage is characterized by *overwhelming fear* that is sometimes masked by the novice acting as if he knows what is going on. At other times his fear is masked by excessive talk or withdrawal into silence. This stage is the most common exit point for clinicians from the field of group therapy; for that reason, adequate supervision of the novice group therapist is imperative from the start to prevent the loss or damage of practitioners before they even begin their career.

Jerry was a new social worker in his first job with clinical responsibility at a staff model HMO in the Midwest. He had received excellent training and supervision in graduate school and felt reasonably prepared to take on the next step in his career path. Within the first month of his employment he was directed to form a therapy group to treat people in crisis.

Although Jerry had experience treating individual patients in crisis, he had minimal preparation in group theory or practice. When he requested group therapy training and supervision from his clinic manager, he was told there was no funding for that sort of activity. A highly conscientious fellow, Jerry felt constrained to learn group on his own as best he could, and asked that he be allowed to postpone his entry into group work until he had contracted with a group specialist in another city for training that he would pay for on his own. His clinic manager informed him that the patients needed groups *now* and that, in effect, they could not wait for him to educate himself. Jerry began his group two weeks later with a collection of patients who had been on a waiting list for a group. Jerry was determined to be a good employee and act as if he knew what he was doing.

Jerry's first group at the clinic was an eye opener. Of the six people who showed up, four had been waiting quite a while for treatment and were very angry at the organization; they proceeded to displace their anger onto Jerry. His finding himself scapegoated in his first leadership assignment was an ordeal. His attempts to defend the HMO and then himself from criticism were futile. The group grew angrier in proportion to his defensiveness. His appeals for help from the two nonangry members were met by an uncomfortable, stony silence. He left the first session dazed and not completely aware of the trauma that the group had inflicted on him.

The following week, a day before the group was to meet again, Jerry developed a migraine headache that led him to cancel his participation in the group. He was petrified of facing the angry group members and deeply ashamed that he was so afraid. He never returned to the group. Although he was temporarily relieved of the pressure to start another group, Jerry found a new job within three months, convinced that he would never do group therapy again.

Stage 2: Beginner

The beginner has reached the level of learning that allows her to accept that she does not know what is going on in a group. Armed with this degree of congruence—that is, clearly acknowledging what she doesn't know—the beginner can control or at least contain some of her fear. She is able to listen in the group, and starts to theorize from her own observations about what might be going on at a rudimentary level. At this point, the beginner may become infatuated with theories and ideas, and often becomes an ardent exponent of one or another school of thought: brief focal therapy, Transactional Analysis, self psychology, object relations, or psychodrama, to name a few. If the beginner is fortunate enough to have a mentor or supervisor who permits stage-appropriate idealization to flourish, the beginner expresses strong admiration for that teacher and begins to nurture the *belief that there are experts in the field.*

Ellen was a third-year student at an institute that prepared candidates for a doctorate in psychology; she obtained a job with a partial hospitalization program for a local hospital. The hospital was attempting to add to the number of patients using its mental health services on an outpatient basis by developing an active group therapy program that treated persons suffering from moderate to severe personality disorders. Groups met frequently at the hospital, and many professionals were involved, although none seemed to have time for peer consultation, and supervision was thought to be a curious notion from another time. Ellen was hired specifically because she was a registered nurse and could receive Medicare payments for the patients she treated in group. She did have the benefit of a professor at her school who was interested in groups and who agreed to supervise her work at the hospital, though he himself had led only one group.

Ellen's introduction to her first group was propitious. Many of the group members assigned to her group had been in groups before, and having considerable knowledge and patience, helped her by assuming various leadership functions. Ellen, following her mentor's lead, had developed a distinct fondness for object relations, and for the first months or so, saw Melanie Klein emerging in every aspect of her group. However, as group members began to leave, and the inevitable turnover of patients occurred, Ellen began to panic. The group members that had fit so well into her favorite theory and had helped her by performing essential maintenance functions in the group were replaced by patients of a different sort. These new patients did not seem to identify or empathize with Ellen's position as a new group therapist. In fact, they challenged her to seek out new theories to understand their behavior in the group. She felt sure that with enough new ideas, she could get a handle on the new group that was forming, and perhaps someday know it all, like the experts.

Stage 3: Beginning Competence

The clinician entering the stage of beginning competence is captivated with techniques and enamored with tricks to use in group. These he may take up and then quickly discard as new devices enter his ken. A therapist may initiate a period of experimentation with his personal style at this time. He may adopt personas in the group the way actors assume roles by changing masks and articles of clothing.

This therapist is still very much afraid of group but is beginning to see how his own personal and family dynamics are being played out in it. Now he is *able to critically question his mentor or supervisor.* A person may begin to feel in competition with other group therapist peers for the first time. This therapist starts to feel accepted by the group and yet is afraid of making mistakes, and so tends to be clinically unassertive and to avoid risks. Often he will feel "exhausted" after a group session.

Dana had been leading groups for two years for a public, nonprofit mental health clinic when he saw the opportunity to advance his career by taking on the new duty of designing a new kind of group for the clinic. To do so, he had to question the authority of his mentor, the chief of mental health, who believed that groups ought to be confined to time-limited formats that specified a certain number of sessions to which all group members would commit. Dana thought that such a philosophy severely restricted the number of patients that would qualify for group treatment in the setting of that particular clinic.

Because many people were too compromised psychologically to be able to make a commitment to regular group attendance, Dana hoped to begin an open-ended group that met each week for patients experiencing anxiety and panic attacks. The chief of mental health acceded to Dana's request to lead such a group, on the condition that he become a team with a co-therapist who had specialized in panic disorders. At first, Dana was intimidated by the thought of collaborating with a co-therapist who would in one sense be supervising his work. He felt a rivalry with the therapist and was afraid he would make foolish mistakes in his presence. However, with the help of the clinic chief, who offered to supervise their work together, Dana was able to allay his apprehensions and implement the group he had conceived.

Stage 4: Competence

The competent group therapist still believes in experts, and secretly wishes that someday she will be one. This person appreciates the wealth of experience that comes of participating in many and varied groups and is now able to formulate her own criteria for what constitutes competent group leadership. She gathers a growing sense of professionalism and camaraderie with other group therapists and is able to temper competitive feelings to a greater extent. This therapist knows that, in general, a group will be more accepting of a member than that same member will be of herself. Building on that feeling of acceptance, she is able to share parts of herself genuinely with a group when appropriate and steadily grows in awareness of what she is willing to share. She is able to model communication for the group as a whole. Although technically competent, this leader often lacks the enthusiasm to generate the interest among patients necessary to start and maintain groups.

Erica had worked for a community-based mental health clinic for five years, during which time she had developed her skill as a leader of groups for women who suffered from various kinds of eating disorders. She had successfully cooperated with her colleagues at the clinic, making the goals of her groups known to them so that they could refer appropriate patients. One year, she had mentored a new therapist who shared leadership of her group in a nequipo team, an unequal team formed for the purpose of training the less experienced member in group therapy. As a person who had suffered from an eating disorder herself, Erica had learned a keen sense of timing and the proper phase of group development in which to share her experiences with her patients— and the knowledge of when it was not appropriate to share.

When Erica wanted to leave the clinic in order to establish a small private practice, she felt confident in her ability as a group therapist and wanted to continue conducting groups for anorexia and bulimia. However, she had underestimated the difficulty associated with forming such groups apart from a system that she had carefully cultivated to supply her referrals. She became quite discouraged when her initial attempts to found a group on her own did not materialize. Senior colleagues had cautioned her about the time needed to start a group, but she had thought she would be an exception because of her degree of specialization in the field. After more than a year of concerted marketing and network building, Erica did succeed in putting a group together.

Stage 5: Mastery

In this stage, the therapist at last understands that there are no experts—that the field is too broad and the complexity of the phenomena in group too vast for any one person to be able to know completely. At this point, a therapist can break with his mentor and obtain full independence as a professional. He is willing to seek consultation when necessary and is willing to be satisfied with imperfect knowledge to arrive at practical solutions. The master has worked out a conceptual framework consistent with his style of leadership. He is able to deal with high levels of abstraction in terms of group interaction models and other paradigms that account for group process, and yet can relate to group members in their own language and in concrete and meaningful terms. As a person, he is now willing to risk mistakes for the sake of group development or an individual member's progress.

The master group therapist is able to appreciate styles of leadership other than his own and to learn from others. The master therapist is able to correct his own weaknesses with preventive measures— for example, the narcissistic leader who chooses to work always with a co-therapist to offset potential damage to a group. This therapist uses empathy astutely and courageously, and is assertive clinically. No longer is he afraid of groups; he is able to accept himself and others fully in the group context.

Austin had studied organizational psychology and business in graduate school and found himself strongly attracted to group therapy when he turned to clinical practice. He studied with as many group practitioners as he could find, in whatever field—cultural anthropology, sociology, criminology, and social psychology—and through a creative synthesis, formulated for himself a theoretical system that matched his open and nondefensive way of being with people in a group setting. His chief mentor had been a group analyst who had encouraged Austin's inquisitive mind and had written several articles with him in professional journals.

The break with his mentor came when Austin, after fifteen years of study and practice, no longer believed that the concept of the unconscious was a useful construct in his work with people in groups. Ironically, he appreciated more than ever the excellent results obtained by his mentor. Yet Austin took his career in the direction of short-term therapy conducted in intensive formats that did not focus on transference or resistance. His proficiency in communicating directly with patients was aided by his capacity to state concisely the import of the sometimes chaotic events in the group without reducing those events to oversimplifications.

Acutely aware of his tendency to be impatient and to want to obtain quick results, Austin was careful to choose people for his intensive groups who were concurrently in individual treatment. This practice allowed him to consult afterwards with their therapists as a follow-up to see if his group members were making changes in their lives or just adapting to his wish for them to change while they participated in his intensive group experience.

Stage 6: Boredom and Existential Anguish

In this stage, a therapist begins to have the feeling that "I am no longer stimulated or excited as I used to be in group." It is most interesting and ironic to note that the absence of the leader's fear in group during Stage 5 is also attended by a loss of her excitement in the group process in general by Stage 6. This individual's panic or anguish reaches a crisis point with questions such as, "Where do I go from here?" and "What does it all mean for me now?" Here is another common exit point for professionals from the field of group therapy. Again, it is most ironic that a clinician will leave the profession at the very height of her knowledge and mastery.

Marion held a faculty appointment at a major medical school and had published extensively in the field of forensic psychiatry, especially in the group treatment of impaired physicians, her area of expertise. She had involved herself fervently in creating physicians' groups both within the hospital setting and in the private sector. Her research had shown very pragmatic results, and her clinical acumen was much admired. She taught group therapy seminars that were well attended. But her heart was no longer with her group work, and she knew it. It became more and more a chore to consult with others about their groups, and, despite her best efforts to remain interested, she found herself thinking of other things while leading her groups with physicians. This break in the everyday continuity of her life was upsetting to her, and she wondered if it meant a permanent shift in the personal foundations of her life. She consulted with her trusted colleagues and her own therapist to see if she harbored some resistance to her work that she had yet to master.

After much exploration and introspection, Marion felt satisfied that there was no psychological barrier that prevented her enthusiasm for what she used to enjoy. She did realize that her anxiety pointed to her need to make a decision. Within a year she had stopped her clinical and research pursuits and had entered a graduate program for medical managers. Her new challenge and goal was to manage physicians in corporate medical practices, building on the insights she had gained from twenty years in the field of group process.

Stage 7: Self-Imposed Challenge

As in the example of the previous stage, a person at this stage often leaves the group therapy business or the therapy business for another line of work involving groups, and may become quite successful in private enterprise, business management, or government.

If this therapist stays in the field, he strikes out on a different course and becomes intensely involved in the training of group therapists or in consultation, research, teaching, or writing. This person may also become politically ambitious in professional organizations.

Seth was a marriage and family therapist who had developed two group therapy programs in his twenty years as a group therapist. In the first program, he expanded the group delivery system for the mental health service of a midsize HMO. In the second, he organized the structure of a hospital-based, intensive group therapy program of three- to six-week duration for the treatment of persons who suffered from personality and mood disorders. His success in these endeavors had brought him consulting jobs with a number of prepaid mental health systems that wanted help in organizing their group therapy programs. He enjoyed the consultation business at first, but soon began to dislike the amount of traveling required and the time spent in other cities and in airports. He wanted to return to working with individuals in small groups but not with patients in psychotherapy groups. The idea of training had always intrigued him, and he had quite a bit of experience training various clinicians as group therapists. However, Seth wanted a new challenge, one that would compel him to grow as a professional.

When he spoke with a former colleague, a physician who had worked with him at the HMO, Seth was delighted to learn that his friend was training for a position in management and incorporating many of the skills he had learned as a group clinician into his practice as a physician manager. It occurred to Seth that he had a lot to offer in such training programs—such skills as group decision making and leadership that could best be learned through specially structured small process groups. He joined with other health educators to develop training systems for doctors in transition to management. In the process, he successfully made the transition to a new career for himself—one that allowed him to continue his work with groups.

Stage 8: Second Mastery—A Return to an Informed Naivete

An understanding of this stage springs from the philosopher Paul Ricoeur's notion of a "second naivete," a human attitude that combines the freshness and exhilaration of discovery with the mature capacity for reverie and judgment. A therapist passing through this stage questions radically her own conceptual framework and forgets the old rules, tears down past models and formulations, and reflects on past experiences in light of her present self. She clearly sees the limitations of both group process and group therapy—and this insight, rather than producing discouragement, propels her to investigate the phenomenon again with renewed interest.

Marjorie had bounced back several times from being burned out during her twenty-five years as a group psychotherapist. Each time, she confronted herself with a new challenge and new goals. Now, she looked at a textbook she had written but a few short years back and was astonished to find that she no longer believed in the tenets she had so carefully laid down. Her questioning of her own wisdom was profound, but instead of disconcerting her, the experience invigorated her intellect. She began systematically to let go of many long-held beliefs, casting them off like so many withered autumn leaves and expectantly awaiting new ideas to flourish in their place. She fully accepted her limitations as a group therapist and viewed her previous intense interest in theory-building as one way she avoided the uneasiness of not-knowing and the floating sensation that comes with surrendering to spontaneity.

Her new approach, Marjorie thought, would be to open her eyes to the ongoing procession of unexpected consequences that seemed forever to emanate from group interactions. She did not know if a new theory might develop from this approach, nor did she care. She was buoyed up by her willingness to remain watchful of unexpected events as they occurred in her groups—and that particular stance inspired her curiosity about groups in unprecedented ways.

Stage 9: Acceptance of Personal Limitations—Humility

An individual may experience this stage as a religious or transcendent moment in his life. In this state of mind, he comes to believe that "the group is larger than myself and dwarfs my attempts to conceptualize it; the group has a life of its own, and I am not indispensable to it; although I am crucial to the movement of a particular group and to the members within, the constructive power of group process exists apart from me, and my presence is not a necessary condition for its development." These thoughts are a spiritual counterpoint to the existential anguish and general irreverence of Stage 6. Some persons may return to Stage 6 from here, especially if in transition or under stress.

The continual collision between feelings of reverence and feelings of irreverence in group leaders and group members leads to their experience of the absurd. The absurd, as experienced by group members, is the sense of the iron-law inevitability that certain causes produce certain effects regardless of human will or intervention. The existentialists raise a simple example: life is absurd because birth leads inevitably to death—and obviously there's no choice involved. Group intensifies the members' sense of mortality and thereby intensifies the experience of the absurd. From this point of view, group members are always faced with at least two options: (1) the faith that there are choices we can make—this is an act of reverence and feeds solemnity: we must choose wisely; and (2) the belief that there are no choices we can make—this is an act of irreverence and feeds hilarity: it doesn't really matter how we choose.

Joy had never given much thought to the spiritual aspect of the healing she helped her patients achieve in her therapy groups. Yet from time to time she was impressed by certain phenomena that appeared repeatedly in group: the psychic connections that patients would make with each other and with her, the synchronistic way in which group members could be there for each other, the ways in which the group could contain great upheavals of emotion or judgment, and the way the group seemed to hold each member in times of crisis or distress. Sometimes she would create conceptual frames to circumscribe these phenomena, and other times she would simply marvel and wonder at the events as they unfolded before her eyes.

Joy became aware that she was not causing these events to occur—it was not her technique nor her knowledge that set them in motion. She might, it was true, inhibit some things from happening, but short of obstructing the group process itself, she knew that as a leader she was not in control of these occurrences. Her trust in that fact seemed to deepen over time until it became almost an absolute belief. Her sense that these phenomena possessed a transcendent or spiritual quality was not an easy one to grasp; she resisted using those terms to describe the sensations she felt when she shared such an experience with members of her group.

Gradually, Joy embraced the idea that she was taking part in something that was larger than herself. Emotionally, she found herself wavering between the notion of herself as an active participant in the life of a group that could never be truly controlled and the notion that she was a rather passive character in a drama that was controlled by unknown and unknowing fates that did not admit the existence of human will. She was surprised that her emotions would shift so much, depending on the point of view she held that day and the degree to which she allowed reverence or irreverence to affect her stance in group.

I have given one model of how the clinician can progress from novice to master in the field—and beyond. There are surely other ways to conceptualize this passage for a group therapist. By whatever design, we must appreciate the complexity of the task and the wide diversity of the individuals who take up the challenge.

Once professionals have dedicated themselves to the study and practice of group psychotherapy, they conscientiously must ask: What are the central ideas that motivate the practice of this art, and what are the reasons that prompt individuals to join groups? The next chapter will respond to these questions.

CHAPTER TEN

The Purpose and Value of Groups

At this point, it would be meaningful to look at the ideas that underlie our thinking about groups, in order to establish a theoretical foundation for the enterprise of group therapy. Both newcomers to the profession and seasoned practitioners must revisit these concepts from time to time to bolster their confidence in what is known and to remind themselves of the need to generate new theory.

Groups have many functions in society. They govern communities and states, complete work tasks, maintain a social network for citizens, provide for the common defense, afford personal support, allow recreational opportunities, sanction religious rite and observation, and establish a common ground in otherwise depersonalized and highly individualistic industrial societies.

In the United States, groups have an additional democratic function: to petition the larger society to address the claims of minority segments of the population. Such a process was anticipated by Alexander Hamilton, James Madison, and John Jay in the eighteenth century, when they published their *Federalist Papers*. The individual could gather with like-minded individuals to amend some grievance owing to a failure of society as a whole.

Every group, therefore, draws on a long history of group relations that stretches into the distant human past. Psychotherapy groups are deeply rooted in this history, but they evoke their uncommon power from the willingness of their members to establish a contract among themselves that is quite distinct from the social contract that obtains in the larger society. Psychotherapy groups exist to explore and alter the behavior and character of their members, and in order to accomplish this task, the members must commit to developing relationships with each other. Understanding how relationships are formed and character revealed in such groups entails a deeper understanding of certain basic concepts.

BASIC CONCEPTS

What are the central ideas that animate group psychotherapy and make it effective? In the following ten sections, I respond to this question by drawing on the concepts of many theorists in the field as well as on the history of ideas, and by providing examples from clinical practice. Although many of the points overlap as they become manifest in group, they remain distinct concepts.

Universalization

Universalization is the realization by the individual that her "private" experience is one that is common for humankind. A person will often express relief when she discovers that she and other group members share similar experiences. It is a common feeling that connects yet also allows for a sense of ambiguity. When a group member says, "I can identify with what you are saying," she means that she can relate to this part of your life. It does not imply that her experience was identical. More precisely, it means that her feeling, reflecting on the situation, is analogous to yours, similar but with important shades of difference. Leaders must use special skill so that real differences between people are not minimized.

Pre-Socratic philosophers spoke of this phenomenon as "the problem of the One and the Many." The paradox is that a person can discover her individuality in a group setting in a way more profound than when she is alone. Universalization is a partial attempt to answer the question: How am I a part of the human family?

At the beginning of a short-term couples' group, as the couples spoke of the conditions of their marriages, each of the males identified with the feeling of being controlled by his female partner. The men complained that their wives brought things to them that required their immediate and undivided attention without first checking to see if the men were available to listen. The men felt especially gratified to learn that each of their experiences were similar yet different in important ways. They bonded around this issue and encouraged each other to express feelings of anger and frustration directly to their spouses in group. In this manner, they were able to overcome passivity in relation to their wives and move toward a stance of action. Humor helped them master their resistance and become more expressive and vocal about their grievances.

As they listened to themselves describe the various ways they felt controlled, they began to understand how each man carried a specific meaning for the experience of being controlled. They named the controlling figures in their past and let each other see how the current situation with their wives differed from the ways they remembered being dominated in their childhood. At an early phase of the group process, they created a male subgroup that allowed them to mobilize their feelings and set the stage for seeing the distinctive methods they used to negotiate power in their relationships.

Differentiation

Groups can help dispel the fantasy of uniqueness that can prove so troublesome in social adaptation and self-acceptance. Yet group members must be prepared to embrace the real differences that distinguish them from others in their group if they are to grasp a full sense of self. By the process of differentiation, I can sort out who I am from who I am not. In group, I can accomplish this as I separate my sense of others from my sense of myself. I can explore my ambiguous feelings about my wish to be you and my wish to be me—or the me I've yet to discover. These steps are essential to creating the personal boundaries necessary to establish an identity.

Laurie was a successful writer who had joined a therapy group to overcome the intense loneliness she experienced. She was well liked by the group despite her tendency to distance herself when she began to feel a connection with someone. When a new man entered group, she took a great interest in him. Jay had just dropped out of an academic program leading to a doctorate and was floundering, uncertain whether to finish his program or pursue another life goal. Laurie was quite vocal and adamant in her approval of his choice to leave school, adding that graduate studies were useless and telling stories of the unhappy grad students she had known. When Jay stated that he still considered school an option, Laurie derided him as "living in an unreal world." Jay responded with anger, saying her opinions seemed one-sided and did not help his decision-making process. The two remained at an impasse until finally Laurie revealed that she, too, had once participated in doctoral studies. Her experience proved so negative to her that it completely colored her perception of Jay's dilemma.

As the group explored the differences they saw between the two members, Laurie began to understand how deeply her judgments prevented her from understanding the lives of others. She was so certain that Jay would suffer if he returned to his program that she zealously made it her job to protect him from that fate. Gradually, she began to see how much she missed of who Jay really was by clinging to her perception of who she thought he was. This failure to see had led to a pattern of isolation from others and a loss of insight into her own personality. As Laurie continued to differentiate herself from Jay, Laurie was able to experience her own boundaries in a way that allowed her to sustain a connection with him.

Experimentation

Learning by trial and error is a large part of the group experience. The individual can experiment with actions and new behavior in a "near to life" setting. This is often referred to as reality testing. The group becomes the arbiter of reality as it is played out among its members. The group therapist has a lot to do in helping the patient face new situations and to shed archaic but now unnecessary defenses. The leader can assist in the constant revision and reformation of the patient's view of the world as she tries new ways to adapt and change in response to the challenge of relating to other group members. The individual must ask herself, "How many risks can I take in becoming the person I want to be?"

Arlen wanted to become more assertive in his transactions with people, and he came to group therapy to develop and practice this part of his ego strength. His first experiments in this direction, however, resulted in disappointment because his efforts to make contact with others were interpreted by group members as self-serving comments or questions. Arlen did make comments that seemed pertinent to the content of what another person said, but his words did not reflect that he had understood the meaning behind the other's statement. It was as if he had not heard the other person accurately. He persisted in trying to listen and frame appropriate responses only to be frustrated by the feeling, voiced by several group members, that he had missed the point of what they were saying.

The group therapist asked Arlen to try an experiment and switch seats in group with a woman, Leslie, who was complaining that Arlen did not get the gist of what she said to him. From Leslie's chair, Arlen expressed what he heard her say to him. Then he listened to Leslie speak the words she had heard him say. In this simple exercise, Arlen learned that he was not listening carefully to others because his anxiety over how he should formulate a response prevented him from doing so. He was able to grasp why others missed feeling connected to him. As a youngster, he had had to be the "man of the house" and always have a ready response to whatever was said to him. He was ready now in group to risk silence and relax his compulsion to speak.

Socialization

Group is a social laboratory that can approximate for each member a new family, which, in contrast to the family of origin, can meet the needs of the individual for nurturance, patience, care, and love. A good deal of what is called *social* in human life is at the same time deeply internal, influencing the structure of the personality dynamically. Personality change begins with the opportunity to explore relations with others and at the same time probe deeper into the self. In the social sphere, democratic ideals compete with the authoritarian uses of fear, mystery, and magic. The essence of authoritarian leadership is eloquently captured by Fyodor Dostoevski in *The Brothers Karamazov*. In the words of the Grand Inquisitor, "We have corrected Your work and have founded it upon miracle, mystery, and authority. And men rejoiced that they were again led like a flock, and that the terrible gift that had brought them such suffering, was, at last, lifted from their hearts."

In contrast, the leader of a therapeutic group must create an atmosphere that lessens the individual's fear and demystifies the group interaction. That means never appealing to intimidation as a means of control and always respecting the powerful events that occur in group, without oversimplifying its subtly complex transactions. It also means letting members know that the wonders of group can be duplicated in the world outside—by powerful, freely acting individuals.

Socialization raises the questions, "Will I be treated as an object in my interactions with others—or will my autonomy be honored? How close can I be to you without losing myself? How much can I compromise without sacrificing my essential integrity?"

Edie was a travel executive who was highly skillful in business contacts but not happy with the social life she had created for herself. She came to group therapy to gain insight into how to improve it. Specifically, after initiating social contact, she found herself being manipulated into constantly doing favors for her new acquaintances. Doing these kindnesses brought her no pleasure but lowered her self-esteem and left her feeling used. In group, she presented herself at first as a lively extrovert, but soon plunged into a depressive state that puzzled the group leaders and baffled the group. How could she shift so quickly from outgoing optimism to a gloomy pessimism? She remained in this state for many weeks, hardly reacting to questions and never offering to help anyone.

At last, a man in group told Edie how powerful she felt to him, refusing to seek the approval of the group leaders or comply with the wishes of group members to engage with them. A light seemed to turn on for her, and she stated very resentfully that she had no desire to please anyone. She told the group how weary she was of giving to people the way she had given to her parents in order to obtain their love. She was dissatisfied with being that way and yet could not envision a way to keep her boundaries without placing a great distance between herself and others. Her depression served to enforce that distance because she simply could not give anything while in such a low-energy state.

The group leaders wondered if Edie could create a level of social contact in group that satisfied her needs so that she might not have to defend her personal boundaries by depressive episodes. This idea intrigued her and offered a way out of her malaise. She would have to trust that the group members would respect her need for separateness as well as affiliation and that they would not punish her by withdrawing as her parents had done.

Communication

Ninety percent of the communication in group is nonverbal, yet the currency of group therapy is words and speech. Gestures, posture, facial expressions, movements, and the images we have of our own bodies—all are potent messages transmitted subtly and indirectly to others. Communication is at the center of all group processes. Its most articulate form is language, which we learned by imitating the speech of our caretakers and yet share with our community. If we begin with the assumption that everything that reaches our awareness is a kind of communication, whether it is an event inside or outside group therapy, we can arrive at some startling realizations. Many events that appear at first sight to have nothing to do with group are, on closer examination, clearly associated with the group. When group leaders employ this hypothesis, they are often led to profound insights.

A group therapist was perplexed when one night none of her patients showed for group. She had been elated just the week before by the extraordinary closeness that seemed to exist between group members and had marveled that such intimacy could surface by only the fourth meeting of the group. Although surprised by how rapidly the group advanced, she moved quickly to keep abreast and challenge its members to go even deeper. Was their absence somehow a reply to her challenge?

When she spoke with each member by phone during the week, most had very legitimate excuses for missing the session. Two members, one man and one woman, said they had reconsidered their commitment to the group and were going to enter other forms of therapy. Several of the members did attend the following week, but the group ended soon thereafter, two months short of the time allotted. The group therapist came away with the impression that she had disappointed her group by giving them the message to "hurry up." In retrospect, she believed the more appropriate message would have been to "slow down and take your time." Paradoxically, the group that attains instant intimacy may swiftly fall apart.

Externalization and Internalization

The human imagination has the capacity to arrange within the mind relationships between images of the self and images of others. These images are preverbal in origin, and throughout our lives they hold power over how we perceive ourselves in relationships with others in the world. How our inner world affects and is affected by external reality is a dynamic that is constantly played out in the relationships we form in groups. From this perspective, the aim of therapy is to alter the inner realm of the individual in order to improve the quality of his relations in the external world.

The process in which internal parts of the self, or representations of the self, are externalized or projected onto group members or the group as a whole is common to group therapy. The attention paid to this process by group therapists is one factor that determines the depth to which the members will go in their work and must be modulated in short-term groups so that the group leader doesn't open up conflicts that would require a long-term commitment to resolve.

Classically, it was believed that projection involved only the externalization of negative parts of the self, that is, the projection of destructive and hateful urges to protect a vulnerable ego from contamination and imagined injury. However, the projection of positive parts of the self allows the individual to trust his surroundings, and in particular, to trust a group.

The internalization of positive experiences leads to loving internal images and ego growth; the internalization of hateful experiences enables the individual to be tolerant of and patient with others, and generally empathic. All of these mechanisms have great import for group interactions.

A complicated dynamic occurs when parts of the self-image and parts of the images a person has of others are split off and projected onto another person, who in turn becomes possessed and controlled by and identified with the projected parts. There is always a confusion and a loss of ego boundaries between self and other when this occurs. A person does this in order to disown vital facets of his personality. By this process of "externalization-internalization," I face the conflict between what I accept as me and what I won't accept as me, and my ambivalence about self-acceptance.

This largely unconscious dynamic is called *projective identification,* because it combines aspects of both externalization and internalization. It happens so often in group that whole theories have been spawned to understand and track its occurrence.

From the start of their group, Jamie and Helene competed with each other for attention. Competition became anger when Jamie accused Helene of constantly interrupting the group process to speak of herself and how she related to the topic of discussion. Jamie stated she would leave the group if Helene did not contain her emotions better. Helene responded by attacking Jamie for manipulating her like her mother did when Mother threatened to abandon Helene if she did not acquiesce to Mother's wants. Jamie insisted that Helene contain her fears, yet she continued to arouse Helene's fears by threatening to leave. Both members viewed each other as hostile people and believed they had to defend themselves from the imagined damage the other could do. Both blamed the group therapists for not protecting them.

When the group therapists began to sort out the projections, it became clear that Helene projected onto Jamie that part of Helene's mother that used to manipulate Helene into giving up what she wanted for herself. In turn, Jamie saw Helene as that punishing part of Jamie's mother that blamed her for injuries that Mother sustained when she gave birth to Jamie. Jamie was impatient with Helene and intolerant of her need for recognition by the group, and in those ways did fulfill Helene's image of a controlling mother. In return, Helene did fulfill Jamie's expectation of a mother who would take vengeance on her daughter by speaking only of the wounds that she, the mother, received. Only after both members became aware of how they acted as containers for their mothers' self-loathing and how they had identified with their mothers' low self-esteem could they begin the painful separation from their mothers and the mourning and reparation of their own disavowed parts.

Recapitulation and Reparation

By their very structure, groups enable each member to recapitulate her family of origin or the institutional milieu in which her caretaking was given. This is a powerful regression to the past for a person to experience; it opens up opportunities to heal and repair many of the wounds that were inflicted on a child during those early years. It is an extraordinary feature of group therapy that this repetition of early life can occur *simultaneously* for all group members. Although each member's relationship to the group as a whole must be considered separately, the ways in which the respective projections and transferences overlap are fascinating and significant. The group leaders must be skillful in pointing out this phenomenon to group members, if other members of the group, adopting leadership roles, have not already done so.

It's important to note that the group will go only as deep as the leaders allow them to. The boundary of psychological depth is set by the group therapists. Although some groups will not choose to go that deep for a number of reasons, the absence of an Emotional Leader is one hindrance; I describe this leadership role in Chapters Eleven and Twelve. Group therapists must take risks in challenging patients to go deeper in their work—especially when that work is circumscribed by time limitations. Given the proper conditions, family-of-origin reparation can be accomplished rapidly, as we saw in Chapter Six, but the leaders must take the initiative in plunging the group to that level.

In this process, the patients' compulsion to repeat the past is confronted by their desire to obtain a new understanding of their past and how it affects them now.

Mary was a bright, hard-working businesswoman who had been physically abused by her father throughout her childhood and adolescence. Her mother had been beaten also and was terrified as she watched passively while her daughter was battered. Mary had succeeded in breaking away from her family of origin at an early age and had become successful in her career. But the emotional scars from the past prevented her from enjoying the company of males in social situations outside the protective boundaries of the work environment. She was frightened of males and had come to group to overcome her fear.

She felt accepted by the men in her group, and bonded with two in ways that helped her explore her feelings about males. But she remained fearful in relation to her male group therapist, onto whom she projected her father's violence. The female co-therapist invited Mary to see that her fear was deeper still and that she feared becoming violent like her father in relation to the group members. A turning point occurred for Mary when she saw a man she respected in group express anger at the male group therapist. It was healing for her to recognize that anger is not the same as rage and that anger did not have to lead to physical abuse, as was the case in her family of origin.

Reorganization

An assumption of group therapy is that individuals will act out their maladaptive behavior in group. And yet the group can set the stage for the individual to reorganize something within himself, if while in the group he has an emotional experience that serves to correct a traumatic or false impression from the past that impedes him from living fully in the present. Depending on a number of conditions, both personality and behavior change is possible. This is usually a relatively long process in which the human psyche is first destructured and then restructured in accordance with a group ethos that permits growth and does not penalize change. This can be a frightening and exhilarating experience of tearing down and building up. It raises the question, "How do I become acquainted with the person I've become?"

Brady was a transvestite male who joined a group to mourn the death of his lover and friend. He suffered from a complex amalgam of personality disorders that kept him in low-paying jobs and constantly eroded his self-esteem. In the group, he transferred very positive feelings to his male therapist yet harbored deep hatred and rage for males in general, on account of the abuse he received at the hands of his stepfather. He had a most ambivalent relationship with his mother, whom he adored and yet despised; she had scapegoated him as a child, telling him he was crazy and evil like his father, who abandoned the family when Brady was a year old. Brady tended to establish relationships with sadistic individuals, both male and female, who would then act the role of his stepfather in degrading him and punishing his already frail ego.

He established a strong attachment to Sasha, a woman in group who as a child had been raped by her father. Sasha reminded Brady of his sister, who had been sexually molested by the same hated stepfather. His bond with Sasha allowed him to break down his distrust for women that undermined his efforts to heal the deep wounds inflicted by his mother's sadism. His inclination to make himself vulnerable to exploitation, either in financial dealings or love relationships, was fed by his masochistic need to experi- ence punishment and relieve his guilt for imagined crimes against his mother and step- father.

When Sasha challenged him to stop associating with people who acted as either sexual predators or racketeers, he was deeply touched. The male group therapist thought he might succumb to a major depression, as Sasha—representing the abused sister he could never protect—was insisting that he take care of himself. Sasha's abil- ity to grieve her losses struck a chord with Brady, who saw her as a healthy model for healing trauma at the hands of neglectful and brutal parents. With the help of Sasha and the group, Brady received for the first time in his life the permission to protect himself from exploitation and invasion. This stimulated a healthy urge within him to acknowledge the part of his personality that would let him be subject to all kinds of degradation and manipulation. The recognition of this part of himself was a major step in choosing to reorganize that element within his personality.

Sublimation

Sublimation involves the redirection of primitive destructive urges into creative, constructive actions that foster ego growth. Groups must be able to tolerate a certain degree of "acting out" behavior from its members, that is, permit the discharge of inner stress through acts of aggression, provocation, or seduction. Group therapists must always confront these acts, but the prevailing attitude should be one of under- standing, not condemnation.

Unless individuals are allowed at some point to discharge their inner stress within the relative security of their group, the chances for them to sublimate their impulses are reduced and the opportu- nity for subsequent ego maturation is lost. This is why conflict and its resolution is such an important therapeutic factor in groups: members experience an increase in self-esteem and confidence as they learn that verbal aggression will neither destroy them nor oth- ers in the group.

Sublimation also implies the letting go of unfulfilled wishes and impossible hopes. In this process, the group can help by offering its acceptance, so that I can celebrate what is true for me. I can rejoice in my achievements, regardless of who they please, and no longer must I live in the shadow of unkept promises to anyone. Sublima- tion raises the question, "How can I become satisfied with the per- son I really am?"

Christine was a successful marketing executive who nevertheless felt discontented with her career. It seemed that the higher she climbed on the corporate ladder, the greater her dissatisfaction. Her disappointment caused her to spark unproductive conflicts with other managers that, if left unchecked, might jeopardize her future with the company. The members of her therapy group could not understand her unhappiness, and their attempts to give her credit were met with sharp rebuttals: "It's still not what I want." When asked what she did want, she responded with vague notions of "being in charge of it all." It did appear she was on track to become the top manager, but that thought did nothing to appease her distress. She had shared with the group that her father, who died when she was four years old, had been the owner and chief executive of his own publishing house, and that she felt destined to lead.

During one group session, Christine remembered a scene from her childhood, sitting on her father's lap in his office, which resembled the cabin of a ship, and promising her father and herself that one day she would be captain, too. Shortly after that, her father died, leaving her with the pledge she had made as her only legacy, as the business was sold by the heirs. A much older man in group said to her, "You know, I always wanted to be a cowboy, but I had to give it up when my father's ranch was sold for a housing development." Christine was visibly moved by his story and began weeping for the loss of her dream. She slowly began to resign herself to the fact that the publishing industry had changed enormously since her father operated his business. Her skills as a team player had brought her to her present position and might in time carry her to the top office. But her dream of leading in the same way her father did would remain unfulfilled. This sober realization let her mourn the lost connection with her father and begin to embrace the life she would make for herself.

Revelation

Groups offer the individual the chance to reveal himself before others. The revelation of character in the presence of a sympathetic audience links group therapy to drama and other forms of art. The individual, as protagonist of his life, must act without complete knowledge of himself. Group members have a great desire to have their characters revealed to them; they look to each other as mirrors to accomplish this. We have both a fear of being seen and a wish to be revealed to others. This paradox is present in all group activities and carries a strong religious connotation: we have a deep human need to be seen as we are, and yet in many religions the one true self is known only to God. Here is a sacred moment filled with passion and primitive desires. Paul promised it to humankind as salvation in his letter to the Corinthians: "We shall know even as we are known."

Clifford was a medical student who entered group in crisis after the breakup of his engagement. Initially, he was quite open with his emotions. Yet as the pain of the split subsided, he became more and more diffident and removed from the group. He was an intelligent and attractive fellow, but when group members made efforts to get closer to him, he put them off by expressing fears that he would not be able to meet their expectations of him. He appeared open, yet there was a large part of his personality that he kept buried. Various group members confronted him for being coy, angling for attention, and then acting as if he did not notice the attention when it was given.

His relationship with his father, a physician, was difficult and estranged. The father made halfhearted attempts to see his son, but never followed through for one reason or another. As Clifford described his father to the group, the members identified father and son as being very much alike. Both went into hiding—and then wished to be found. At first, Clifford denied any similarity and reacted with shame that he would be anything like someone for whom he had such negative feelings.

The next group session, Clifford was absent. He returned the following week, and group members felt he had gone away from them as his father had absented himself from his son. Clifford responded with anger, as if he had been accused of some misconduct. The group did not relent, but continued to reflect back to him their impressions. Clifford expressed shame. "I'm afraid of finding out that both my father and I are incapable of making relationships," he said.

He became aware that he had missed a session to test whether the group cared about him. Like his father, he wanted to go and hide—yet secretly wished that we would come and find him. With the group's help, he was able to see that his behavior was not reprehensible but understandable in light of his loneliness and his need for extraordinary assurances that he would not be rejected once contact with a person was established. The picture of himself that the group held up to Clifford was not one he wanted to see, but it was an authentic likeness around which he could form genuine relationships.

The central ideas presented here form a common language that permits group therapists to speak about their work and formulate new theory. One of the most interesting theories to emerge in the field of group process in the last thirty years is the seminal work of Ariadne P. Beck. In the next chapter, I present her phases of group therapy development as a powerful instrument for understanding how a group can progress over time and how the group therapist ought to behave to assist the maturation of the group.

CHAPTER ELEVEN

Phases of Group Therapy Development

~~~ T here have been many theories proposed to account for the evolution and maturation of group processes. Of these theories, one stands out in its clarity and completeness for the purpose of understanding the profusion of events that unfold in time-limited psychotherapy groups.

AN INTRODUCTION TO THE THEORY OF ARIADNE P. BECK

In this chapter, I will apply the theory developed by Ariadne P. Beck and her colleagues in the Chicago Group Development Research Team, James M. Dugo, Albert M. Eng, and Carol M. Lewis. This theory has been derived from the study of group process over the past thirty-six years. It presents an analysis of group members' behavior as that behavior contributes to a group's passage through nine distinct phases of development, as shown in Table 11.1. The theory describes the emergence of four leadership roles, shown in Table 11.2. The theory stems from a systems orientation that stresses the isomorphy of processes characteristic of all living systems. As stated earlier in this book, isomorphy means that beneath the diverse content of systems there exist identical structures and organizing processes. Thus, intrapsychic, interpersonal, and group-as-a-whole phenomena find parallel expression during the life of the group.

Beck also defines the group as an organism. "As an organism, it evolves in an orderly way over time unless obstructed; it defines rules and methods for interacting with the world around it and for protecting its boundaries; it regulates its own internal processes and has its own form of organization that gives it coherence, identity, continuity, and a characteristic emotional tone or atmosphere" (1981, p. 63).

Distributed Leadership

One chief assumption in Beck's theory is the notion of distributed leadership, that is, the idea that leadership in group does not always, nor should it always, emanate from the designated leader or leaders. Leadership can and does emerge spontaneously in a group in response to the specific needs of the group—with each leader expressing these needs either explicitly or implicitly for the group as a whole. These leadership roles are part of the informal structure of the group. Various group members perform these leadership functions in order to accomplish the developmental tasks associated with the group issues characteristic of each phase. A member can be said to assume a leadership role when he is perceived to carry out a certain set of leadership functions that define the role. In the context of group, a therapist must become closely attuned to the behavior of these leaders as they emerge so as to observe how they facilitate the group process and to keep himself from getting in the way of the work performed by these leaders.

Necessary Conditions for
the Application of This Model

In order to see the orderly progression of phases clearly, a group must have a time limit that all members know in advance. The group must also have a fixed membership during its time together, meaning no members will be added or lost and thus change the original constellation. Membership changes often lead to leadership changes and recycling to Phase 1.

In ongoing groups in which new members join frequently and in which there is an indefinite time commitment (such as the depressed

1   Creating a contract to become a group/making an initial assessment of each other/forming an initial bond.

2   Forming a basic group structure: personal influence and survival in group and the resolution of competitive needs while forging a group identity/establishing group norms and goals and selecting leaders.

3   Disclosure of individual identity/defining individual goals to be pursued in the group/establishing a group work style/work on early life or authority relationships.

4   Exploration of intimacy and closeness in relationships outside of group and in relationships inside the group/challenging the authority of the Task Leader, if necessary.

5   Establishment of mutuality/negotiation of the management of dependency, personal limitations, and differences in needs.

6   Ownership of the group by the members/sharing power and influence with Task Leader.

7   Self-confrontation in the context of interdependence and ownership of one's own problems/resolving core issues.

8   Review of gains made and work still to be done/application of what was learned to other contexts.

9   Coping with separation and termination/acknowledging the meaning of the experience and the role that others played in it.

Table 11.1. Major Themes in Phases of Group Development.
Source: Copyright © 1996 by Ariadne P. Beck.

group I describe in Chapter Three), I have found that Beck's theory applies with significant modifications. For example, Phase 3 is usually the highest level of group functioning that is possible under changing conditions of membership, and is the goal toward which the group therapist strives. Moving rapidly through Phase 2, while allowing necessary differentiation and conflict to occur, becomes a major goal for the clinician leading such groups.

The number of members must be sufficient to engender a process (no less than six) but small enough to allow the exploration of individual issues in the group (no more than ten). The purpose of the group must be understood by the members to be personal and behavioral change, whether each of the members can verbalize his particular goals or not. External influence on the organizational structure of the group must be kept to a minimum. For example, the boundary of the group must be safe from intrusion by nonmembers, and any pressure to increase the size of the group above a certain number must be resisted. In the context of managed care, the group therapists must monitor both of these circumstances closely.

Leader	Role Function	Conflict Modeled
Task Leader	Convenes the group; guides the task: expert in communication and therapy processes; influences norm and goal development; handles interface of group and its organizational context, group and world outside; is usually the therapist.	Struggles with using or sharing power.
Emotional Leader	Prepared and motivated to participate in group task; monitors emotional processing in group; models the therapeutic change process; best-liked person in the group; most important support person to peers and Task Leader.	Struggles with denying or acknowledging the importance of close bonds with others.
Scapegoat Leader	Crystalizes group-level issues regarding norms; is perceived as "different" during early group phases; expresses deep commitment to group in the face of being misunderstood; is the object of negative feelings in early phases; monitors the clarity of normative and emotional issues.	Struggles with conformity and autonomy.
Defiant Leader	Expresses considerable vulnerability in group; challenges and questions the trust level in group; expresses ambivalence about participation in group.	Struggles with merging and fleeing.

Table 11.2. Emergent, Ongoing Leadership Roles.
Source: Copyright © 1996 by Ariadne P. Beck.

Finally, the group therapist must agree conceptually with the notion of distributed leadership, be able to share the leadership of the group, and welcome the various leadership roles as they emerge. As I noted in Chapter Nine, it's a sign of maturity and mastery for a group therapist to be able to follow the lead of group members who carry leadership functions for the benefit of the group. The acting out of envy or rivalry has no place in the repertoire of the competent group therapist.

Special Application to Short-Term Groups

In my opinion, Beck's work has special relevance and immediate application to short-term group therapy as it is practiced in managed mental health settings. This is true for five reasons:

1.   The nine phases of group therapy development adapt well to the structured format of short-term group therapy and can help the practitioner identify key elements of group process as they occur as well as anticipate salient events to come.

2.   The emergent leadership roles, which I will illustrate in greater detail in Chapter Twelve, can help guide the group therapist as she adopts and develops a leadership style appropriate to the short-term format and specific group she is conducting. The group therapist can "read" the leadership functions provided by the members and see what functions are not being supplied.

3.   Using Beck's theory can let the group leader assess early on what is possible for a particular group to attain, given its composition and stated goals. The depth to which the members will go and how ambitious the group can be in achieving goals can be predicted as the leadership roles emerge to propel the group into new phases of development. In other cases, where the leadership roles do not emerge, the group therapist can predict how limited the progress of the group will be.

4.   Beck's theory, though subtle and complex, can be taught by knowledgeable clinicians and by the use of videotapes, which allow the practitioner to see the behavioral characteristics of the emergent leadership roles and identify the explicit behavioral markers that distinguish the passage through one phase into another.

5.   For my fifth reason, I quote Beck's work:

A developmental conception of group process can help the group therapist by giving him a context for understanding individual, interpersonal, and group level phenomena which might otherwise be perplexing, misleading, or completely misunderstood. The therapist who chooses to work with individuals in a group takes on a much more difficult task than that of treating individuals alone. The difficulty comes from the concern with facilitating a healthy group process for each member. The therapist must learn to move comfortably between the individual, interpersonal and group level experiences and not get lost in the process. An understanding of the function of distributed leadership aids the therapist in maintaining this delicate balance [1981, p. 64].

Analysis of a Videotape Group

Ariadne Beck and her colleagues will write the definitive work on their conceptions of group developmental theory. She and Carol Lewis have edited a new book, *Process in Therapeutic Groups: A Handbook of Systems of Analysis,* in which one chapter is devoted to their current research into this theory, and I trust they will follow that with a volume dedicated solely to their work. In this chapter and the next, I intend to illustrate some of the most striking features of their observations by means of a videotape of a time-limited group that Vivian Nelson and I conducted, live and unscripted, for ten sessions. Participants volunteered to interact spontaneously with each other with the goal of "discovering the emotional connections between them" as a training experience for their own study of groups. Our videotape is an opportunity to investigate the work of Beck and other systems theorists; it is also a practical guide to viewing transference, projective identification, and many other psychodynamic processes that emerge in time-limited groups. I invite clinicians to use it as a starting point to test and apply these theories for themselves. (Videotape ordering information appears following Chapter Thirteen.)

Six members of our videotape group were either therapists or therapists in training, and one was an attorney. Vivian and I approached our task not as researchers but as clinicians intent on applying the research of Beck and her associates for the benefit of our group members. In that process, it is as important to see where the theory does not apply as where it does. Because group therapists often find the use of theory in their practice a daunting prospect, it is refreshing and encouraging to find ideas that have practical value to group treatment. This chapter is not meant to be an exhaustive analysis of our videotape group, and will touch only the highlights of Beck's theory. Although clear and cogent, Beck's theory is complex and merits further study to appreciate its fullness and depth.

In considering group developmental theory—as with all theories—we must be careful not to attempt to fit all phenomena into the theory. A theory is best used to illuminate the data of a group. It is poorly used when a clinician seeks to explain all that happens in light of one perspective. Ideally, a theory can give shape to disparate and often contradictory experiences, but to impose a theory where the data do not warrant is a misuse of theory. No single theory encompasses the scope of all the activities portrayed in a group. In our videotape, I employ a variety of theories, including object relations, systems theory, and psychodynamic ideas, to understand and conceptualize the process of our group. In this chapter and in Chapter Twelve, however, I will direct my comments almost exclusively to Beck's ideas.

Our videotape group had special characteristics that made it atypical and therefore somewhat difficult to apply Beck's model to. The presence of an "outer group" of eight individuals responsible for video production created an external environment that interacted with us constantly on a nonverbal, sensory level. Often the group would sit for as long as three-quarters of an hour prior to the start of a session, while production team members arranged light and sound variables. Our group was never sure when the end of the group might occur, as factors in the control room or the studio might overrule the prerogative of our group.

Given these conditions, our videotape participants demonstrated much integrity, maturity, and courage as they disclosed themselves in the process that unfolded. As a group, we succeeded in capturing seven of Beck's nine phases and illustrating all four of the emergent leadership roles. Vivian and I remained cognizant of the isomorphy between the two group processes: the anxiety, cooperation, and conflict of the group in front of the cameras; and the tensions, disputes, and camaraderie of the group behind the cameras. Both groups functioned superbly, under quite extraordinary conditions. In view of my admiration and affection for the members of our videotape group and their candor and trust of the process that we explored together, I can do no less than present myself with the same candor. I will therefore show my own face in the following summary of the group's process, without the usual authorial mask, letting myself be open to public scrutiny as well.

NINE PHASES OF GROUP THERAPY DEVELOPMENT

The nine phases of group therapy development highlight group-level issues that are critical to the group as a whole at specific points in its development. According to Beck, the phases will evolve in sequence and be unvarying in their order of appearance, so long as group membership remains unaltered and the task does not change. The loss or addition of members will tend to revert the process to the beginning phase. Not every group will progress through all or even most of the phases, and groups may spend long intervals of time in a single phase as a result of positive or negative events. As was the case with our videotaped group, many time-limited groups will complete only some of the phases before moving toward closure and termination.

I will describe the nine phases of group therapy development and then bring them to life with scenes taken from our videotape group to illustrate the central ideas and show how the various developmental tasks can be accomplished. When possible, specific attention will be given to behavioral markers that define the boundaries between phases. Leadership roles play a special part in phase transitions, and I will point these out when they are apparent. A more detailed description of leadership roles, and the way they are revealed by the members of our videotape group, will be given in Chapter Twelve.

Phase 1: Making a Contract

Initially, a gathering of people must agree to become a functional group. This means they must elucidate both individual and group goals, clarify expectations, and thereby commence the early norming process. The questions, "Can I accept the others?" and "Will they accept me?" are prominent in the members' minds. They must find some degree of similarity among themselves in order to have a minimum level of cohesion. The question, "Will I get my needs met?" touches on the theme of survival, and evokes a primitive fear that is shared by most members and often the therapist as well. Although the first bond felt is usually with the therapist, that is not sufficient to sustain membership in the group. Unless the members discover connections with each other, they will not remain as a collectivity. An incipient group identity begins to surface as the members agree on informal norms of operation.

Our videotape group participants inaugurated Phase 1 by stating why they had come to our group. Joanna wanted to observe and learn about group process. Tony was an experienced group leader himself, yet wanted "to be more expressive and open" with a group in which he was a member. Robert wished to address his family-of-origin issues as they came up in group. Patricia wanted to learn more about how she functions in relation to the group process, with an eye toward leading groups someday. Victoria wanted to learn about group process. John did not know what to expect but wanted an "adventure." Judy had specific things to work out: she wanted to practice taking her time and space in the group, something that had been proscribed in her family of origin.

In an early attempt at bond formation, Judy and Robert explored the similarities in how they perceived their relationships with their mothers. Robert shared a memory of being with his mother in the kitchen, forced to listen to her as her confidante but unable to get her to listen to him. Judy related a time when her mother angrily demanded a response from her, and her frustration at having to repress her own anger, knowing she would not be heard. I emphasized both the similarities and the differences in their experiences with their mothers and asked Judy, "Have you and Robert worked out a way to be with each other?" In this way, I helped facilitate the member-to-member bonding.

Later in the first session, Tony expressed the desire for acceptance with a question to Patricia: "If you and I were to disagree, how could we do that without you writing me off?"

Patricia said, "If we could have respect in our disagreement . . ." Then she described her customary way of dealing with intractable conflict: "The only way to break the dynamic is to get out of it. . . . I don't know any other way to protect myself." She pointed to a defensive pattern that arises for her in a later phase of the group. In so doing, she raised the important issue of how we as a group might defend ourselves, and opened the door to the possibility of experimenting with new ways to act. This kind of initial testing of how each might react in conflict paves the way for the exploration of differences in Phase 2.

Phase 2: Establishing a Group Identity

In this phase, the group seeks to clarify its identity by defining its purpose, deciding on a style of communication—whether authoritarian or egalitarian, competitive or cooperative—setting the conditions for member participation, and allowing leadership to emerge. The group members must identify mutually acceptable norms by grappling with their differences and resolving them. The process of scapegoating is common to this phase; it permits the differentiation of group members into polarized positions or sometimes into opposing subgroups. The Scapegoat Leader emerges at this time as a focal point for conflict and galvanizes the group's energy. Often, the Scapegoat Leader's appropriateness for the group is questioned. The emotional tone of the group is characterized by stereotypical relating and competitive maneuvering. Therapists must prove their skills by assisting the group toward a level of abstraction that encompasses their differences, and must be particularly active in stressing the inclusion of all members. This phase is successfully concluded when the polarities are reconciled, resulting in greater group cohesion. In this process, the members must face their anxiety about differences without resorting to attempts to control others.

Early in Phase 1, Judy had disclosed certain frustrations in her life and what she described as her "wound" in the hope that others would respond in kind, exposing their flaws. The group members did not respond at that level because her disclosures came too early in the life of the group. It is difficult to determine the exact moments of transition between phases, but I believe the sequence that begins with Patricia's confrontation of Judy in Session 2 was one of the key points of passage for our group as it moved from Phase 1 to Phase 2. Here is a portion of that interaction:

JUDY: There's trust of other people and there's trust of myself . . . and there's distrust of my own level of "urrghh." (*Guttural nonverbal expression*)

PATRICIA: You're talking about your anger. . . . I think it happened to me yesterday, this feeling. . . . I really went toward you and I loved your openness . . . but at the same time . . . I did feel some anger and felt put upon. . . . you were talking about your wound and I'm thinking, "OK, she's a therapist, now how much work has been done on this?" Or do you continue to talk and talk about the same thing and not go anywhere with it?

JUDY: (*A few moments later*) You're putting me in touch with this other side . . . which is passive-aggressive . . . and I think your response is an appropriate response to passive-aggression.

The willingness to confront differences and dislikes, especially to a person who emerges, as Judy does, in the role of the Scapegoat Leader, signals the passage into Phase 2 behavior, in which judgments are made explicit and the limits of toleration are tested. The members of the group took the opportunity to examine their opinions and feelings about Judy's initial presentation to the group. By their reactions to her, they were able to explore their individual tendencies to categorize others by first impressions and opened the discussion about the phenomenon of stereotyping.

The group remained in Phase 2 throughout Session 3. Patricia was absent for this session. The further elaboration of the conflict between Patricia and Judy in the previous session was truncated and postponed until Session 4. Early in Session 3, Joanna emerged strongly as a leader, rallied to action by the tensions in Phase 2 and possibly by a fear that Vivian and I would not adequately contain the anger in the group. She challenged both Vivian and myself and masterfully orchestrated support for her subgroup, which included those who wanted the style of communication, at least initially, to be cognitively framed, and anger to be contained. Judy had allied herself with an opposing subgroup that endorsed high personal disclosure by members, and slowly watched support for that position ebb. There was competition between Joanna and Judy to determine which norm would be accepted at this early phase of group; Joanna's subgroup won. Judy lost support in her bid because most of the members were interested in a training experience, not a therapy experience. She was faced with an internal crisis that she did not share immediately with the group: she must either adapt to the informal norm being advocated, or leave.

After the third session, Judy called Vivian and me to discuss her leaving the group. We gave her permission to take care of herself in any way she needed to—including coming to the next session and letting the group know she would not complete the ten-session commitment. As Task Leaders, it was important that we did not take an authoritarian position with the Scapegoat Leader, as we discuss in detail in Chapter Twelve. Paradoxically, our permission for her to leave allowed her to stay.

Our group was fortunate enough to have in Judy a Scapegoat Leader strong enough to contain the negative projections of the members—and to resist the temptation to leave the group after the third session before the resolution of Phase 2. Her decision to stay helped propel the group into Phase 3.

During these first two phases both Robert and Joanna were quite active in providing cognitively stated guidelines to other members about group process and expectations. They were providing the didactic aspect of the Task Leader role.

Phase 3: The Exploration of Individuals in the Group

In this phase, the group must develop effective work and communication skills. Individuals must be recognized for their differences and how they will each potentially contribute to the life of the group. The group must establish a cooperative mode of interaction that allows room for each person to express his own perspective in an atmosphere of equality and respect. Space must also be created for members to experiment with diverse communication styles and discover how certain styles affect others. The Task Leaders strongly influence the group's experiments with communication and therapeutic change. In contrast to Phase 2, where conflicts are acted out, in Phase 3 the group's capacity for intrapsychic examination is tested. These processes lead to higher trust among members and greater cohesion, lessening to a degree the group's anxiety about closeness. Peer bonds are formed as members disclose fragments of their personal histories, helping others understand their particular circumstances and awakening feelings of empathy within the group. In a therapy group, Phase 3 is a time when parent-child and authority issues are explored.

At the beginning of Session 4, Judy returned to our group and shared how "alienated and regressed" she had been the previous session. In compliance with the formal norm to report contact outside the group, she said that she had called Vivian and me with the expectation of leaving the group. That morning, however, she had decided not to leave. She realized that she had tried to be intimate right away, but added that maybe she could switch and participate from a different part of herself.

Patricia came back to group in Session 4 and found the resolution the group had achieved sufficiently comfortable at least for the time being.

I believe a number of events converged at about the same time during this session that helped the group advance to Phase 3. It began when Judy interacted with John, who had implied she was trying to control the group. She said to John, "I'm not trying to control the group. I'm shifting my perspective." John, who shared Emotional Leadership with Robert in our group, began to adapt to Judy's shift and, in a sense, helped the group adapt also. As the group moved out of Phase 2, members had to claim their own projective processes that contributed so much to the scapegoating phenomenon. John began that process, evoking a strong emotional response. The following is a good example of how he took responsibility for his own behavior and in that process contributed to the acceptance of the Scapegoat Leader and to her own self-acceptance:

JOHN: (*To Judy*) When I left this group last week, it was with the resolve to do no harm, and I was concerned that I had.

JOANNA: John, can I interrupt you for a minute? (*Judy is crying at this point.*) I want to give Judy a chance to respond. (*To Judy*) Take your time . . . the cameras are rolling, but we're all here.

JUDY: (*To John*) When you said to me, "Your face looks controlled," you handed me the knife and I did like that (*Hand gesture of stabbing herself*) with it. What I heard was "I'm looking the way that I hate looking.". . . My face does feel like a mask sometimes.

Joanna's act had great import for healing in the group, because by making space for Judy's emotional response, she was recognizing and accepting the leader of the opposing subgroup. Her gesture removed the tone of competition between these two leaders and helped resolve that issue for the group as a whole. Joanna also acknowledged her contribution to Judy's experience of alienation by explaining, "When I'm not sure that someone understands me, I repeat myself. I was talking for quite some time without Judy interacting with me." The implication was that by her behavior Joanna was reminding Judy of what her own mother had done, creating further understanding of how the Scapegoat Leader had been alienated.

As a result of this sequence of events, Judy and Patricia made a provisional peace surrounding the conflict that began Phase 2, allowing the group to move fully into Phase 3. In this phase, individuals spoke more freely of their family-of-origin issues, with Robert and Tony leading the way. As they shared, they developed a peer bond. Robert and Patricia also began to work out a peer bond, but this broke down later in the group's life.

At the close of Session 4, John expressed his resentment at being interrupted by Joanna. He began Session 5 with the same theme by asking, "Do we have to stay at a nurturing level and not go back to dealing with conflict?" John watched the passage of the group into Phase 3 and wondered if he would be able to express his anger in such a harmonious atmosphere. This is a good example of how one group member may lag behind following a phase transition—and may need to test whether the new norm of cooperation works in resolving conflict.

Early in Session 5, John conceded that he needed to change his way of communication so that he was more direct and clear. Judy said to John that she appreciated his sharpness and opposition, adding, "I don't want us to become a mutual comfort organization." John confessed that he tended to be a bit blunt, stating that he wanted to modulate that. With this openness to change and a greater sense of trust, the group approached the next phase.

Phase 4: The Establishment of Intimacy

Attention to the individuality of members in Phase 3 opens the possibility for intimacy during this phase in two important respects: (1) the members can express closeness and tenderness, and (2) they can discuss sexuality as it affects their lives. New informal norms are established about emotional closeness and distance, such that a level of self-revealing behavior is now appropriate that would not have been earlier. Expressions of warmth and attraction let members bond at a deeper level. Group members are more relaxed and able to enjoy each other as a result of the relaxation of interpersonal tensions. The cohesion experienced at the close of this phase creates an openness for a new commitment by the group members. Members begin bonding more deeply with each other, becoming less dependent on their therapists, viewing them less as authorities and more as persons. If there are co-therapists, their degree of unanimity regarding the shift in power and their comfort with the expression of positive feelings facilitate the transition into this phase. Humor and playfulness come to the surface and move the group in a direction of greater creativity.

A half hour into Session 5, Victoria initiated an intimate exchange with John that carried us partway into Phase 4. In this one instance, she was expressing both her own and the group's feeling toward the Emotional Leader about his being warm and giving.

VICTORIA: When I think about you, John, I get this image of Friar Tuck in Robin Hood. Somebody that has a lot of humor and a very big heart. . . . The way you protect yourself is intellectually . . . but you're protecting a very big heart. (*There is a fifteen-second interval of silence in which Victoria and John maintain eye contact; John nods and his eyes swell with tears.*)

JOHN: (*Softly*) I appreciate . . . it's beyond words for me . . . (*Ten more seconds of silence with eye contact*) It is intense for me, that type of exposure. . . .

VICTORIA: My heart's beating really fast, too. I just want you to know that I see you.

John and Tony generously gave credit to Victoria for helping the group see John at a deeper level and opening up the possibility for greater closeness. John commented on how quiet Victoria had been up to this point. She replied that "being seen is vulnerable for me," and verbalized the anxiety that comes with intimacy: "What's the timing? . . . How long can you go on staring into somebody's eyes lovingly?"

Later in the session, Robert picked up on the issue of timing, admitting that his timing is off when he speaks and how much this is a liability for him. This insight allowed him to be more quiet in subsequent sessions. Judy related to having bad timing also, from the position of being overly impulsive, whereas Victoria was not spontaneous enough.

The group commenced to speak of the need to be seen and to have one's hopes and aspirations mirrored back. Tony shared a memory of his childhood in which he was given two games by his father. But Father ignored the game Tony wanted to play, and played the one that entertained himself, causing Tony to withdraw and suffer alone. Judy stated, "I'm struck by the continuing need and hunger that is left in us when we are not seen." This theme becomes the basis of a conflict between Judy and Patricia in the next phase. In temporary unanimity, both of them appeal to Joanna to show greater emotional expression—and are rebuffed. Joanna felt comfortable with the way she expressed herself.

Joanna showed her greatest emotional expression in Phase 4, especially in relation to Tony's story about his father. At the close of Session 5, Joanna commented that "I felt very connected to Victoria. . . . [*Looking at Victoria*] what I said seems to be enough for you."

When Vivian asked, "How do you feel that others are asking you for more?" Joanna said, "I'm trying to absorb that."

Joanna began Session 6 feeling Victoria's absence acutely. It seemed that Joanna felt less support and sensed the shift of the group to a new phase of development, one in which she would lose some of her authority established earlier in group, and be challenged to conform to a new informal norm about closeness worked out in Phase 4. Joanna said, "I get a sense that there is something going on that is more than the content of what people are actually saying to me, and I don't understand this level of process. I get this very strong feeling that anything I say in direct response to the individual comments isn't going to resolve this. There is something going on here that is a group question."

Joanna turned to me for a sense of direction and how she could respond to the request that she reveal more of who she is. As Task Leader, I found myself in a double bind, wanting to support the group's progress and yet not wanting Joanna to be isolated as the group moved toward a new norm of closeness.

Joanna continued to take an observant, analytic stance by identifying the two subgroups divided along the dimension of disclosure-nondisclosure: Judy, Patricia, John, and Robert versus Victoria, Tony, and her. She was aware of the differences in these subgroups but did not name them. Robert came to her aid, as Emotional Leader, making statements that integrated her observations with his. Speaking for his subgroup, he said, "The two levels intermesh. There really was something that got triggered in Judy, John, and Patricia that was related to the way you [Joanna] are—and there was also a dynamic reason why it happened."

John became very active during this portion of the group. He confronted Joanna concerning her "leadership function of distancing and defending," and continued to press her as others had done. When Vivian questioned her regarding her emotional response, Joanna answered in a way characteristic of her style in group: "An emotional response, I don't stick with. . . . I try to actually detach myself . . . to see what's going on." From this point until the beginning of closure in Phase 8, Joanna withdraws for the most part from group interaction.

What followed was a period of intermember bonding, in which some members risked verbalizing their hostile feelings and their affection, generally making themselves more vulnerable. John initiated a deeper bonding with Robert, using direct and authentic communication, a norm worked out in the previous phase.

Judy tearfully acknowledged her trust for John by saying, "You are so open. Your honesty is refreshing."

John admitted that his perception of Judy had changed: "I see you now as three-dimensional . . . not superficial." This was an example of how the Scapegoat Leader is seen more positively in the later phases of group development.

Judy and Robert made an attempt to bond beyond merely project-ing their mothers onto each other. Tony divulged how healing it was for him to watch John and Robert work through their conflict to a res-olution. John again took the initiative and invited Tony to negotiate a new agreement on how to be closer to each other.

Phase 5: The Exploration of Mutuality

Vulnerability is the key word to describe this phase. The positive expression of feeling in the previous phase suggests a mutual com-mitment to create deeper relationships in the context of the group. The members will test how their dependency needs will be handled and how their frustration and hostility will be abided when those needs are not met or understood. A major achievement is the direct expression of animosity without the experience of rejection. These developments lead to mutual relationships based on equality and the acceptance of mutual responsibility for each other. Often the Task Leaders are challenged by the Defiant Leader, who bargains for a spe-cial agreement regarding norms that have been established. In this way, the diversity of the group can be embraced as the Task Leaders demonstrate flexibility in their consideration of one person's needs. A dominant norm of equality emerges based on the allowance for individual difference. If the group cannot achieve mutuality among its members, it cannot proceed to the next phase, that of reorganizing its structure.

Our group spent more time in this phase than in any other, con-suming the end of Session 6 and all of Sessions 7 and 8. We seemed very stuck on the issues of vulnerability and establishing mutuality, and in the end, Vivian and I had to evoke the time boundary as a way to move out of this phase and into the later phases, signifying the clo-sure of our group.

Toward the end of Session 6, buoyed by the successful bonding accomplished by the males during Phase 4, Judy returned to the unre-solved conflict with Patricia.

JUDY: Last week I talked about letting out raw, ugly feelings and (*To Patricia*) you really didn't like that. . . . I also had a mother [who] was the only one allowed to express anger in the family. If I were to express anger. . . . (*She strikes her fist against her hand indicating the wrath of Mother.*) It feels really great to let that out. . . .

PATRICIA: My heart's beating. . . . my response to you is whoa, I just want to run away. I had a mother who was just totally out of control with her anger. My response to you is to stay away. . . .

BILL: I get this powerful image when both of you speak. It's as if there is this witch mother that's hanging over us. . . .

I believe this was a crisis for Patricia, our Defiant Leader. At this point we entered a period of intense projective identification between Judy and Patricia that approached the level of group illusion and fantasy, as if the past were actually being played out before our eyes. As Task Leader, I made this interpretation, but we were not able to get beyond this impasse. It kept us squarely locked in Phase 5 until both Task Leaders began to structure a process of closure at the beginning of Session 9. I believe that the visual image of Judy striking her fist against her hand triggered a traumatic memory in Patricia that sent her into the past. In similar fashion, Judy had acted out her fear and anger in relation to her mother.

I stated a belief that I repeated several times over the next two sessions: that this interaction was exactly what we hope to achieve by group therapy. "We bring to group our memories from the past and by such interactions, we can understand how our memories get in the way of our being in the here and now."

Judy demonstrated growth in Session 7 by realizing that she had used some of Joanna's ability to detach during her conflict with Patricia. She had heard her own internal voice in Patricia's criticism of her, and she discovered that she could detach from it. The group showed patience with Patricia in letting her recapitulate the conflict of the last session. At the close of this session, Joanna, in a Task Leader way, connected with both Vivian and me, supporting our contention that the group was holding Patricia's pain and that she was not ready to deal with it yet. As Joanna put it: "When you have that [pain], the group takes it on. [*To Patricia*] And when you said, 'talking about it helps,' that seems to me to be the first step. And with this amount of pain that was triggered, it's not going to go away in one session."

The following exchange late in Session 8 summarized the frustration and vulnerability that the Defiant Leader experienced in Phase 5 and the Emotional Leader's reminder of the positive connections she made.

JOHN: I hear everyone connecting and being seen almost at a deeper level . . . being seen for who we are. . . .

ROBERT: When you said "everyone," my thoughts went to you, Patricia. I'm wondering how you're feeling and what this has been like for you?

In her reply, Patricia showed that she was least ambivalent about the ending of the group.

PATRICIA: It's been uncomfortable being here, and I will welcome the end of this group. I have somewhat mixed feelings. . . . It would be nice to continue on, but in a different group.

ROBERT: When you said that, you sounded hurt and angry.

PATRICIA: I'm not sure that's entirely what's going on, but I'm not comfortable with some members of the group. . . . I've felt that coming here has been a burden. . . .

ROBERT: Am I one of the people you feel uncomfortable with?

PATRICIA: Yes, definitely. . . . I feel like every connection we've had or I've tried to make with you, the end has become negative. . . .

ROBERT: I'm feeling some sadness as you say this. . . . I think there is a reality about that and . . . it's a Mother projection. My relationship with my mother always ended with my rejecting her. You and I have had nice connections, touching your shoulder. Even though I tend to push you away, there's a part of me that really cares about you.

PATRICIA: Thank you, I've felt your caring.

At the close of Session 8, Patricia and Judy made another attempt at bridging the gulf between them, but time ran out before they could completely do so.

This group was not able to achieve complete mutuality, in part due to the unresolved conflict between Judy and Patricia, which precluded their regarding each other as peers and embracing their diversity. Also, for reasons I do not completely understand, neither Vivian nor I were invited to move from positions of authority to join the group in a different capacity, as members with special expertise. Such a move is a necessary step for entering Phase 6. It is possible that our minimal Task Leadership at the beginning caused the group to view us less as authorities from the start.

Phase 6: The Achievement of Autonomy Through Reorganization of the Group's Structure

In this phase, the leadership structure of the group is altered, with the Emotional Leader taking over initiation and support functions from the Task Leader. The Task Leader is invited to become a member of the group with special expertise. All the leadership roles become more fluid. The group achieves separateness from the therapist as an authority and revels in a sense of self-directedness. The members take "ownership" of their group, resulting in a heightened sense of accomplishment and autonomy. The sense of group identity now reaches its peak. Because many interpersonal conflicts have been resolved in Phase 5, the self-esteem of members has increased and the ambience is more friendly. The members deepen their commitment to the group, with the therapist now acting as a collaborator, changing the informal norms of how the group will be managed. This change in role functions among members and therapists sets the stage for a different quality and kind of therapy work in the next phase.

Our videotape group did not proceed to Phase 6.

Phase 7: Self-Confrontation and the Achievement of Interdependence

This is a highly collaborative, creative, and interdependent period during which mutual commitment and responsibility for each other is the rule. The group is now ready to engage in intense work on individual issues. The deepest therapy can occur in this phase as members face the regressive aspects of their behavior and encounter their ambivalence about giving up defensive patterns established in early childhood. Another level of differentiation occurs based on the cohesion achieved in earlier phases. There is an awareness of each member's profound complexity and a sense of sharing the struggle that is involved in personal change. In an ongoing group, the individuals achieve the kind of functional interdependence that facilitates a high level of productivity over sustained periods of time. In time-limited groups, the individuals confront a pivotal issue: the relevance of what they have learned in group to their life outside the group.

Our videotape group did not proceed to Phase 7.

Phase 8: Independence, the Transfer of Learning

In this phase, the group considers the possibility of close relationships outside the context of the group. The question, "Can I do elsewhere what I've accomplished here?" becomes a central concern. The members review the issues they confronted in group with an eye to transferring what they learned to their daily life. They reflect on the meaning of the experience they have shared and think of ways to experiment with their growing independence from the group. They begin to cope with the fact of impending separation and look at the unfinished business between pairs of individuals.

Some members will make efforts to complete interactions or resolve conflicts still outstanding, or alternatively, accept that they will not be resolved. Sometimes members will ask for feedback about their participation in group, as they evaluate their progress and that of the group as a whole.

One of the fascinating aspects of writing this chapter was the isomorphy of the writing process. I struggled to write about Phase 5, much as our group struggled to move through it, and coming to Phases 8 and 9, like our group, I was somewhat reluctant to let go of the process and bring it to a close.

At the beginning of Session 9, Vivian and I set the tone for termination and reflection about what had happened in the group. This would be the last session for both Joanna and Patricia, and we wanted to structure a closure for them as well as create space for the members to acknowledge their importance to each other. As Task Leaders of a time-limited group, we were cognizant of our responsibility to help the group say goodbye and to gently but firmly move through resistances to do so.

Following our reminder of the time boundary, the group entered a fifty-second period of silence. It was as if this abrupt shift to a new phase was gradually being absorbed and processed. Joanna broke the silence with a statement that she had found the group worthwhile. Her statement was followed by a forty-second interval of silence. Then Robert, as Emotional Leader, began the process by addressing Joanna: "I thought about saying goodbye to you." He reflected on an earlier exchange between them and expressed regret that he had not listened better to her comments.

Vivian supported Robert's movement toward change outside the group by sharing her impression of him in group: "You said earlier you wanted to talk less and listen more. And you did. I hear you are not finished with that, but I did see some change." Vivian reminded Robert of what he had said in the first group session, when he described how angry he was, having to listen to his mother. "You wanted to listen to Joanna because she had something worthwhile to say."

Robert reached out to Tony, admiring his listening skills and remembering their moment of closeness. Tony responded, "For me, it's rare to feel that level of connection with a male." Then Tony reflected on an incident that stood out for him in group, when John expressed his anger directly at Robert. "They were both simultaneously modeling something for me: John was congruent in his emotional tone . . . saying angry words, and Robert was sitting there, soaking it in with curiosity. Both of those would be hard for me to do. I learned that if two people can do that, there can be a cleansing and a working through it. . . . it was healing and counter-conditioning. . . . I imagine myself doing both of those. . . . the next thing is to practice each."

Robert made an attempt to clarify for himself what transpired in the conflict between Judy and Patricia. "What I saw happen in this group was, Judy gave a clear expression of anger, and [*To Patricia*] your heart started beating [fast], whatever emotion that was, and then [you gave] a really heavy judgment about how therapists should have their shit together."

Patricia spoke to correct Robert's narrative, but I interrupted, setting the limits appropriate for the phase of group. I said, "We don't have time to resolve this issue. This is the last time that you [Patricia] and Joanna will be here. We must look very clearly at what we can accomplish and what we have to let go. I think this is one we'll have to let go." Judy and Patricia returned to the impasse once more, and Vivian and I stopped them again.

With less than an hour remaining in the session, the group began the Phase 9 process of saying goodbye to Joanna and Patricia. Robert stated his appreciation for Joanna, complimenting "the qualities of love and sensitivity" she brought to the group. He acknowledged Patricia's struggle and attempted, rather awkwardly, to give her credit, but she was much too vulnerable to hear it. Robert only seemed to awaken negative transferences to her family of origin, so their imbroglio was left unresolved.

Victoria praised Patricia's willingness to take risks and added: "For me, if there is conflict, I'll usually withdraw, rather than keep coming back. So, you've modeled that for me." Patricia responded that she was learning to do the opposite, that is, when to withdraw. Patricia thanked Vivian and me for our "minimal style" of leadership.

I acknowledged the special bond she felt toward me, and voiced my appreciation for the vulnerability she displayed. Vivian and I said our goodbyes to Joanna and then spoke to each other, commending the group on the fine work they had done and reminding them that one session still remained.

Following a silence near the end, Robert shared his experience during the quiet interval. "I was back at the deathbed of my mom, because in some ways this seems a similar process." He explained what was different for him in this situation. "My mom was less and less there, while you are all very present." With four minutes remaining, Judy attempted to find closure with Patricia.

JUDY: I'd like to try something.

VIVIAN: This is the very last try. (*The group laughs, indicating their exhaustion with the process over the last few sessions.*)

JUDY: (*To Patricia*) I want to see if I can accurately see how you've been seeing me. . . . If I were going to start this group all over again, I'd do it differently. I put stuff out before there was any base [for understanding]. I put out the victim part of myself, and you were uncomfortable with it because . . . it felt to you like I was identifying with it. . . .

PATRICIA: Yes, identifying with it. That you were believing this about yourself. And that part made me want to move away because you weren't struggling. . . .

JUDY: So, you saw me as not struggling?

PATRICIA: Yes, yes.

This appeared to be the beginning of an understanding between our Scapegoat Leader and our Defiant Leader, coming, ironically, at the close of their experience together.

Phase 9: Terminating

The process of saying goodbye to significant persons, and sharing how they have been important to one's growth, is one of the richest moments in group therapy. If the group has been relatively successful, the group will be ready for termination as a natural consequence of the phases of development that have gone before. The task is to stay open to one's own feelings and to others, expressing the warmth and meaning that was shared. It is possible that some members will deny the impact that others have made on their lives, as a way of defending against the pain of loss and separation. In these cases, the Task Leader may have to structure the termination so that members can face that pain and move through it. There must also be room for the expression of regrets for what was not accomplished—regrets that were not fully addressed in the previous phase. Members will participate in historical reviews of what happened in group, highlighting salient moments and incidents that bring both laughter and tears. Some people will explore the possibility of postgroup relationships. Others will share their perceptions of the therapists and the bond they formed or did not form with them. The therapists can positively reinforce the changes participants have made as well as indicate directions for future development and growth.

With only five members remaining, we entered the final session of our group. Victoria began with a well-thought-out, twelve-minute presentation. She demonstrated how well she could give when the giving is structured. She gave gifts to each member of the group, much as an Emotional Leader might have done. She shared with Vivian and me how we had not met her expectations, as well as her appreciation of us. Vivian and I both responded to Victoria, followed by a thirty-three-second silent interval. The members then responded to Victoria. This was Tony's response: "I can't imagine doing what you just did. It's the process of saying goodbye that's always been hard for me. Part of it is the sadness that I don't want to feel. Whenever I could orchestrate it, I would just drift away."

The group spent a good amount of time helping Tony structure his goodbye. Vivian gave encouragement to Tony, reinforcing the positive steps he had taken and how he might act differently in the world.

TONY: I don't acknowledge my friends unambiguously and overtly what they mean to me. I somehow experienced that in my family. . . . That's how we were with each other. . . . That's what I'm projecting now onto this experience.

VIVIAN: Not fully, Tony. [You're doing something different.]

Robert explored with Tony the possibility of a friendship after the group ended, and Tony, breaking his family rule, was open to that.

John, apprehensive that he might say the wrong thing in the last session, now spoke with my encouragement to take a risk. John reviewed how much he had thought of the group between sessions and how much he had let go of judgments that he had earlier harbored about group members. He made connections with Tony and Judy, and Vivian and me, using humor as a vehicle to reach out. Then he and Robert had this exchange:

JOHN: Is there something going on with you, Robert, or is it just me?

ROBERT: I often feel annoyed when you speak, and I'm trying to figure out what that's about. . . . I sense a great dis-ease, married to your humor. When I get in touch with that it makes me quite sad. . . . My father was always joking my mother out of her pain.

A genuine dialogue ensued between the two men, leading to a deeper understanding of each other. Concerned that others needed to say their goodbyes, I brought their exchange to a close, saying: "I've seen an openness between you two today that I haven't seen before, and I realized that we'll not be able to fully appreciate it. We won't have the time."

The preceding narrative is one analysis of a very complex and absorbing group. There are many other ways to analyze the process of a small, time-limited group, and some of these we address in the commentary that accompanies the videotape we produced from these sessions. On viewing the videotape, many clinicians will undoubtedly arrive at interpretations different than ours. One of the great beauties and satisfactions of group process is the understanding that we will never fully explain or grasp all that occurs. Yet our perspective, limited as it is, remains vital, because it allows us to fully engage with the group—and as group therapists we must remain engaged with our groups.

For me, the value of Beck's theory lies not in the precision with which we can make demarcations between phases or even our exactness in naming the leadership roles. What seems of greater significance is how her theory illuminates some of the dynamics of a group amid the rich abundance of data that are present. Also—much like previews of coming attractions—the theory helps us predict a few events, so we can adjust our behavior as group therapists to meet the expected challenges. In the next chapter, I examine in more detail those aspects of the emergent leadership roles that can help us foresee the direction a group may take.

CHAPTER TWELVE

Emergent Leadership Roles

—~~~— The idea of leadership raises the question of character, a question that pervades the history of drama, philosophy, and psychology. It is a question of great complexity and depth, asked by many great thinkers. Who am I that acts?

In the history of Western tragedy, character defines a person who acts without complete knowledge of himself and without knowing the ultimate consequences of his actions. As the audience, we approach the drama of Oedipus with knowledge that he does not have about himself; we experience our grief for him as we watch him discover the truth that becomes his own undoing. In each performance of Hamlet, we keep hoping he won't go into his mother's bedroom. But he does—again and again—in search of deeper knowledge of self, even though it brings him to ruin.

As participants in group therapy, we too act without complete knowledge of who we are and without knowing the ultimate impact of what we do. We are assisted by our fellow group members, who perceive us doing things either in character with what we usually do or radically different from our standard behavior. By our actions, we may become so disproportionately influential in the life of the group that we are assigned a leadership role, sometimes much to our aston-ishment.

We have all experienced the power of one character to propel the dramatic action of a play. The person who assumes a leadership role also propels the movement of the group to new levels of action and understanding. However, the leadership role, as it emerges in a psy-chotherapy group, does not depend entirely on the personality of the individual who assumes the role. It is possible that any group mem-ber could take on any of the four leadership roles, depending on the configuration of the group and the needs of the group as a whole.

Thus it may be that I'm the Task Leader in one group while the Scapegoat Leader in another. In some groups, I may not figure as a leader at all. Aspects of my personality, my ambition, or my family of origin will not be the ultimate factors that determine the leader-ship role I assume, but rather the context and circumstances of the group itself.

In spontaneous groups, parts are not scripted, so I may play a role in one group that explores an aspect of who I am, then find myself in a second group exploring another aspect of myself in a new lead-ership role. Only the change of group composition will call into ques-tion the assignment of leadership roles. It is true that one person may in time play many parts—but only as the context of the group changes.

THE MATRIX FROM WHICH LEADERSHIP ARISES

At the beginning of each of the phases of group therapy development, various group-level issues are raised that demand an action or reac-tion from each member, who differentiates himself from the others by his response. The challenge to the group is to work out a solution that will embrace the varying responses. As this happens, the group becomes more integrated and cohesive, and achieves some closure on that phase of the process. The emergence of leadership roles makes possible the transition from one phase to the next.

In each phase, certain members become more active because they are directly challenged or strongly motivated by the issues raised. Mem-bers who take up diametrically opposed positions in response to the issues become the leaders who perform characteristic functions throughout the life of the group. Their consistent behavior in carrying out their leadership functions distinguishes them from others who are highly active during a particular phase but do not sustain that activity over the course of the members' time together.

Leadership Roles Have Significance

As I've indicated in earlier chapters, the group therapist must learn to rely on the emergent leadership roles as a key to success in short-term groups. For example, in the absence of a Scapegoat Leader, a group will resist moving beyond a superficial and stereotypical way of relating that will consign the group to a rather shallow experience. The group therapist must confront the group members on their tendency to be "nice" and play it "safe," pointing out how the group is avoiding its work. Groups that see only similarities and refuse to see sharp differences among its members often fit this description.

In the absence of an Emotional Leader, I've been perplexed to see groups become mired in negativity, caught up in Phase 2 conflicts that seem never to subside, let alone find resolution. In such groups, there is no one who conjures an all-embracing, positive view of the group or discloses personal material that opens the boundaries of others to the possibility of intimacy as a shared group experience. The result is a group in which the Task Leaders must work doubly hard to draw out the emotional lives of its members.

As a sea captain employs compass and sextant, the savvy group therapist can use the emergent leadership roles to determine the position of the group relative to the phases of its development and assess its progress over time. Many times I've lamented to my co-therapist how much I miss the direction provided by one of the leadership roles, when the group seems lost in a fog or imperiled by some danger. Why certain roles fail to appear in some short-term groups remains a puzzle to me, and an important question that is beyond the scope of this chapter. The relevance of the leadership roles, when they are manifest, is obvious to the clinician who is wise to the service they perform in groups.

Therapists Must Facilitate Emergence of Leaders

In short-term groups, the therapists must watch for the signs of leaders who assume the necessary functions that propel group development. Group therapists must be careful not to take the initiative away from leaders as they start to carry out tasks appropriate to their nascent role. An anxious group therapist may be too eager to be all things to the group and thereby dominate its operation. For example, she may be unable to resist making an observation that a group member would have made had she not "stolen" it away from him. In doing so, she inhibits the person from expressing himself spontaneously in group.

The patience a group therapist must demonstrate in allowing the leaders to emerge may sometimes run counter to the therapist's understandable desire to "get things moving" in a group that is time limited. Ironically, the therapist that is so driven may close down the affective life of the group entirely, or call the hostility of the group down upon himself and find himself "scapegoated" as an authoritarian or patronizing leader.

On the other hand, a Task Leader who is too inactive in the first two phases of group development may hamper the smooth processing of feelings of anxiety and competition and dampen the emergence of other leaders by not providing an atmosphere of safety. It is also possible that members will fill the void and assume certain aspects of the Task Leader role. In many training group experiences this is seen as a way to facilitate greater awareness of group dynamics and to encourage participants to experience the primitive anxieties that lead a group to form a structure in the first place.

THE FOUR EMERGENT LEADERS

Ariadne P. Beck has identified four emergent informal leadership roles in psychotherapy groups. These leaders arise spontaneously in conjunction with the progress of a group through the nine phases of development, under the conditions specified in Chapter Eleven. More recently the Chicago Group Development Research Team has identified a variant pattern of leadership in some training groups. This variant pattern includes members who share the Task Leader role, members who share the other leadership roles, members who become the Task Leaders, and a new role identified as the Ambivalent Emotional Leader. There may be other leadership roles, as I suspect there are—the most ill member and the premature leader being two favorite candidates Vivian and I have noticed in our clinical observations.

I shall list the salient characteristics of each leadership role and then track the progress of each through our videotape group as a way to highlight our passage through the phases. These descriptions of leadership roles may be read along with the group narrative given in Chapter Eleven as a counterpoint to deepen the meaning of both. A greater comprehension of these roles will be obtained, of course, by watching our videotape of a time-limited group (see information following Chapter Thirteen).

Task Leader

In therapy groups, the Task Leader is the therapist. In groups co-led by a team equal in training and experience, the Task Leader role is shared. These leaders bring the group together and function as guides to the task of the group, regulating the time and limiting the scope of the task when necessary. They monitor the boundary between the group and the environment in which it meets, dealing with all the external factors that surround it. They are masters in communication, influencing how deeply the members will explore intrapsychically. They are the arbiters of what constitutes fantasy and what constitutes reality in the many projective processes that occur throughout the life of the group. Ideally, they model the exercising of power and the sharing of authority. In each of these role functions, they influence the creation of group norms.

Beck's theory has recently been used in a study of training groups for psychotherapists, and that has led to a variation on the theory for groups in that context. This study of leadership in forty training workshops showed that many roles were duplicated, especially when the groups were larger than eight to ten persons. Sometimes two or three persons shared one of the leadership roles. Also, when the Designated Leader was relatively inactive in the early phases of the group—or throughout the life of the group—a member emerged to share the Task Leader role, and the Emotional Leader expressed fairly strong ambivalence. This led the Beck research team to identify a new role named the Ambivalent Emotional Leader. In this study, members who became Task Leaders were perceived in similar ways to Designated Leaders.

In our videotape group, Vivian and I shared the role of Task Leader. Our equal sharing of the role did not mean we did the same activities, and I shall point out a few of the subtleties of our work as a co-therapy team. Prior to entering the group, all members had agreed to attend each of the ten sessions unless prevented by unavoidable conflicts with vacations or work schedules. Of course, all members had signed waivers of their right to confidentiality so that videotaping could occur. The absence of a formal norm to preserve confidentiality was one of the most unusual features of our group.

Vivian and I could have been more active as Task Leaders in the early phases of the group. In some ways, regarding information-giving and asking questions of members, we did not fulfill the requirements of Task Leader, especially for a time-limited therapy group. This was true for two reasons.

First, because of the televised nature of our group, the task of the group had been left intentionally ambiguous and the question left open: Was this a therapy group, in which people were supposed to make changes? Or was this a training group, whose purpose was to study its own behavior? As we see in the video, this ambiguity caused great difficulty for Judy, our Scapegoat Leader, when she exposed herself so early and then had to draw back in conformity with the developing group norm. The group did take on the characteristics of a training group in many respects.

Second, the pressure Vivian and I felt "leading" the eight people on our production team, just outside the view of the cameras, took our attention at the beginning, and we were not able to be there totally for the group in front of the cameras. As the videotaping proceeded, we became more comfortable with the operation of the production team and could focus our attention on our task as leaders of the group. The experience of being in a videotaped group is rather intimidating, and we were no more immune to this factor than were our group members. In a videotaped group, the task of monitoring the boundary between the group and the external environment is complex and time consuming.

In the videotape, we see Joanna and Robert fill the gap early on and share the Task Leadership role with us. We will see some examples of how they did this.

In Phase 1, I led off the group by stating the formal norms for its operation: the members must report all absences in advance to the other members, and they must report all contact with other members that occurred outside the actual meeting times of our sessions, including the content of what was said, so that no secrets were harbored by external subgroups. I stated the task of the group simply: to discover the deeper emotional connections between us.

Vivian stated that it was her belief that members would learn more about themselves through the process of our group. She invited the group members to introduce themselves and the goals they wanted to accomplish during our sessions together. This was a very active group from the start and did not require much assistance from us in Phase 1, in contrast to groups that openly depend on their Task Leaders to guide them. Twenty minutes into our first session, I asked Judy how she felt about being the focus of attention. She replied, "Ambivalent." Then Vivian asked for information about Judy's family of origin to elicit memories of the competitive feelings she felt in the presence of her mother, who monopolized attention for herself. To which I added, "Perhaps Mother's here in the group?"

A bit later, Vivian asked Judy to experiment by saying, "I'm not going to take care of you" to Robert, a member onto whom she had transferred feelings about her mother. The purpose of these spare interventions was to help Judy examine her feelings and explore the parallels she experienced between her own family and our group. The themes of Mother and competition were raised and became very important in the next phase.

When I asked Patricia, following her confrontation of Judy at the start of Phase 2, if she could trust the group enough to show her passive-aggression, it set the stage for Joanna to challenge me.

JOANNA: That's a loaded question.

BILL: That's spoken like a lawyer.

JOANNA: Maybe it's not an issue of trust. (*Then, a few moments later, to Patricia*) You were talking about something and I thought that Bill was leading you. . . . I kind of jumped in there and you [Bill] jumped right back at me . . . and then said that's a typical question [for a lawyer].

BILL: That's my aggression at lawyers coming out.

JOANNA: What did you feel when I said, "That's a loaded question?"

BILL: I think you were right, and I felt, "Boy, she's really going to stop me. . . . she won't let me get away with too much." (*Joanna laughs.*)

It was important for me, in this case, to be congruent with what I was feeling and to acknowledge the rightness of her challenge without defending from a position of authority ("I know better") or acceding to alter my style of questioning. The Task Leaders communicate a powerful message to the group by the way they respond to the challenges to their authority. This was especially true with Joanna, who had taken on some of the Task Leader role up to that point and continued to share that role with us to some degree throughout the life of the group. Hanging in the balance are the questions of how egalitarian a group will become and how appropriate it is to question authority and to eventually take ownership of the group. Vivian and I conveyed to this group a sense of collegiality and equality from the start, so establishing equality, a Phase 3 operation, was a relatively easy process. In this way, also, our group resembled a training group of therapists. It is interesting to note that Joanna was the only person to ask direct questions of either Task Leader during the life of our group.

The group was delighted with Joanna's challenge, telling her she seemed more animated, with color in her face, and her voice louder. Robert, who also appeared to assume some Emotional Leader functions, pointed to the establishment of a new informal norm: "It's a trust issue. . . . Who's leading this group and what are the rules? . . . Can we challenge? Is that OK? Do we get reprisals if we challenge?" Robert also seemed to be speaking from his anxiety about a lack of Task Leadership, and filling in the gap.

A little later, Robert, in a very peer-like statement, moved to open the intrapsychic boundaries between members and the Task Leader by giving his interpretation of my behavior when I said "I outed you" to Joanna (when I revealed to the group that she was a lawyer): "Bill, you acknowledged you had some hostility to lawyers and it occurs to me that the assertion, 'I outed you' means 'I have some power over an attorney,' and my thought is maybe you've experienced situations in your life when it was the other way around . . . and you have some feelings about that. . . ." This led to some useful discussion of stereotyping, appropriate to Phase 2.

In the midst of Judy's struggle in Phase 2 to find an entry into the group by winning the acceptance of a norm that sanctions the expression of strong emotions, Vivian lent support by saying, "I think this is one of the differences [between] a therapy group whose goal is to learn how people really are . . . and a social group where we don't usually challenge people with whom we're trying to get along." This is a clear example of how the Task Leader can help the group remain intact while it negotiates the formation of enough norms to be capable of cooperative work and allow for the emergence of individuals.

During Phase 3, the Task Leaders needed to supply only minimal support to the group's experiments at communication, as the cooperative mode was in full operation. Vivian nurtured Robert in a way that allowed him to connect to her as a good mother. When John, who shared the Emotional Leader role with Robert, voiced his resentment of Joanna's interrupting him, I validated the appropriateness of his expression of feeling. I also noted that the members of more mature groups can postpone meeting their needs until a later time, when waiting is called for. This is a teaching function appropriate to the Task Leader role.

Following the group's passage into Phase 4, when Victoria gave her gifts to John, I positively reinforced her speaking up in group. I also reminded the group that she would be absent the next session, and told her I would miss her presence.

Contrary to what Beck predicts in Phase 4, neither Vivian nor I experienced a shift from "authority" to "person" during this time, chiefly because we believe we had relinquished that authority position much earlier in the life of the group.

At the close of Session 5, while still in Phase 4, I made the time limitation explicit, stating that having completed the halfway mark in our group, the members should be asking themselves if they are accomplishing what they set out to do.

At the beginning of Session 6, still in Phase 4, Joanna was puzzled about requests from Judy and Patricia that she reveal more of herself. Joanna looked to me as Task Leader and guide to answer certain questions about how she should proceed in group.

JOANNA: (To Bill) I don't know if it requires a certain amount of knowledge or expertise. . . .

BILL: I don't think it requires expertise, but it does require that we look into ourselves and notice how we feel at any particular time. . . .

During Phase 5, in Session 7, Joanna helped interpret to Patricia the degree of pain that the group was experiencing in light of her traumatic memories being awakened. Also, at the beginning of Session B, Vivian and I used effective co-therapy skills to help Judy, who had set a therapy contract with us in Phase 1, come to a redecision.

JUDY: Now at this point I start to feel like I'm taking up too much time and space and I'd better shut up. That I shouldn't be doing this.

VIVIAN: Sounds like the message you got from your mother when you did take time and space. . . . I imagine this little preverbal child. . . .

how scary it must have been, because you knew what you needed and you weren't getting it. If you dared to try and get it, you got smashed.

JUDY: Yeah, yeah. (*Softly*)

BILL: The little girl decision that you described last time was that you would be a really good little girl . . . but here it sounds like you're wanting to do something different . . . and that involves a redecision.

VIVIAN: And it's not being a bad little girl. It's being a natural child who wants attention and wants time and space for herself.

JUDY: (*Responding emotionally, hand covering her mouth*) When you said the words, "want some time and space" I. . . . (*A shudder passes through her body*)

VIVIAN: It's OK for you to want that.

JUDY: I'm just going to say it. I want time and space. I'm going to say it again. I want time and space (*Laughing*).

Vivian and I were quite active structuring the termination process in Phases 8 and 9, as I have described in Chapter Eleven.

Scapegoat Leader

Early in a group's life, this leader becomes either the target of attack or the container for negative projections by other group members who perceive that this leader is quite different on some dimension of membership. (It is often the Task Leader's function to help the group see whether this difference is real or a projective fantasy.) In this way, the Scapegoat Leader tests what is acceptable behavior in the group and the degree to which group members will tolerate difference, helping clarify the norms of inclusion. The Scapegoat Leader models the conflict between self-assertion and conformity to the group, making room for individual uniqueness. She exposes herself in a vulnerable way and must be strong enough to hold the negative perceptions of others. During her crisis in Phase 2, she must maintain a sense of loyalty to the group, even while feeling separated from it.

In our videotape group, Judy occupied the role of Scapegoat Leader. She struggled with impulses toward aggression on one hand and submission on the other. She introduced herself in Phase 1 in this way: "I don't want to be diffident, I don't want to be good, I don't want to hold back and give everybody their chance, I want to take my space, which is not easy for me to do. . . ." She approached the group with a readiness to disclose and an impatience to have others disclose as well. Her impatience was perceived initially by group members as an attempt to control them or shape their behavior in a particular way. Robert confirmed this perception when he said, "I heard Judy saying . . . 'Look, I'm putting stuff in the pot, now if you guys don't put stuff in the pot, I'm going to get really pissed at you.'"

Judy was also quite frank about her own internal conflicts: "I feel a real distrust of a group like this. . . . I immediately feel there is competition for attention and time. . . . I want to really hear others . . . yet I so much want to be known and seen." Her willingness to be vulnerable set her up as a target for others.

Patricia, our Defiant Leader, had confronted Judy one hour into Session 2, and I described that scene as part of my discussion of Phase 2 in Chapter Eleven. Following that confrontation, Judy remained silent for a while and then returned to Patricia and the topic of passive-aggression.

JUDY: I feel like you really nailed me when you said you felt angry at my putting out this victim thing. . . .

BILL: How did you feel being nailed?

JUDY: I felt defensive at first, I felt critical of you [Patricia] . . . my response was, "You don't understand. . . . (*Raising her voice in anger and grimacing her face*) I've done all those things!" . . . and then somebody else stepped in and said, "She's right." . . . In fact there's some internal reason that I'm stuck in this way, so I felt respectful of what you said. It was bracing to have you say it.

In this way, the Scapegoat Leader demonstrated considerable strength in being able to hear criticism and yet remain open and willing to engage. As is often the case with this leadership role, this person's openness is not perceived right away by the rest of the group. Patricia was unable to hear that Judy was acknowledging her astute observation, and she focused instead on the word *nailed* and the nonverbal expressions Judy used to convey her message, all of which carried negative connotations for Patricia. Unfortunately, this pattern of failing to hear the other person characterized the relations between these two group members during most of the group. An intense kind of projective identification involving each woman's mother distorted their communication to the degree that I had to name it as a projective fantasy on several occasions in my role as one of the Task Leaders.

As I recounted in Chapter Eleven in the section on Phase 3, Judy's positive interaction with Joanna in Session 4 helped propel the group into Phase 3 cooperation. Throughout this phase, Judy became more integrated as a member of the group, adapting to its norms and remaining engaged and committed to the process.

Early in Session 8, while still in Phase 5, Judy made an important change involving a redecision about time and space, which was quoted earlier in this chapter in the section describing the functions of the Task Leaders.

In the closing moments of Session 8, after the Task Leader reminded the group of the time boundary and the absences that would occur in the next two final sessions, Judy clarified for herself the transference of her mother onto Patricia. She said: "I feel unfinished. . . . I want to do something different in response to the ways you remind me of my mother. . . . I get into situations where I feel that someone else is taking the floor and dominating and that there's no space for me. . . . And you happen to be that person in this group."

In Phases 8 and 9, Judy continued to be recognized for the changes she had made in the group. From Phase 5 and on to the end, she contained herself in a way that contrasted sharply from the way she had entered group.

Defiant Leader

This leader's name comes from her stance in relation to the group: she challenges one or more of its informal norms. In this way, she demonstrates the power of an autonomous individual to retain a degree of independence in relation to the group. She resists the pull toward cohesiveness by insisting on space for individual variation, preventing the loss of self in togetherness. She carries considerable vulnerability throughout the life of the group, although her vulnerability may be hidden beneath a veneer of strength. The issue of trust is paramount, and she tends to pull away from intense involvement or deep self-disclosure. Conflicting within her are the temptation to merge and the impulse to flee. In her behavior, we see the desire to be open and learn from others compete with the urge to protect herself from others. Often she is ambivalent about participating in the group from the start, and this ambivalence continues to be reflected in her

response to the development of closeness in the group. She models
the struggle between dependence and independence for the group as
a whole.

In our videotape group, Patricia emerged as our Defiant Leader. In
contrast to the rest of the group, Patricia never fully accepted Judy as
a member of the group, because Judy's behavior in the group did not
meet her standards for how a therapist should act. In that way, she
challenged the informal norm of accepting other members despite
their imperfections. She challenged it by strongly implying how therapists should behave in this group. This was important in a group that
consisted of therapists or therapists in training (save one member,
Joanna). Patricia's first confrontation of Judy is recorded in part in
Chapter Eleven, in the description of Phase 2.

Early in Phase 5, after Judy struck her hand with her fist, Patricia
seemed to reach a crisis, and returned to this theme with renewed
vigor. She addresses Judy: "I appreciate your releasing the energy, but
I wonder in my mind, knowing you are a [therapist]. . . . By the time
we reach a stage of being able to help others, we should have worked
through some of that stuff." When the group embraced mutuality,
Patricia, in keeping with her role as Defiant Leader, could not.

At one point during Phase 5, midway into Session 7, in the role of
Task Leader I try to lead the group to an empathic response to Patricia, referring to how much of her pain I was picking up as she made
subtle hints of the abuse she had suffered in her life. My attempt was
heard and echoed by Robert.

BILL: (*To Patricia*) I think that the memories of your mother and step-
mother came up very strongly. . . .

ROBERT: Were you hit?

PATRICIA: Oh, yeah.

BILL: And that's a very painful thing (*Ten-second silence during which
the entire group nods in understanding*).

This was as vulnerable as Patricia allowed herself to be. The group
members saw her pain, showed empathy, and very gently carried her
pain. Together they created a new norm regarding the inevitable diversity in the group.

At the close of Session 8, with the group still mired in Phase 5,
John, in the role of Emotional Leader, acknowledged the "relief of ten-

sion" between Robert and Patricia, and then addressed Judy with the hope that she might find some resolution with Patricia also. Judy responded, addressing Patricia.

JUDY: I feel an adversarial energy between us, and I'm wondering how we can acknowledge each other and not have to make it different . . . not have to want the other person to change.

PATRICIA: I don't feel adversarial. I feel discomfort. And I feel a lack of trust. . . . I appreciate the fact that you can name and touch your emotional levels because that is something I can't do. . . . it's something I'm working on.

In Session 9, Phase 8, I asked Patricia whether she had learned something in the interaction with Judy. Patricia replied, "The one thing that I missed was not being able to support [Judy] in that process of being stuck and blaming and being quite negative. . . . (*To Judy*) I felt badly that I was not there for you on that level."

Later in the session, in contrast to Patricia's stance, other members acknowledged the changes Judy had made. Tony spoke for many when he said, "I've seen real shifts in you, Judy. . . . I've seen you consciously do that."

Emotional Leader

This leader enters the group as the individual most prepared and motivated to engage in the group task. He focuses on emotional issues, expressing concern for others and becoming the most important peer support person to other members throughout the life of the group. By forming strong bonds with the Task Leaders, he oversees the opening of boundaries between therapists and members in the group. He models the conflict between forming deep bonds with others and denying the need for deep bonds. Generally, he is well liked by others and becomes a positive focus for group interaction, working hard to accurately perceive and represent his reality to himself and the members. He often comes ready to make a developmental change and models that process for others.

In our videotape group, Robert shared the role of Emotional Leader with John. Although Robert's tendency to talk too much prevented his full participation in that role, he formed strong bonds with Vivian and me, and focused on emotional issues.

John's absence in Sessions 7 and 9 limited his full participation in the group, and his inclination to speak in a circular fashion distanced him from members at times. He may initially at least have been an Ambivalent Emotional Leader—an Emotional Leader who shows ambivalence about participating in the group. Although not active in Session 1, he gradually emerged as an Emotional Leader as he became more direct in his style of speaking.

Victoria, who was very well liked, might also have been a candidate for this role had she been more forthcoming with her *feelings* about events, not just her observations. When she did speak, she had a strong influence on the group. However, her acute concern for managing her image and how she was perceived by the group prevented her from taking a more active role in the emotional life of members.

In Phase 1, Robert became the first to elaborate a memory from his family of origin. He recalled being in the kitchen with his mother, having to listen to her monologues, and how angry he was during those times. In a later phase of group, he had the insight that he himself was subject to talking at length, and how that inhibited his ability to listen. He did try from the beginning to provide support for Judy, and yet his projection of his mother onto her prevented him from doing so as the group progressed. In relations with others in group, Robert's projections obstructed his ability to express empathy and be unambiguously liked in return. This became quite apparent in Phase 9, when he revealed that he projected his father onto John, whenever John used humor in a way that attempted to cover over pain.

Robert did work hard at accurately perceiving and representing verbally what happened in group, as in this example, when he summarized at the close of the first session the group's process of vacillating between emotional and intellectual expressions: "It's a process of including people wherever they're at. . . . It's a process I'm willing to tolerate as we get to know each other."

Again, as a prelude to entering Phase 2, Robert expressed his concern for others: "As I want to be safe, so I want everyone else to feel safe. . . . I want for people to feel accepted . . . acknowledging how different [we are]. . . ."

During Judy and Patricia's altercation in Phase 2, Robert attempted to present integratively a view of what was happening between them. His attempt was largely ignored, but his strong wish for the two to come to an understanding is characteristic of an Emotional Leader. Late in Phase 2, following his interpretation of my statement to

Joanna, Robert made an emotional connection with me, during which I acknowledged, mostly nonverbally, his need to be listened to and seen. This included a fifteen-second interval of eye contact without words being spoken.

Robert invited Joanna to share more of her deeper emotions. She responded, but very skillfully maneuvered Robert into speaking again of himself. At this phase of development, the heart of Phase 3, the group did not push Joanna and accepted her difference and desire to reveal no more.

In Phase 3, Robert revealed that he carried the pain for his family. In part, this explains why he believed he must be the container for the pain of the group. Tony noted Robert's impact on the group by admitting that he felt close to Robert as he spoke, and "vicariously" experienced what Robert said. In the middle of the phase, Robert drew an interesting parallel between Judy's desire to leave our group and his own desire as a young man to leave his family. In this way, he continued to try to form bonds with group members. He also stated that he tended to fall in love when entering groups. We witnessed some of that tendency in the admiring gazes he gave Victoria in later phases of the group.

In Phase 4, Robert made an important shift to withholding speech until necessary and practicing the delivery of words when appropriate. In Phase 5, Robert expressed his awareness of the time slipping away and the change he wanted for himself: "In the time we've got left . . . I really would like to slow things down . . . so I could really be expressive of what's happening with me in a whole way . . . what I'm thinking, what I feel, and what I want. . . ."

In this way, Robert worked hard to integrate thinking and feeling, bridging the two subgroups organized around these dimensions. He also made explicit the group-level questions: How can we get closer? How can we connect at a deeper level? In Session 8, Robert stated, "I don't want to say goodbye to this group," reflecting his strong attachment for the group.

John, as Emotional Leader, got off to a slow start. In Session 2 and near the beginning of Phase 2, he indirectly confronted Judy, our Scapegoat Leader.

JOHN: (*To Judy*) My experience of victims is that they tend to be the most powerful people, and that's why I tend to back off from them.

JUDY: Can we get back to the level of process here and now?

BILL: Are you addressing her as a victim?

JOHN: In that role.

John emerged as an Emotional Leader when he began to change his posture and speech patterns toward greater directness in Session 3. When Judy interrupts his dialogue with Robert, he flashes at her in anger.

JOHN: Do you think he can ask his own questions?

JUDY: I would rather that you—

JOHN: You can "rather" . . . but I'm speaking with you. (*Indicates Robert with his hand.*)

Later, John said, "I felt like it was controlling. . . . I hear 'I want something different.' What's that about?"

Judy responded, "Thank you. Now I'm getting what I wanted. I wanted you to do just what you're doing now." She seemed to be relieved that there was finally strong emotional expression from John, even though it was negative and coming in her direction as Scapegoat Leader.

Nearly one hour into Session 3, with the group still in Phase 2, Vivian, as Task Leader, said to Judy, "I wonder if there is something between you and John that needs to be talked about. John? You're shaking your head yes."

John replied, "I'm just sorting it out myself. . . . (*To Judy*) I am experiencing some anger. . . . I do notice I'm tending to be very skeptical of what I hear when it comes from you. . . . It's almost like one can almost complete the thought of the other sometimes between Robert and you. . . . The fur on my back goes up when I see other people anticipating or answering questions [for others] . . . I heard questioning of my internal experience, and I'm wondering 'How could you know?' . . . Part of me is angry."

John kept the pressure on Judy, but early in Session 4 came back to own his projections onto her, as I have described under Phase 3 in Chapter Eleven. After Joanna interrupted him, John remained silent for over an hour, being respectful of the emotional connections being formed in the group, before expressing his appreciation and resentment. John said, "On the one hand I'm moved by the profundity and the depth [here] . . . setting the agenda for nurturing. I've learned a great deal just listening. . . . I'm reluctant to draw away from that because it feels very nice and very good for me. But there's another side of me that wonders. . . . I felt a little at the beginning, censored, censured, or sanctioned. I was having a dialogue with Judy and . . . I wasn't noticing something. . . . I appreciated my attention being drawn to that. On the other hand, I noticed how rapidly it moved away from what I'd brought up. . . . *[Group reacts with surprise.]* There was not an opportunity for Judy to address what I had been saying. . . ."

In this way John drew the attention of the group to its process and his need to resolve something for himself. I closed the session, commenting that it was appropriate for John to bring us back to the incident. Making a teaching comment, in my role as Task Leader, I said: "The only way we get to depth is to not ignore negative feelings."

As we began Session 5, I asked John if he had noticed my eye contact as an invitation to speak during his silence in the previous session. John replied, "I think I was getting that invitation. Frankly, I see I need to change how I'm communicating . . . so that there's greater clarity . . . and brevity."

Later, John added that he was in the group to learn and that he would welcome interruptions even though they felt uncomfortable to him. This marked a shift in John's verbal behavior; he was becoming more direct and clear in his communication and more effective as an Emotional Leader. After this, he formed an emotional bond with Victoria that I described under Phase 4 in Chapter Eleven.

Early in Session 6, still in Phase 4, John demonstrated his new directness by initiating a deeper bond with Robert based on authenticity.

JOHN: (*To Robert*) The intensity is increasing between the two of us, and I wonder what that's about.

ROBERT: (*To John*) There was a moment when you seemed to get really angry. . . . You seemed to be saying, "Get off my back." . . . It was around your tendency to speak circularly.

JOHN: It was pissing you off?

ROBERT: I was getting frustrated. . . . I wanted you to be speaking so much simpler and straighter . . . and that's exactly what you've been doing today.

A half hour later, John initiated an important exchange with Tony in which they worked out a new agreement of how to be with each other. His question to Tony, "What can we do to open it up between the two of us?" seemed to open the way for the entire group to bond with each other.

As we have seen, identifying emergent leaders can help the group therapist be mindful of the many leadership functions that must be served in the course of a time-limited group experience. In some cases, clinicians can predict hazards that could throw the therapy off course if they are not addressed. The next chapter catalogs some of these hazards, and shows how the group therapist can respond effectively and empathically to better meet the patients' needs.

CHAPTER THIRTEEN

The Limits and Hazards of Practice

⟣⟣⟣ In a practice as powerful as group therapy, clinicians must be aware of the potential damage that can be done to patients in their groups. Often the damage is iatrogenic; that is, it can be traced to errors by group therapists, either through ignorance, omission, or lack of attention. Other wounds can spring from risks inherent in the process itself; these wounds can be minimized by rigorous training, the practice of co-therapy, personal psychotherapy, peer supervision, and therapist self-evaluation.

I want to distinguish between mistakes that can be useful to the movement of a group, when acknowledged by the leaders, and errors that lead to the injury of group members. Mistakes are important to the development of group leaders, as I emphasize in Chapter Nine. However, the dictum "Do no harm" remains the chief principle that must guide us in our pursuit of corrective emotional experiences for our patients.

Errors that lead to injury often result from arrogance, that is, the therapist's need to arrogate powers to himself that are beyond the scope of his competency or capacity as healer. Some of these are obvious—such as the power to make predictions about future behavior or the belief that one can help just about anyone—but others are more subtle, enticing the clinician to assume that he can practice without recognizing clearly both his limitations and the limitations that are frequently a part of the practice of group therapy.

HAZARDS AND REMEDIES

The following sections delineate situations in which the conscientious group therapist must exercise discretion and prudence. They in no way exhaust the possible hazards that professionals face, but they will alert clinicians to likely trouble spots.

The Therapist Misapplies a Good Theory

There are many fine theories to apply as a group therapist. However, the therapist can employ a sound theory at the wrong time or in an inappropriate context.

Transference, for example, is an excellent theory. The idea that patients will transfer feelings they had for parental figures and siblings onto group therapists and group members is a powerful way to understand how patients bring their memories to life in group. The interpretation of transference by the group therapist allows the patient to begin a process of personality change by letting him consciously identify with "new" parents and siblings that can provide him with healthier messages and more wholesome internalizations.

If interpretations of transference are premature, they are often simply ignored by the patient until such time as she is ready to assimilate the information. Other times, group members themselves can deliver the message in such a way that the patient is able to hear and comprehend. There are times, however, when the group therapist must not interpret transference at peril of damaging the threads that hold a person's life together. The following case is an example.

Bodie was a disturbed young man who drove a truck for a living. He was psychologically unsophisticated relative to his group, yet perceptive and alert. He put his observations in the form of references to movies that had influenced him; movies seemed to be the prime source of learning for him, as he had been grossly deprived both culturally and educationally in a neglectful family.

He developed a strong attachment to Hannah, an older woman in group whom he identified with the tragic heroine in a European film. It was obvious to the therapist that he had made a sibling transference to Hannah and saw her as the older sister who attempted to shield him from the criticisms of his stepfather. Because his sister had died as a teenager, the victim of a botched abortion, he was filled with both rage toward his stepfather (the presumed father of the child) and guilt that he had not been big enough to protect his sister.

Bodie was currently embroiled in a battle with his boss, who he said was "just as mean as my stepfather." The group, including Hannah, was helping to defuse Bodie's rage and encouraging him to dispose of his gun, which he might be tempted to use either on himself or his boss. The therapist refrained from naming the transference to Hannah because it could have intensified the murderous feelings Bodie was experiencing toward his boss and further destabilized his grasp on the here and now. When the potential danger was past, there would be time to analyze the meaning of his relationship to Hannah.

It Is Time to Act, But the Therapist Applies the Wrong Theory

The notion that resistance on the part of the patient ought to be confronted by the group therapist is another theory worthy of application, because the rather unconscious actions that serve to keep a patient locked into self-defeating behavior must be brought to the patient's awareness. However, timing and the patient's readiness to receive the information are pertinent factors to be considered. The situation is further complicated in the cases where the patient needs a response from the leader—but what response? Sometimes, when the group therapist is called on to act, he takes the wrong action, as the following example shows.

Wakefield was a young man, born in the South, the only child of an unmarried mother who pampered him and smothered him with attention as she raised him alone. He had done well at school and had made a life for himself in a respected profession, but had been unable to sustain any relationship with a woman for more than a year. He spoke of his mother in rather idealized terms and never criticized her for any part of his upbringing. Although it was clear to the group that she had seduced him into being her "little husband," he was resistant to any suggestion that she had done anything inappropriate.

On one occasion, the group became particularly adamant in their reproach of Wakefield's mother, insisting that Wakefield admit she had been a bad parent. Wakefield turned to the group therapist and asked him directly for his opinion. The therapist responded by agreeing with the group's assessment of his mother and urging him to see her in a different light. Wakefield fell silent for the remainder of the group and was absent the following week. When the therapist spoke with him on the phone,

Wakefield said he was too embarrassed to return to the group because obviously the group members could not respect him for being so naive and such a "mama's boy."

In supervision, the therapist learned that to point out the patient's resistance in such a direct way was especially shaming for Wakefield, considering that the whole group seemed to be maligning the view he had constructed of his mother. Wakefield had turned to his therapist for protection—exactly what he had needed in his family of origin—and needed to hear something about how painful it must have been for him, trying as he did to be a good son. Confrontation by the therapist was not indicated because of the early phase of the group development (Beck's Phase 2). Also, the tenuous bond Wakefield had formed with the therapist was not strong enough to allow that sort of intervention and keep the patient in treatment.

No One Theory or Technique Works All the Time

One of the fondest dreams of science in general and the social sciences in particular is that of an all-encompassing theory, one that will apply under all circumstances and contexts. Of course, no one theory suffices, however well constructed. In fact, the group therapist must be prepared to implement several theories, including some that may be contradictory, if she is to adequately grasp the phenomena that occur simultaneously at many different levels in group.

For example, there are times when the Emotional Leader (one of Ariadne Beck's emergent leadership roles described in Chapters Eleven and Twelve) does not emerge, and the members of the group are slow to pick up the Emotional Leader functions—such as modeling the opening of intrapsychic boundaries between the self and the rest of the group, or accurately perceiving and representing verbally the group process—as part of their behavior. When this happens, other complementary if not competing theoretical perspectives can be called on. The following instance in group serves as an illustration.

In a time-limited group consisting of individuals with inadequate ego development, there was a great reluctance to engage with one another either in drawing out emotional responses or in probing meaningful connections with each other. Group members spoke at a superficial level and did not seem to listen or respond to what other members said, neither supporting each other nor making use of supportive statements when they were proffered. It was as if the members were waiting for someone else to initiate something. Yet when the therapist suggested that they could go deeper, they acted as if they did not understand what she was saying.

In the absence of an Emotional Leader, the therapist viewed the group through the lens of Wilfred Bion's Basic Assumptions, perceiving that the group as a whole was avoiding its work by assuming that all demands by the therapist would be ignored that did not allow them to fight or take flight. In other words, they would either express aggression or evade psychological difficulty. The therapist then made an intervention based on the strength of her own emotional reaction to the group. She stated that she felt as though she did not exist for the group except as an accomplice in their efforts to run away. She was therefore willing to maintain a state of nonexistence, although very uncomfortable for her, until the group tired of its plans to escape.

The Therapist May Need to Refrain from Acting

Group therapists sometimes must be prepared to contain the impulse to act: they must hold back from interventions that might prove intrusive or patronizing and creatively explore the uses of silence. Defending a person in group that does not need defending is one way of infantilizing the individual and belittling the vigor of her defenses.

Joyce was a middle-aged woman who had come to group to recover from being scapegoated as the youngest child in her large family of origin. Her father had considered her incompetent, ridiculing her attempts to be autonomous and making verbal predictions that she would fail to make friends when she grew up because she lacked social skills. He did defend his daughter when she was attacked by her mother, not on the grounds that the mother's criticisms were unfair but on the basis that Joyce was "weak" and needed propping up.

During one group session, Joyce was censured by another woman in group for acting too sweet and nice, claiming that she could not trust Joyce to be genuine while she maintained a facade of pleasantness. When Joyce responded that she was not aware of hiding rancor beneath the surface, the woman increased her attack on her, calling her agreeableness merely an excuse for being "spineless." The co-therapists in the group were experienced at leading women's groups together, and they patiently observed the conflict as it escalated. Both understood that the group was in a mature phase of its development (Beck's Phase 5), and Joyce had formed a more than adequate trust bond with them as leaders. They correctly assessed that Joyce could sustain this challenge without their interference, and they remained silent.

Joyce did defend her position, although not without difficulty. She later thanked her therapists for staying out of the fray: "Nobody ever believed that I could handle something like that." Joyce increased her self-esteem by facing up to conflict.

There Are Times When the Task Leader Must Act

This imperative is especially true when a particular illusion has taken root in the group's imagination and must be dispelled before it threatens to damage its members. As Wilfred Bion noted, the group therapist can easily become caught up in the projective fiction of her patient, so much so that it can seem to her that she is playing a role in the patient's fantasy. Projective identifications that go unrecognized, unacknowledged, and unrepaired are especially hazardous. What seems dangerous to group members in this case is the possibility that the illusion will become real and that their worst nightmares will come true. The following is an illustration.

Virginia was leading a group for men and women with her longtime co-therapist, Jacob. The group had been in progress for six months when Jacob had to miss several sessions due to illness. At the first session without her co-therapist, Virginia was accused of having a special relationship with a man in group named Giros. "You care for him more than the rest of us," said Kelly, whose history of incest with his older sister gave him the inclination to see relationships in terms of sexual misconduct.

Kelly was well respected by others in the group for his astute intuition, and they demanded that Virginia say whether Kelly's jealousy had any basis in fact. Virginia said she felt especially close to Giros because he reminded her of her own brother, whom she loved very much.

With that admission, Kelly began feeling nauseated in group, saying he was about to throw up. He left the room, mumbling that the "smell of incest in the group" was too much for him to handle. The group reacted as if the fact of incest had been proven by the sudden appearance of Kelly's symptoms. One group member said she was very angry that the therapist had stepped out of her role as therapist and that her boundaries couldn't be trusted.

It seemed to Virginia that she could not say anything that could break the spell of illusion that had mesmerized the group, and she herself felt as if in a dream, unable to awaken.

At last, Giros said he felt guilty for what happened, because he both wanted and feared a special connection with Virginia. He wished that Jacob had been present as a "reality check" to help them see they had done nothing wrong by expressing affection for each other. As it was, the group regressed deeply in the face of inaction.

Although Virginia was in the thrall of projective identification, she should have acted. At the very least, she could have stated that she was feeling strange and that something highly unusual was occurring. She could have speculated that a memory was being acted out in the group as though the memory were true in the here and now.

A strong statement, such as "We are all living someone else's memory at this moment, and we're not in touch with the reality of the situation," might have slowed the pace of the group's regression. The presence of the co-therapist would have helped Virginia take such action, yet we can surmise that the incident might never have happened if Jacob had been present.

Openly Recognize Damage That Has Been Done

One of the greatest tests of group therapist integrity is the ability to admit that she has made an error. This is especially difficult when a patient has suffered a narcissistic injury as a result. Often the group therapist must overcome barriers within herself in order to go to this deep level with a patient. In the following example, the therapist initially was blinded to the harm she did to her patient by her own difficulty with maternal caring.

Rachel had been a successful group leader for many years, and so was very pleased and honored when a respected colleague chose to enter her group for treatment. The colleague, Ann, was a group therapist herself; she had returned to therapy to work through issues following the death of her mother, who had been in constant competition with Ann throughout Ann's childhood. Ann needed a strong attachment to her group therapist in order to accomplish her treatment goals, and yet her attempts to bond with Rachel were thwarted by Rachel's tendency to keep their relationship at a collegial level. At a poignant moment in group, when Ann was most vulnerable and requesting a nurturing response from her therapist, Rachel rebuffed her with the statement, "You're the last person I'd expect to ask for that." Ann visibly withdrew into silent despair.

Later, in peer supervision, Rachel realized her error. Because her own mother would switch from being the nurturer to being a needy child so swiftly, Rachel distrusted the sincerity of the maternal nurturing she could summon for someone so obviously competent to care for herself. Rachel's mother had been unable to tolerate such neediness and had taken advantage of Rachel's willingness to let go of her needs. Now Rachel seemed to be getting back at her mother by withholding from her patient.

Rachel returned to her group and let Ann know how sorry she was to have said what she did. "It must have felt so injurious to you—repeating your mother's message to be strong." Ann was surprised and gratified by her therapist's candor and was able to let go of some of the guilt she felt for letting herself have needs. By frankly admitting her mistake and expressing empathy, Rachel was able, over time, to form a bond with Ann that was emotionally corrective and mutually satisfying.

Revelations by Patients Go Unrecognized

Risk-taking behavior is one of the great gambles in group therapy. The individual wants to experiment with a novel approach in a familiar context or to test practiced behavior in an unusual context. The highest risk is responding spontaneously in a strange setting. When a patient in group takes a risk and receives no affirmation by the treatment group, she can feel the rejection acutely. This pain is exacerbated if the group therapist also ignores her, as he customarily encourages people to take chances in the service of personal growth. In the following vignette, the patient tried on a new role in a group that refused to receive what she revealed to them.

Roberta was the oldest of eight children, and she joked about the group exactly replicating the number and gender of the children in her family of origin. A very isolated and private person, she did not reveal much about herself for many months in group. She occupied the Defiant Leader role by remaining aloof from group involvement, and her frequent questions of the group leader established a special relationship with him based on the nearly opposite points of view they held concerning group matters. Her group therapist, Detrich, took a rather ambivalent stance relative to Roberta, sometimes praising her courage to state her opposing views and other times lamenting her contrariness. He was irritated by her threats to leave group unless it gave her more support and acted less like her big family that gave her none.

During the next group session, Roberta made a shift in her approach to other members by sharing her feelings for a man she had met through work. She invited them to give her feedback on her budding relationship, but was met by a diffident silence, as though people were wondering what she was up to. One man thought what she was doing was "interesting," but no one affirmed the risk she was taking by her encounter with the man. They also failed to understand that her asking for feedback was not just another call for "support" but a change in her relationship to the group. Detrich, too, remained quiet, and could not muster so much as a word of encouragement, being caught up in his own ambivalence. Roberta was devastated, and withdrew deeply into herself. It was several weeks before Detrich grasped how gravely he had blundered with his patient. An independent group therapy supervisor pointed out how painful it was for Roberta to have her vulnerability ignored and how negligent Detrich had been as a group leader not to emphasize the importance of the event in the presence of the other group members. The group did finally realize what Roberta had done, but their recognition came too late to avoid injuring her.

Scapegoating of an Individual Member Goes Unchallenged

Of all the processes that attend groups, the scapegoating phenomenon is one of the most persistent and troubling for members. Yet, as we've seen in the account of Beck's Scapegoat Leader role in Chapter Twelve and the description of her Phase 2 of group development in Chapter Eleven, coming to terms with and resolving the many issues that emerge around the scapegoat is a prerequisite for taking the group to a deeper psychological level. Although scapegoating to some degree may be an inevitable event in groups, it does not have to be, nor should it be, a destructive one.

The group therapist must prepare herself, through training and supervision, to address the primitive emotions unleashed as group members are caught in the vortex of negative projections. She must be able to turn the occasion for attacking into an opportunity for learning. Her first responsibility is to protect the scapegoat, but how and when to do that requires artful practice. Too much protection and the person is infantilized; too little and he may be damaged.

Yvonne Agazarian, as a way to manage this sort of conflict, promotes the formation of subsets in a group, called functional subgroups. These subgroups contain differences in the group until the group is ready to integrate them. In her theory, subgrouping can contain the negative projections and splits within a group, thereby obviating the need for a single member to be encumbered with the role of scapegoat. And if the scapegoat does not find a subgroup of her own, the therapist must join with her in order that she not be isolated.

In the example that follows, the therapist neither helps the emergent Scapegoat Leader find a subgroup with which to identify nor joins with the scapegoat to protect her while the group uses her to discover the range of differences it will tolerate. As a result, the patient becomes a casualty of group therapy.

Daniela was an impeccably dressed Latina who held a high-powered job as a professional in corporate finance. She had come to a therapy group of men and women to find out why she had so much difficulty making a love relationship with a man. Although verbally adroit and insightful in her observations of others, she tended to make overly intellectual statements and never referred to her own emotions. At first, the group countenanced her manner of speaking because she filled the uncomfortable silences. But they soon wearied of her constant questions and began to attack her. One woman said that Daniela was holding the group back by interrupting the process whenever group members started to express their feelings.

Another woman thought that Daniela was not ready for group therapy and needed individual work instead. The criticisms took on the character of racial stereotyping when one man queried, "I thought Spanish women were usually more subservient?"

The group therapist, Christy, was bewildered by the sudden onset of the group's hostility. She had brought Daniela to group so that she could profit from the members' feedback, especially that of the males. But it was not turning out the way Christy had planned.

The group was much less accepting than she had expected. She wanted Daniela to get an accurate picture of how others perceived her, yet the image they were reflecting back to her seemed so distorted that Christy quietly wondered how helpful it could be. The group therapist identified closely with the patient's conflict over how to integrate intellect and feelings. She concluded that Daniela was strong enough to endure the assaults of the group and would probably resent as an intrusion any attempts she as a clinician might make to defend her. Christy believed that Daniela would eventually benefit from the ordeal, perhaps even getting in touch with her feelings, as the members began to take back their projections.

Clearly, the group therapist was misreading the situation through the filter of her own experience. The group was becoming even less open minded about Daniela, issuing calls for her to leave the group because they could not move forward as long as she remained.

Christy was alarmed by the animosity displayed toward the patient, and belatedly attempted to correct their impressions of her and interpret their projections. The members turned on their therapist and bitterly accused her of sabotaging the group by letting such a person in the door. When the group began attacking her, Christy's worst fear had been realized, and she felt impotent before its censure. She had, in effect, relinquished her leadership of the group.

After Daniela saw her group therapist collapse, she felt betrayed and powerless to help herself. When a group member maliciously told her to leave, she walked out of the room and never came back.

The Therapist Opens Wounds and Doesn't Close Them

There is often a great temptation, especially among less experienced group therapists, to push hard for quick results. Especially galling is the compulsion to extract emotions from people at almost any price.

In a time when the call for rapid treatment is de rigueur among psychotherapists, we must not display professional hubris and succumb to the clinically questionable practice of hurrying the healing process. The following account is a testimony of this sort of mistaken practice.

Joan, a middle-aged housewife, had come into a crisis group that treated individuals who were suffering from emerging problems that produced high stress and anxious depression. She introduced herself as "an accident that's waiting to happen." She said her marriage was in trouble, and her married daughter, who had just become pregnant, was having marital difficulties also. Never having had therapy before, she had called the crisis number that week, received an interview, and was referred to group. The group had its full complement of members that night, and Warren, the group therapist, was working alone, as his co-therapist was away on vacation.

The group members had many things to talk about but kept focusing their attention on Joan, whose sense of desperation evoked the group's concern. Warren noticed how much time Joan was monopolizing but did not attempt to refocus the group's attention or modulate the affect that Joan was pouring out. Rather, he shifted his scrutiny to her, probing Joan's psyche and concentrating on peeling back layers of her memory. Warren was impressed that she went deep very fast and did not seem alarmed when old memories broke through to her consciousness. She spoke of an abortion she underwent as an adolescent, and a subsequent suicide attempt. She reeled off images and pictures in sweeping flourishes of speech, with hardly a pause to breathe or integrate her emotions with her recollections. Warren did nothing to slow her process and had some difficulty stopping her when the group came to an end, although he did commend her for "sharing and making so much progress" her first night in group. The patient seemed to collect her thoughts before she left the treatment room, saying that she looked forward to next week's group.

Within thirty-six hours, Joan had admitted herself to the emergency room, completely distraught, having not slept for two nights. When Warren conferred with a more experienced group therapist, he conceded that he had overestimated the ego strength of the patient and had used poor judgment in her care. She was psychologically unsophisticated and highly susceptible to the encouragement of group members to disclose more of herself than prudent. Warren did not take heed of the warning signs in how she presented herself nor did he take measures to protect her from the galvanizing effects of group. It was as if the group therapist had performed surgery without anesthetic and without sufficient time to suture the incision.

The Patient Is Prematurely Opened to Vulnerability Before Adequate Defenses Are in Place

A limitation inherent to group therapy is the discrepancy between the often intense pressure the peer group places on the individual to change and the relatively slow pace that people take in making their changes. To enter group therapy is to enter a realm of unpredictability and unexpected consequences, the very stuff that helps to loosen defenses and makes personal transformation possible. It is judicious to slow the process down so that the individual can integrate changes within his personality structure and organize new defenses to replace the old. A poignant example of how an astute group demonstrates the wisdom of keeping defensive structures in place is provided in a clinical story that Don Shaskan was fond of telling.

A patient had suffered a conversion reaction—a paralysis of the right arm while in a battle in which his best friend was killed. He suffered acutely from survivor guilt but did not relate that to the "injury" to his arm, which he maintained was nonfunctional despite no evidence of neuromuscular lesion. He was treated in a psychotherapy group for male veterans on an outpatient basis. During one session, he related a dream about his friend who had been killed. As he told the dream—in which his friend had returned to him alive and well—he moved his right arm freely. Neither the therapist nor anyone in the group pointed this out to him. He was simply not ready to have his symptom taken away; he had no defenses yet to replace it. As the group therapist said later, "We all knew that he might become psychotic if we did."

The Therapist Sets Inadequate Boundaries

Unrecognized countertransference is one of the many ways a group therapist can fail to set appropriate boundaries between himself and the members of the group. Countertransference, or therapist responses that have their source in the therapist's internal object relations or his family-of-origin issues, are an inevitable part of group therapy practice. In one sense, this projective phenomenon gives the therapist access to the patient's inner life, and particularly that aspect of the patient's life that can become the focus for a therapeutic relationship. It is, however, the hallmark of a well-trained group therapist to have a deep awareness and knowledge of his own projective tendencies; he knows how to contain them and keep them from overshadowing the very different experiences of group members.

For this reason, some group therapists choose to work only with co-therapists so that they can monitor each other's boundaries and avoid infringing on the group. Unrecognized countertransference can lead to premature termination, as the example here indicates.

Justin was the newest member in an ongoing group of men and women. His group therapist, Peter, had given him a list of rules prior to entering group, as part of the initial interviewing process.

At that time, Justin had described the goals he wanted to accomplish, and they included being more assertive in groups. He mentioned that his father had shamed him as a boy whenever he attempted to take the initiative or differ from his father's opinions. He wanted to practice beginning dialogues in a relatively safe atmosphere.

During his fourth session in group, Justin noticed that people were coming late each week, in direct opposition to the rules, and the group therapist said nothing. Justin challenged Peter to enforce the rules and take charge of the group. "I want you to be powerful here—so I can learn from you."

Peter was peeved by Justin's unexpected directness yet decided to humor him with the notion that being flexible in the application of rules was part of the art of group therapy. Justin was resolute and repeated his request that Peter show him how to take control of the group.

Although careful not to show it, Peter became quietly angry at Justin. Justin reminded Peter of his younger brother, who was a pest and a stickler for compulsively following regulations. Yet this awareness did not inform his response to Justin. Instead, he launched into a speech about the virtues of spontaneity and adaptability and missed entirely Justin's appeal that he teach him to be powerful.

Justin came away from the session feeling maddened and ashamed, and he never returned to therapy. He had come to group to discover a new way to assert himself, and when he did he encountered a new version of his father.

The Therapist Fails to Establish Closure and Allow Termination

How a person leaves the group often determines his willingness to embark on a course of group therapy in the future. Not everyone will complete the work they have set out to do, and this fact must be accepted by the group therapist. In ongoing groups, the group therapist must expect a turnover rate of about 30 percent during the first twelve sessions. Some of these are patients who may have been inappropriate for the group to which they were assigned and are opting for another form of treatment or no treatment. Others may be responding to their own internal resistance to the process of change that the group represents.

In time-limited groups, group therapists can expect that a certain number of patients will not complete their commitment, often without their showing any outward sign of dissatisfaction. Paradoxically, a person's willingness to speak of her ambivalence toward the group is one of the better indications that a patient is committed to the process.

How the group therapist reacts to the termination of one of his members is revealing of how well he has worked through the primitive emotions aroused by loss, abandonment, separation, and death, all of which may appear as themes during the termination process. The group therapist may be tempted—especially if unaccustomed to positive terminations, in which the gains the patient has made are quite visible—to presume that he knows what is best for the patient, including whether she should leave or not.

This is a complicated issue, because the group therapist has a responsibility to confront the patient's resistance to treatment. But the appropriateness and timing of such confrontation is part of the art of being a group therapist, as the next case shows.

Bennett had been a member of a long-term group for thirteen months and had achieved some of the goals he had set out to accomplish. His announcement of termination took everyone in group, including the therapist, by surprise. As the youngest member of a highly abusive and chaotic family, he had been suffering from severe symptoms of delayed posttraumatic stress syndrome, including hypervigilance and scanning with his eyes, chronic insomnia, and reexperiencing traumatic events in response to external stimuli (such as the sudden application of brakes by cars in the street). Bennett commonly experienced dissociative flashbacks as well as disturbing dreams with violent images. During his course of treatment, he had been able to reduce the frequency of some of these symptoms, yet still isolated himself in the social sphere apart from his job.

His reason for leaving group was to "take a rest from therapy." However, his therapist did not accept that explanation as a sufficient reason to stop and let him know immediately, by calling what he was doing a sabotage of the progress he had made. Bennett made no attempt to defend his position but just remained silent and stared at the floor.

Bonnie, the Emotional Leader of the group, broke the tense silence by reminding everyone of the termination of a person who had previously been a member of the group. Bonnie said, "I thought at the time that she should have stayed in group, but I've seen her since, and she has done remarkably well without us." Bonnie's statement allowed Bennett to say how grateful he felt for all the help he had received and to wonder whether he should continue as an expression of his indebtedness to the group.

The group therapist was nodding in agreement with that sentiment when the Defiant Leader challenged her, saying, "I think your inability to accept Bennett's departure has more to do with your stuff than his." This assertion led to a series of reflections by other group members on the therapist's tendency to hold on too tightly, like a mother afraid to lose her children. By listening carefully to the group, the group therapist was able to see how she might perpetuate Bennett's history of mistreatment by failing to acknowledge his wish to conclude his treatment.

It is neither my wish nor intention to frighten able clinicians away from the practice of group psychotherapy. However, I want them to enter the field with guarded enthusiasm, fully cognizant of the contingencies that affect outcomes and especially attuned to the damage they can do as group leaders. I recommend a modest approach to leading groups; we need always to learn anew from our patients and not be lulled into complacency by our treasured assumptions and other "things we know to be true." Each new patient and each new group is a fresh start. Our own arrogance is our greatest enemy. We must proceed with both caution and exuberance, as do our group members, looking forward to reshaping our lives with insights into the lives of others.

⎯⋙⎯ Videotape Ordering Information

On the next page (p. 202) you will find ordering details for the six-hour videotape *The Promise of Group Therapy: A Live to Tape Demonstration of a Time-Limited Group,* which has been produced as a companion to this book. The video is edited from a ten-session group that Vivian Nelson and Bill Roller co-led with individuals who volunteered to participate in order to learn more about the group process and themselves. In the video, we see demonstrated Ariadne P. Beck's phases of group therapy development and emergent leadership roles. With the aid of commentary by Nelson and Roller, the viewer learns how object relations can be applied to the group therapy setting. The work of other systems theorists is also introduced, providing a practical method to contain conflict and intense affect by the skillful use of subgroups.

Nelson and Roller point out the mistakes that group therapists commonly make and the ways those mistakes can be employed in the service of the patients' progress. They also show the ways a mature co-therapy team can advance the group's movement through the various phases of development. Many of the basic concepts of group psychotherapy outlined in this book are given visual representation, with helpful annotation provided by the co-therapists.

The viewer will find the video beneficial in a number of ways: as a practical guide to conducting short-term group therapy, as a way to learn the skills of group leadership, as a means of teaching others the craft of group therapy, and as a means of anticipating the potential hazards that await the group leader. The video consists of three VHS tapes, which may be purchased singly or as a package. The three tapes trace the beginning, middle, and end phases of the group.

HOW TO ORDER YOUR COPY
OF THE VIDEOTAPE

The Promise of Group Therapy: A Live to Tape Demonstration of a Time-Limited Group, by Vivian Nelson and Bill Roller, is a practical guide to conducting short-term group therapy, a useful tool for learning the techniques of group leadership, and an invaluable resource for teaching the craft of group therapy. The three tapes are as follows:

Videotape 1:   The Beginning Phases   Price: $150.00
                     (2 hours with commentary)   Item 0–9999–0181–8

Videotape 2:   The Middle Phases   Price: $150.00
                     (2 hours with commentary)   Item 0–9999–0182–6

Videotape 3:   The End Phases   Price: $150.00
                     (2 hours with commentary)   Item 0–9999–0183–4

Purchase the complete set of three videotapes for only $350.00. Item 0–9999–0184–2
(Prices do not include cost of shipping and sales tax, where applicable.)

To order *The Promise of Group Therapy: A Live to Tape Demonstration of a Time-Limited Group,* contact Jossey-Bass Publishers:

CALL toll free: 1–800–956–7739
FAX toll free: 1–800–605–2665
Or write:
Jossey-Bass Publishers
350 Sansome Street
San Francisco, California 94104

For more detailed information about the videotape presentation *The Promise of Group Therapy: A Live to Tape Demonstration of a Time-Limited Group,* you may call or write:

Berkeley Group Therapy Education Foundation
1104 Shattuck Avenue
Berkeley, California 94707
Phone: (510) 525–9215
Fax: (510) 525–4651

—ᵕᵕ— Bibliography

Frontispiece

Tolstoy, Leo. *Resurrection*. Book II, *World Classics*. Oxford: Oxford University Press, 1994.

Introduction

Anthony, E. James. "The History of Group Psychotherapy." In Harold Kaplan and Benjamin Sadock (eds.), *The Origins of Group Psychoanalysis*. Northvale, N.J.: Aronson, 1972.

Burrow, Trigant. *The Social Basis of Consciousness*. Orlando: Harcourt Brace, 1927.

Dies, Robert. *The Efficacy and Cost-Effectiveness of Group Treatments*. New York: American Group Psychotherapy Association.

Freud, Sigmund. "Group Psychology and the Analysis of the Ego." In James Strachey (ed.), *Standard Edition of the Complete Psychological Works of Sigmund Freud* (vol. 18). London: Hogarth Press, 1921.

Moreno, Jacob. *Psychodrama*. Beacon, N.Y.: Beacon House, 1946.

Pratt, Joseph H. "The Principles of Class Treatment and Their Application To Various Chronic Diseases." *Hospital Social Service*, 1922, 6, 401.

"Rhode Island Ruling." *Family Therapy News*, 1995, *26*(6).

Roller, Bill. "Group Therapy Marks Fiftieth Birthday." *Small Group Behavior*, 1986, *17*(4), 472–474.

Roller, Bill. "Group Therapy Will Make a Big Difference in the Age of Managed Care." *California Therapist*, Mar.-Apr. 1994, pp. 34–35.

Scheidlinger, Saul. "History of Group Psychotherapy." In Harold Kaplan and Benjamin Sadock (eds.), *Comprehensive Group Psychotherapy*. (3rd ed.) Baltimore: Williams & Wilkins, 1993.

Schilder, Paul. "The Analysis of Ideologies as a Psychotherapeutic Method, Especially in Group Treatment." *American Journal of Psychiatry*, 1936, *93*, 601.

Shaskan, Donald A., and Roller, William L. *Paul Schilder: Mind Explorer.* New York: Human Sciences Press, 1985.

Starr, Paul. *The Social Transformation of American Medicine.* New York: Basic Books, 1982.

Wender, Louis. "Dynamics of Group Psychotherapy and Its Application," *Journal of Nervous and Mental Diseases,* 1936, *84,* 54.

Chapter One

Feldman, Saul. "Leadership in Mental Health: Changing of the Guard for the 1980's." *American Journal of Psychiatry,* 1981, *138*(9), 1152.

Roller, Bill. "Organization and Development of Group Psychotherapy Programs in an HMO." *Proceedings of the 1982 Group Health Institute,* Detroit, Mich., June 20–23, 1982. Washington, D.C.: Group Health Association of America.

Roller, Bill, and Nelson, Vivian. *The Art of Co-Therapy: How Therapists Work Together.* New York: Guilford Press, 1991, p. 20.

Chapter Two

de Tocqueville, Alexis. *Democracy in America* (vols. 1 and 2). New York: Vintage Books, 1945. (Originally published 1835)

Hamilton, Alexander, Madison, James, and Jay, John. *The Federalist Papers.* New York: NAL/Dutton, 1961. (Originally published 1787)

Roller, Bill, and Lankester, Dina. "Characteristic Processes and Therapeutic Strategies in a Homogeneous Group for Depressed Outpatients." *Small Group Behavior,* 1987, *18*(4), 565–576.

Roller, William L., and Shaskan, Donald A. "Patients' Perception of Distance: The Same Therapist in Group Therapy Compared to Individual Treatment." *Small Group Behavior,* 1982, *13*(1), 117–124.

Rosen, David, Asimos, Chris, Motto, Jerome, and Billings, James. "Group Psychotherapy with a Homogeneous Group of Suicidal Patients." *Group Therapy and Social Environment.* Proceedings of the 5th International Congress for Group Psychotherapy, Zurich, Aug. 19–24, 1973. Bern: Verlag Hans Huber.

Chapter Three

MacKenzie, Roy. *Effective Use of Group Therapy in Managed Care.* Washington, D.C.: American Psychiatric Press, 1995.

McKay, Matthew, and Paleg, Kim. *Focal Group Psychotherapy.* Oakland: New Harbinger, 1992.

Roth, David, and Covi, Lino. "Cognitive Group Psychotherapy of Depression: The Open-Ended Group." *International Journal of Group Psychotherapy,* 1984, *34*(1), 68.

Spitz, Henry. *Group Psychotherapy and Managed Mental Health Care.* New York: Brunner/Mazel, 1996.

Tolstoy, Leo. *Anna Karenina.* New York: Bantam Classics, 1981.

von Bertalanffy, Ludwig. *General Systems Theory: Foundations, Developments, Applications.* New York: Brazilier, 1968.

Chapter Four

Agazarian, Yvonne, and Janoff, Sandra. "Systems Theory and Small Groups." In Harold Kaplan and Benjamin Sadock (eds.), *Comprehensive Group Psychotherapy.* (3rd ed.) Baltimore: Williams & Wilkins, 1993.

Budman, Simon H., and Gurman, Alan S. *Theory and Practice of Brief Therapy.* New York: Guilford Press, 1988.

Chapter Five

Boland, Peter. "The Role of Reengineering in Healthcare Delivery." *Redesigning Healthcare Delivery.* Berkeley, Calif: Boland Healthcare, 1996.

Maslach, Christina, and Jackson, S. E. "Burnout in the Health Professions: A Social Psychological Analysis." In G. Sanders and J. Suls (eds.), *Social Psychology of Health and Illness.* Hillsdale, N.J.: Erlbaum, 1982.

Roller, Bill, and Nelson, Vivian. *The Art of Co-Therapy.* New York: Guilford Press, 1991.

Roller, Bill, and Nelson, Vivian. "Co-Therapy." In Harold Kaplan and Benjamin Sadock (eds.), *Comprehensive Group Psychotherapy.* (3rd ed.) Baltimore: Williams & Wilkins, 1993.

Shaskan, Donald. "Treatment of a Borderline Case with Group Analytically Oriented Psychotherapy." *Journal of Forensic Sciences,* 1957, *2*(2), 195–202.

Chapter Six

Goulding, Mary McClure, and Goulding, Robert L. *Changing Lives Through Redecision Therapy.* New York: Grove Atlantic, 1979.

Goulding, Robert L., and Goulding, Mary McClure. *The Power Is in the Patient.* San Francisco: Transactional Analysis Press, 1978.

Hoyt, Michael F. *Brief Therapy and Managed Care: Readings for Contemporary Practice.* San Francisco: Jossey-Bass, 1995.

Chapter Seven

Cummings, Nicholas A. "The Successful Application of Medical Offset in Program Planning and Clinical Delivery." *Managed Care Quarterly,* 1994, *2*(2), 1–6.

Cummings, Nicholas A. "Does Managed Mental Health Care Offset Costs Related to Medical Treatment?" In A. Lazarus (ed.), *Controversies in Managed Mental Health Care.* Washington, D.C.: American Psychiatric Press, 1996.

Follette, William T., and Cummings, Nicholas A. "Psychiatric Services and Medical Utilization in a Prepaid Health Plan Setting." *Medical Care,* 1967, *5*(1), 25–35.

Friedman, Richard, and others. "Behavioral Medicine, Clinical Health Psychology, and Cost Offset." *Health Psychology,* 1995, *14*, 509–518.

Kogan, William S., and others. "Impact of Integration of Mental Health Service and Comprehensive Medical Care." *Medical Care,* 1975, *13*(11).

MacKenzie, Roy. *Effective Use of Group Therapy in Managed Care.* Washington, D.C.: American Psychiatric Press, 1995.

Roller, William L., and Kanofsky, David. "Medical Utilization Review of Group Psychotherapy Patients: The Offset Effect." *Proceedings of the 1985 Group Health Institute,* San Diego, Calif. Washington, D.C.: Group Health Association of America, 1985, pp. 269–277.

Tillitski, Christopher J. "A Meta-Analysis of Estimated Effect Sizes for Group vs. Individual vs. Control Treatments." *International Journal of Group Psychotherapy,* 1990, *40*, 215–224.

Toseland, Ronald W., and Siporin, Max. "When to Recommend Group Treatment: A Review of the Clinical and the Research Literature." *International Journal of Group Psychotherapy,* 1986, *36*, 471–201.

Chapter Eight

Clapp, Jane. *Professional Ethics and Insignia.* Metuchen, N.J.: Scarecrow Press, 1974.

Katze, Jennifer. *Harvard Women's Health Watch,* 1996, *3*(10). Boston, Mass: Presidents and Fellows of Harvard College, 1996.

Locke, John. "On Civil Government." *Two Tracts on Government.* Cambridge: Cambridge University Press, 1967. (Originally published 1690.)

"Questions of Patient Privacy." *New York Times,* May 22, 1996.

Chapter Nine

Feldman, Saul (ed.). *Managed Mental Health Services.* Springfield, Ill.: Thomas, 1992.

Ricoeur, Paul. *Freedom and Nature: The Voluntary and the Involuntary.* Evanston, Ill.: Northwestern University Press, 1966.

Ricoeur, Paul. *Freud and Philosophy: An Essay on Interpretation.* New Haven, Conn.: Yale University Press, 1970.

Roller, Bill. "The Group Therapist: Stages of Personal and Professional Development." *Small Group Behavior,* 1984, *15*(2), 265–269.

Whitehead, Alfred North. *Process and Reality.* New York: Free Press, 1929.

Chapter Ten

Bion, Wilfred. *Experiences in Groups.* New York: Basic Books, 1961.

Bridger, Harold. "The Northfield Experiment." *Bulletin of the Menninger Clinic,* May 1946, *10*.

Burrow, Trignant. *The Biology of Human Conflict.* Old Tappan, N.J.: MacMillan, 1937.

Dostoevski, Fyodor. "The Grand Inquisitor." *The Brothers Karamazov.* New York: Dutton, 1960. (Originally published 1879)

Foulkes, Sigmund H. *Therapeutic Group Analysis.* Madison, Conn.: International Universities Press, 1964.

Goldstein, Kurt. *The Organism: A Holistic Approach to Biology Derived from Pathological Data in Man.* New York: American Book Company, 1939.

Jones, Maxwell. *Social Psychiatry.* London: Tavistock, 1952.

Kibel, Howard. "Object Relations Theory and Group Psychotherapy." In Harold Kaplan and Benjamin Sadock (eds.), *Comprehensive Group Psychotherapy.* (3rd ed.) Baltimore: Williams & Wilkins, 1993.

Lewin, Kurt. *Resolving Social Conflicts: Selected Papers on Group Dynamics.* (Gertrud Weiss Lewin, ed.). New York: HarperCollins, 1948.

Powdermaker, Florence B., and Frank, Jerome D. *Group Psychotherapy.* Cambridge, Mass.: Harvard University Press, 1953.

Rosenbaum, Max, and Berger, Milton (eds.). *Group Psychotherapy and Group Function.* New York: Basic Books, 1963.

Schilder, Paul. *Psychotherapy.* New York: Norton, 1938.

Schilder, Paul. *The Image and Appearance of the Human Body.* Madison, Conn.: International Universities Press, 1950.

Segal, H. *Introduction to the Work of Melanie Klein.* (2nd ed.) New York: Basic Books, 1973.

Slavson, Samuel R. *Analytic Group Psychotherapy.* New York: Columbia University Press, 1950.

Slavson, Samuel R. *A Textbook in Analytic Group Psychotherapy.* Madison, Conn.: International Universities Press, 1964.

Wolf, Alexander, and Schwartz, Emanuel. *Psychoanalysis in Groups.* Philadelphia: Grune & Stratton, 1962.

Yalom, Irvin. *The Theory and Practice of Group Psychotherapy.* New York: Basic Books, 1970.

Chapters Eleven and Twelve

Beck, Ariadne P., Dugo, James, Eng, Albert, and Lewis, Carol. "The Phases in the Development of Group Structure." Presentation at the American Group Psychotherapy Association, 1993, and at the American Psychological Association, Toronto, 1996.

Beck, Ariadne P., and Lewis, Carol M. (eds.). *Process in Therapeutic Groups: A Handbook of Systems of Analysis.* Washington, D.C.: American Psychological Association, in press.

Beck, Ariadne P., and Peters, Lana. "The Research Evidence for Distributed Leadership in Therapy Groups." *International Journal of Group Psychotherapy,* 1981, *31*(1), 43–71.

Beck, Ariadne P., Eng, Albert M., and Brusa, Jo Ann. "The Evolution of Leadership During Group Development." *Group,* 1989, *13*(3/4), 155–164.

Chapter Thirteen

Agazarian, Yvonne, and Janoff, Sandra. "Systems Theory and Small Groups." In Harold Kaplan and Benjamin Sadock (eds.), *Comprehensive Group Psychotherapy.* (3rd ed.) Baltimore: Williams & Wilkins, 1993.

Bion, Wilfred. *Experiences in Groups.* New York: Basic Books, 1961.

Lothstein, Leslie. "Termination Processes in Group Psychotherapy." In Harold Kaplan and Benjamin Sadock (eds.), *Comprehensive Group Psychotherapy.* (3rd ed.) Baltimore: Williams & Wilkins, 1993.

━ₘₘ━ About the Author

BILL ROLLER is a licensed Marriage, Family, and Child Counselor in private practice as a group and family psychotherapist in Berkeley, California. He is a fellow of the American Group Psychotherapy Association, and co-chairman of the Group Therapy Symposium, presented by the Department of Psychiatry at the University of California School of Medicine in San Francisco.

As a consultant to healthcare organizations in the development of mental health delivery systems, Roller focuses on the planning and implementation of group psychotherapy programs. The originator of Group Therapy Grand Rounds at the Center for Psychological Studies in Albany, California, he trains group therapists in a variety of settings. He is chairman of the Berkeley Group Therapy Education Foundation, which has produced the video *The Promise of Group Therapy: A Live to Tape Demonstration of a Time-Limited Group*, a companion to this volume.

Roller and his wife, Vivian Nelson, design and conduct comprehensive training seminars in physician leadership development for medical managers on the West Coast. They have coauthored *The Art of Co-Therapy: How Therapists Work Together* (1991), and a chapter in *Comprehensive Group Psychotherapy*, Third Edition (Kaplan and Sadock, 1993).

Index

A

Absurd, 124–125
"Acceptance of personal limitations" stage, 124–125
Acting out, 137
Action research, *xvi*
Acute care delivery model, 99
Adler, A., *xvi*
Affiliation, 65
Agazarian, Y., 61, 193
Age-related groups, 33
Ambivalent Emotional Leader, 180
American Association of Health Plans, *xiv*
American Group Psychotherapy Association, *xiv–xv*, 12
Analytic-expressive method, 42–45
Anger, 25, 44, 136, 137, 150, 161
Anxiety disorder, 119
Asimos, C., 26
Assertiveness training, 41
Attitudes about group psychotherapy, 21–25
Attrition, 48–49
Authoritarian leadership, 131
Autonomy, achievement of (Phase 6), 159. *See also* Group therapy development

B

Basic Assumptions, 189
Bay Area Rapid Transit (BART), 113–114
Beck, A. P., *xxi, xxii*, 35, 61, 64, 139, 140–145, 169, 188, 193, 201
Beck Depression Inventory, 45

Beck's theory. *See* Group therapy development; Leadership roles
Beginner stage, 118–119
Beginning-competence stage, 119
Behavioral healthcare, 97
Beliefs about group psychotherapy, 21–25
Benefit packages: choosing, 107; and long-term therapy, 104; for stimulating group therapy, 56–57
Bereavement groups, 34, 37, 51
Billings, J., 26
Bion, W., 189, 190
Body image, *xvi*, 132
Body movements, 132
Boland, P., 67
Bonding, 81, 153, 156
Borderline personality disorder patients, 26, 36, 76–77, 97–98. *See also* Personality disorder patients
"Boredom and existential anguish" stage, 122
Boundaries: ego, 134; organizational, 10; personal, 5, 9, 129–130; therapist, 196–197
Brothers Karamazov, The (Dostoevsky), 131
Budman, S. H., 59
Burnout, 10, 124; prevention of, 72–73
Burrow, T., *xvi*

C

Camus, M., 101–102
Capacity maintenance, 54, 62–63
Capitation, *xii–xiii*; and group therapy specialization, 56, 57

⸺ᴠᴠᴠ⸺ COPYRIGHT ACKNOWLEDGMENTS